LLEWELLYN'S

2025

Magical Almanac

Featur

Elizabeth Barrette, Kir Beau...
Blake Octavian Blair, Chic ...
Monica Crosson, Majorie Gatson, Laura Gonzalez,
James Kambos, Opal Luna, Lupa, Sara Mellas,
Mo of Austral-Taur, Shana Nunnelly, Diana Rajchel,
Mhara Starling, Melissa Tipton, JD Walker, Charlynn Walls,
Brandon Weston, Angela A. Wix, Charlie Rainbow Wolf,
Stephanie Woodfield, and Natalie Zaman

ISBN: 978-0-7387-7194-6

Editing and layout by Lauryn Heineman
Cover illustration © Faryn Hughes
Calendar pages design by Llewellyn Art Department
Calendar pages illustrations © Fiona King

Interior illustrations: © Elisabeth Alba: pages 48, 81, 84, 187, 192, 206, 249, and 253; © R. Brasington: pages 9, 14, 197, 200, 232, 238, and 271; © Wen Hsu: pages 1, 34, 39, 43, 88, 93, 107, 116, 121, 183, 228, 259, and 263; © Mickie Mueller: pages 29, 67, 74, 99, 102, 210, 215, and 267; © Tara Schueller: pages 5, 19, 21, 23, 218, 222, and 244; © Angela A. Wix: page 275

Tarot cards on pages 61–63 from *Llewellyn's Classic Tarot* by Barbara Moore and Eugene Smith Copyright © 2014 Llewellyn Worldwide Ltd. All rights reserved, used by permission.

All other art by Dover Publications and Llewellyn Art Department

Special thanks to Amber Wolfe for the use of daily color and incense correspondences. For more detailed information, please see *Personal Alchemy* by Amber Wolfe.

You can order Llewellyn annuals and books from *New Worlds*, Llewellyn's catalog. To request a free copy of the catalog, call 1-877-NEW-WRLD toll-free or visit www .llewellyn.com.

Astrological data compiled and programmed by Rique Pottenger. Based on the earlier work of Neil F. Michelsen.

Llewellyn Worldwide Ltd.
2143 Wooddale Drive
Woodbury, MN 55125

Printed in China

FSC
www.fsc.org

MIX
Paper | Supporting
responsible forestry
FSC® C007683

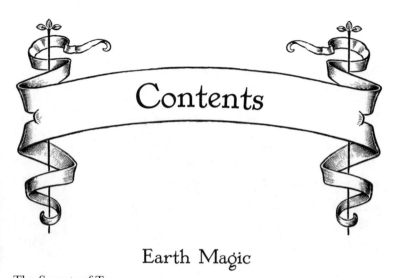

Contents

Earth Magic

The Secrets of Trees
by James Kambos. 2

Green Witchery in Small Spaces
by Monica Crosson 9

Fiber Magick Wheel of the Year: Crocheting into the Dark
by Opal Luna. 17

Standing Stones
by Charlynn Walls 26

All-Weather Spirituality
by Blake Octavian Blair 34

Air Magic

Playing Card Divination
by Charlie Rainbow Wolf. 44

A Deep Dive into Divination with Decans Using Tarot
by Mo of Austral-Taur. 56

The Air Dagger
by Chic and S. Tabatha Cicero. 67

Treasure Mapping
by Sara Mellas 77

Magic of the Spoken Word
  by Mhara Starling 87

Evolving Our Soul through Sabian Symbols
  by Majorie Gatson 96

2025 Almanac

Date, Day, Lunar Phase, Moon's Sign, Color and Incense
  of the Day, Holidays and Festivals, and Time Zones 108

2025 Sabbats, Full Moons, and Eclipses 112

2025 Energetic Forecast
  by Charlie Rainbow Wolf 114

2025 Calendar 124

Fire Magic

Ozark Faery Curses
  by Brandon Weston 184

Temazcales
  by Laura González 195

Creating and Running a Pagan Festival or Event
  by Stephanie Woodfield 203

Hearth Magic
  by Elizabeth Barrette 210

The Magical Nature of Natural Hair
  by Stephanie Rose Bird 217

Water Magic

When Meditation Becomes Shadow Work
  by Diana Rajchel 226

Queer Ancestral Connection
  by Kir Beaux 232

Will the Real Medusa Please Stand Up?
  by JD Walker 240

Tuning In to the Presence of Ancestors
  by Angela A. Wix 247
Rest and Dreaming: A Portal to Power
  by Shana Nunnelly 255

Coloring Magic

Color Correspondences 264
Activating the Magician's Manifestation Tools
  by Melissa Tipton 265
The Self-Care Menagerie Meter
  by Natalie Zaman 269
One Beautiful Thing Each Day
  by Angela A. Wix 273

Contributors 277

Earth Magic

The Secrets of Trees

James Kambos

Before the first human or beast walked this earth, the trees were here. They were already the ancients of our planet—and they were already wise. They had already witnessed the earth convulse. They had seen the land masses rise, the valleys being carved, and the mountains thrusting their massive peaks skyward. Through it all, the noble trees survived. Many trees were scarred by wind, ice, storm or lightning, but they healed themselves. By the time our ancient ancestors trudged across the plains, deserts, and mountains, the trees had already marked more seasons than any of us will ever see.

They have witnessed empires rise and fall. Through the great forests they have formed, conquering armies have marched. Battles have been lost and won. Human and beast have sought refuge amid their steadfast trunks and have been cooled by their shade.

The trees are wise. Hidden in their wood, bark, sap, buds, blossoms, and leaves are the secrets of the ages. For those of us who believe in magic and feel a kinship with the earth, the trees are our magical partners! We only need to listen and watch them. They will share their secrets with us. When their leaves rustle in a breeze, when their branches creak during a storm, or when their bare limbs rattle on a cold windy night, they are speaking to us.

Sometimes we need to watch them instead. In the spring when the sap rises and the vital juices bring about the buds and eventually the leaves, the trees go about this extraordinary transformation silently, but they are still speaking to us. They are showing us the life force of our Earth is still here.

The maple, oak, pine, and hawthorn—all trees have secrets to share with us. Using trees in our magic will enrich our lives. Just connecting to a tree or meditating with a tree nearby will ground and center us.

In short, trees are ancient living beings. They have much to teach us.

The Breath of Life

Trees aren't just our magical partners; they're also our partners for a healthy environment. With the miracle known as *photosynthesis*, leaves draw in carbon dioxide released by our bodies as well as our factories and machines. With the aid of sunlight, the lush green leaves release life-giving oxygen back into the atmosphere. This process enables trees to cool and cleanse the environment, which is essential to our survival.

Driving down a country lane on a late spring or summer day, we take the canopy of green we see for granted. The leaves look commonplace. Not exciting at all. But each leaf you see is performing the miraculous job of purifying our planet by keeping it oxygen rich. Each leaf enables every creature on Earth to survive. Without trees we would perish—all of us.

Trees aren't just magical. They're essential to our survival. So as you work your magic with trees, any part of trees—wood, bark, leaves, pine cones, nuts—do so mindfully.

Trees make our very existence possible. Their leaves are truly the breath of life.

Tree Etiquette

Trees help us make our lives better. Besides allowing us to breathe and cleansing our air, trees provide us with comforts: wood to build our structures, food, and logs to burn to heat our homes. It's necessary at times to cut down a tree. Perhaps the tree is diseased or has been damaged by a storm and could fall, causing injury to people living nearby. If this happens, try to plant a tree to take its place—trees are a renewable resource.

If you're like me and heat your home with wood, please purchase your firewood from a responsible firewood dealer or logger.

They cut only what is needed and don't strip the land. When possible, they also utilize damaged or fallen trees first. Remember to say thank you to your logs as you start a fire. Be grateful. As it burns, the firewood is returning the energy it received from Mother Earth and Father Sun when it was a living tree.

The Magical Energies of Trees

Our ancient ancestors knew and understood the secrets of trees. They know that each variety of tree possessed particular magical properties. In their magic, our ancestors used the necessary parts of a tree to suit their magical intent. When you need to remove different parts of a tree for magic, such as the leaves, bark, or a branch, remember to thank the tree.

Here is a list of some trees and their magical energies:

Apple: All parts of the apple tree are powerful magical ingredients when used in spellcasting and divination. The bark, wood, buds, blossoms, and fruit have been used as magical aids since ancient times. Parts of the apple tree, especially the fruit, are said to grant love and immortality and aid in divination. Use the apple fruit in love spell or when trying to scry to see a future love. When burned, apple logs, including crab apple, are wonderfully fragrant.

Ash: Ash trees are associated with male energy. The wood is very strong and is good for making wands and Witches' broomsticks. The wood burns very hot. This makes it useful to burn during rituals or spellcasting when you need an extra burst of energy. Old folk magic practitioners believed in carrying ash leaves with them for protection.

Cherry: Love, luck, and good fortune all come under the domain of the cherry tree. The bark of the wild cherry tree is especially useful for love spells and to generally attract love. Burning the bark as an incense is useful during a love spell. It's also good to burn as an aid to divination. The cherry tree is associated with feminine energies. Any

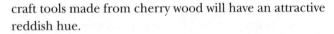

craft tools made from cherry wood will have an attractive reddish hue.

Hawthorn: The hawthorn tree is associated with fertility, the faery realm, protection, and good luck. To attract faeries to the garden, place a hawthorn branch in a secluded spot. Include a bit of hawthorn bark in spells calling for protection or good luck. In the spring, cut one or two hawthorn branches and place them over your front door to protect your home from evil spirits.

Locust: Here I'm speaking of the wild black locust. This tall, slender tree has wood that is slow to rot, hence its use in America since colonial times for homes and other structures. In the spring, long fragrant clusters of white flowers adorn the tree. I remember this from my childhood; my family had one growing by our back door. In magic burning a small amount of its bark is said to aid contact with the spirit realm.

Maple: The magnificent maple tree in all its forms is a tree symbolizing peace, beauty, and balance. Use its leaves or wood in spells calling for peace or love. It's also useful in spells when you need to center yourself. Since the maple grows in such diverse locations, it can also help you adapt to changes in your life. Ruled by Jupiter, the maple tree can also be used to draw happiness to you.

Oak: Long-lived, the oak is associated with the God and masculine power. Use its leaves, acorns, bark, and wood to cast spells for which great energy is required. Since its leaves are slow to fall in the autumn and sometimes remain on the tree into winter, the oak is a good tree to use in spells when you want the results to last a long time. The oak is also a good choice to use when seeking a job or promotion or to achieve a goal in business.

Pine: When I talk about the pines, I'm including the entire evergreen family—the white pines, firs, etc. The pines gave comfort to ancient peoples. When they experienced their first winter, they were afraid. It seemed that nature was dying. But the pines remained green and alive. Hope filled these ancestors. Ever since, the pines have had a special place in magic because they represent eternal life. This is why we bring evergreens into our homes at Yule and Christmas. Use pine when you are working magic for health, lifelong dreams, or cleansing and clearing.

Tree Spells

Here is some tree magic you may wish to try.

Connect to a Tree Spell

Since trees are living beings, you can form a partnership with a tree of your choice. This will give you a spiritual connection. You can use the tree as a focal point for meditation, for example. Go to a quiet area. Begin by approaching a tree that appeals to you. Ask it permission to form a relationship with it. If you receive a positive reaction from it, begin this ritual.

Place your palms upon its trunk. Breathe deeply. Gaze up at its branches and speak these words softly:

Mighty tree, regal and strong
Allow us to connect and let us bond
From toe to crown, from sky to ground
Together you and I belong

Meditate on a question or simply step back and admire your tree. You and your tree are now soul mates.

A Wheel of the Year Ritual

Use this ritual to honor your tree for the year. There are times you need to let your tree know that you think about it all year round. You may perform this ritual during any season. To do this, respectfully cut a flexible twig from your tree. Cut it off cleanly with a ritual knife or a small garden pruner. Next, weave it into a small wreath to represent the Wheel of the Year. Hold the wreath, look at your tree and say,

Spring shall come, buds shall swell
Summer's leaves will shade you well
Autumn comes, the leaves will fall
Winter winds will blow, still you'll stand tall

Lay the wreath at the base of the tree's trunk as an offering. Walk away.

A Spell for Patience

Silently, stoically, trees have witnessed the passing of time. They have observed countless sunrises and sunsets. Their branches have endlessly felt the burden of wind, snow, and ice. They have marked the never-ending cycle of the seasons, the years, the ages. And, they have done so quietly—patiently. Of all the living entities on this planet, trees can teach us the most about patience. Try the following ritual. It will calm and center you.

Go to a grove of trees or a forest. Find a spot and stand silently. Visualize roots growing from your feet down deep into the earth. Feel your heart rate slow. Your breathing should be steady. Now say,

Trees so mighty, patiently you've marked the passing of time
Teach me to make patience a virtue of mine
Through endless seasons you've learned to wait
Show me, a humble human, how to accept time and fate

Slowly return to an everyday state of mind. Slowly move your legs. Listen to the wind, the movement of leaves and branches. Are the trees sending you any messages? Slowly make your way out of the forest. Remember this moment the next time you begin to feel impatient.

Entire forests have been wiped out by wildfires, but the trees return. The trees will be here after we are gone. The trees have secrets. The trees will endure.

A Little Bit of Magic

THE DRUIDS LOVED NATURE
AND TREES SO MUCH THAT THEY
HELD THEIR MEETINGS IN
GROVES AND FORESTS.

Green Witchery in Small Spaces

Monica Crosson

Slip through the garden gate and follow the shady path lined with belladonna, foxglove, and wolfsbane to a ramshackle cottage with protectives tendrils of honeysuckle clinging to its walls. Willow guards the entrance to let one know that Hecate is the goddess who watches over this domain. Mullein stalks stand at the ready to be dipped in beeswax and lit to guide one to their sacred rites. There is mandrake and fern, lavender and hellebore, and hollyhock that stands tall along the fence line where the Sun lingers well into the afternoon. There, just under the quivering birch, you may spy the bright red mushroom caps of the fly agaric and lacy ferns to draw fae energy.

In this Witch's garden, there is everything one would need for any ailment or magickal intent. Comfrey to knit the bone, violets to ease a broken heart, nettle to lessen the pain of arthritis, and dill to increase wealth. A breeze tickles the chimes to let the Witch who calls this dwelling home know we are near her porch, but do not fear, for the broom is propped near the front door with its bristles up, an indication that friends are welcome. Tea is at the ready and wisdom is freely shared as wisps of magick rise from a bubbling kitchen cauldron.

This is a Green Witch's garden only of dreams, you might think—not necessarily, for anywhere a Witch dwells and plants are present (whether a cottage in the country or an apartment in an urban setting), magick grows.

Size Doesn't Matter

When thinking about the quintessential Green Witch's garden, one may ponder those classic fairy-tale images of our childhood dreams and sigh. But as grown-ups, we know far too well that the reality of living in the middle of nowhere in a crooked cottage surrounded by plants may not be a practical option. Some of us live in urban areas without the time or the space to maintain a large garden. Others have chosen tiny homes or other small-space living options as a means to simplify and lower their carbon footprint. But it doesn't mean we can't practice Green Witchery, nor does it mean we can't grow all our herbs for our magickal needs even in the smallest of spaces. With a little planning and creativity, you can grow just about anything anywhere you live, be it an apartment, condo, tiny home, boat, RV, or even a rented room.

When it comes to Green Witchery, the size of the garden plot isn't what's important, but rather how we utilize the garden spaces we have. But before we get started, there are few things even the craftiest of Green Witches needs to consider:

Light: How much light does your area receive? Sun-loving herbs like lavender, rosemary, and tomatoes require between six and eight hours of sun. If your growing area receives less, you may want to consider shadier favorites, like violets, columbine, or ferns.

Wind: Take note of what direction and how hard the wind blows across your growing area. If you're in a high wind area, you may want to consider a windbreak (available at most garden centers), trellis, or other natural woven material to help block and protect your plants. You may also consider low-growing or dwarf herbs.

Start Simply: If you're new to gardening, start with easy-to-grow herbs such as oregano, basil, thyme, lavender, sage, mint, and rosemary. These are all wonderful for medicinal, magickal, and culinary uses.

Embrace Your Space: Don't let a tiny space hold you back. Any space can be made more magickal by using texture, color, and form to create your perfect Witchy oasis.

Container Gardening

No matter the size of your property, using containers is a versatile and accessible way to garden. Especially for Green Witches who have small outdoor spaces. And with a little bit of planning, container gardens can create multiseason appeal. For busy Green Witches, containers offer a low-maintenance form of gardening that is portable (for our van-dwelling Witches) and flexible, as plants can be easily changed seasonally and moved to suit their growing needs.

The great thing about container gardening is that almost anything can be used as a planter, including buckets, salvaged pieces (think of teacups or a child's wagon), canvas bags, and cardboard boxes. One of the most interesting containers I have come across is railing planters. They are adjustable pots that fit between standard fence rails. Not only do they extend your gardening area, but they act as a privacy screen as well.

A basic rule of thumb for successful container gardening is to not overplant your container. Squeezing too many plants in one container is going to limit the amount space and nutrition for proper root development and growth.

Follow these guidelines:

- Less than 10 inches in diameter, limit to 1 plant
- 10–12 inches in diameter, limit to 3–4 plants
- 14–16 inches in diameter, limit to 5–7 plants
- 16–20 inches in diameter, limit to 6–9 plants

Elemental Plant Favorites

I've included some favorites for each of the elements. Pot one from each of the elements individually, or group them in a way that reflects the beauty of your spiritual path. Small potted plants are a lovely way to mark cardinal points in ritual.

Earth: Work with these plants in magick for abundance, fertility, growth, and grounding: fern, vervain, beets, sweet pea, ivy, tulips, mugwort, patchouli, honesty, moneywort, honeysuckle, and primrose.

Air: Use these in magick for intellect, spirituality, knowledge, and communication: parsley, sage, borage, bergamot, hops, lavender, yarrow, marjoram, rue, verbena, bean, and goldenrod.

Fire: Work with these plants in magick for strength, courage, defense, and protection: cactus, sunflower, basil, bay, ginger, peppermint, tobacco, snapdragon, carnations, calendula, peppers, cinquefoil, rosemary, mullein, dill, and wood betony.

Water: Work with these plants for intuition, dreams, divination, and healing: lilies, belladonna, catnip, daffodils, lettuce, comfrey, lemon balm, crocus, bleeding heart, apple, lilac, violets, thyme, strawberry, morning glory, cucumbers, tomato, jasmine, orchid, and hellebore.

Companion Planting

Polyculture is the practice of planting more than one species of plant (or animal) in a growing area. It is a way for large-scale farms to better emulate nature and naturally control pests and disease. When working on a smaller scale, we call it companion planting. It is a little more complicated than just planting pretty plants together, but if done properly, it saves precious growing space, helps control pests and disease, keeps soil moist, aids in weed control, and can be used to attract pollinators to your small-scale or container garden.

Some great companion plants that work naturally to repel garden pests include basil, parsley, cosmos, or borage with tomatoes; garlic with salad greens or potatoes; nasturtiums with brassicas; and dill or calendula with squash.

Kitchen Witch's Container

This container is perfect to set outside the kitchen door, as all the plants have protective energy. They also can be used in kitchen witchery to invoke lust. Easy to grow, basil and parsley make great companion plants for tomatoes, as the basil deters pests and the parsley attracts beneficial pollinators. The varieties below are only suggestions; feel free to substitute with your favorite varieties.

- 1 'Sungold' tomato (*Solanum lycopersicum*)
- 2 sweet basil (*Ocimum basilicum*)
- 2 Italian flat-leaf parsley (*Petroselinum crispum*)

Fill a container at least twenty-four inches in diameter with potting soil. Gently remove plants from nursery containers and loosen the roots to promote growth. Plant the tomato in the middle of the container and basil and parsley around the tomato. Water your new container.

Vertical Gardening

Your Green Witch dreams shouldn't be tethered to the horizontal. When limited in space, why not grow up instead of out? Going vertical is a great way to extend your gardening area. Using trellising, hanging baskets, tripods, and the like is also good for the plants, as it provides better air circulation, resulting in plants that are less susceptible to disease and therefore improved growth.

Some of my favorite vertical space-savers for a patio or balcony are made from discarded items, including old rain gutters mounted on walls or suspended from a chain. Pallets leaned against an outer wall and fitted with brackets to hold small pots of herbs, and vintage step ladders tucked in a corner to shelve potted plants.

Easy Herbal Spell Wall

Growing plants in a shoe organizer is an easy solution to small-space gardening. And for a fun, magickal twist, attach tags to each pocket that provide the plant's name and magickal correspondences.

You will need:

Adjustable industrial or heavy-duty curtain rod (with brackets and screws)
Canvas shoe organizer
4-inch S-hooks (2–4, depending on the width of your organizer)
Potting soil
Herbs of your choice
Permanent marker
Waterproof tags
Small binder clips

Hang your curtain rod 4 inches higher than the desired height of the top of the shoe organizer. Use the S-hooks to hang the organizer from the rod (you can also use the hooks to hang the organizer over a fence or railing as well).

Test drainage by pouring water into a pocket you'll be placing a plant. If the pocket holds water, poke a few small drainage holes at the bottom of each one. Add your soil, leaving approximately 1 inch between the top of the pocket and the soil. Next, add a plant to each pocket and water them in.

Use a permanent marker to write the plant's name and any magickal correspondences you wish to include onto the tag. Use binder clips to attach tags to the front of each pocket.

Indoor Hydroponic Garden Systems

So you want to grow magickal herbs, but you have little to no outdoor space and your home is too small for large plants. I've got you covered: indoor hydroponic garden systems are portable and compact, are easy to use, and will keep you in fresh herbs all year long. Small grow kits start at around $40, with larger systems selling for up to $200. Most have automatic LED grow lights and a digital display to remind you when to water and fertilize your plants.

Because hydroponic systems require no soil, they are clean and fuss-free. Seed pod kits are available, including culinary herb kits, tea kits, salad kits, and more. You can also purchase pod blanks and drop your own favorite seeds into them. Hydroponic garden systems can also be used to propagate starts for your outdoor garden too. For your own mini healing garden, try growing lavender, lemon balm, and thyme.

Your Sacred Space

Even the tiniest of gardens can awaken our connection to the sacred. As Green Witches, our gardens, no matter the size, are a place for ritual, healing, and communing with our natural world. All our senses are stimulated—our sense of smell is our strongest connection to memory. Fill your garden with scented herbs and flowers that stimulate comforting memories. The sound of the soft babble of a tabletop water feature or the gentle harmonics of wind chimes hung near a window can ease us into an inward rhythm. Awaken your taste buds with the flavorsome delights of your garden. What better way to commune with nature than to partake of the fruits of your labor? While in your sacred garden space, use your sight and touch to appreciate every nuance: droplets of water after the rain, the silkiness of a rose petal, the intricate patterns of the veins of leaves. Remember, these intimate insights draw us closer to the Divine.

Witches' gardens come in many forms. Some of us may have the classic Witch's garden from fairy tales. Some of us have large cottage gardens with rambling perennials that threaten to escape the boundaries of their beds, while others have structured gardens where every plant is neatly trimmed and perfectly placed. Still others may have a few potted plants on a windowsill or tucked along a fire escape. But no matter the Green Witch nor the size of their garden, we all have something in common: the desire to manifest the Divine through cultivation. The power of magick is in the palm of our dirt-stained hands.

Fiber Magick Wheel of the Year: Crocheting into the Dark

Opal Luna

Sit back and relax. Take a deep breath and picture yourself hiking a very familiar path. The leaves on the oak and maple are turning the most beautiful shades of autumn. Rich orange hues and toasty golden highlights are everywhere. You can smell the earthy scents of leaves in the crisp morning air, hanging by a thread overhead and crunching under your feet, The Mother is beginning her long winter's nap of rest and repose in the dark half of the year. Breathe deeply and experience the earth's rest, and when you are ready, come back to the here and now.

I live in South Florida, so this meditation is as close as I get to the crispness of fall. The Wheel of the Year still turns here, though, and in addition to local milestones like the hurricane and tourist seasons, I like to include the more traditional sabbats in my crafting. My craft of choice is crochet.

The days grow shorter after Litha even if the temperatures are not taking the hint. Minutes turn to hours until it is dark out long before bedtime. By the middle of September, you are ready to grab a pumpkin spice latte and pick up that yarn with the warm colorway. It is time to crochet into the dark of the year.

Mabon, or the autumn equinox, happens as the day and night hours balance. It is opposite the spring equinox on the wheel and, therefore, will produce the opposite emotion. Instead of life being reborn and springing forward, we see life fall back, regroup, and rest. Never say die, though, because new life

A LITTLE BIT OF MAGIC

Using a handmade item again and again in ritual increases the power of that item.

comes from that temporary death. It is a necessary step in the transformation of energy. Regardless of where we are geographically, this is when we can stop and relax and enjoy the fruits of our personal harvests—if not actual crops, then accomplishments at our jobs, successes in our families, or just being able to cope with the everyday life.

Crochet Abbreviations Key

While teaching how to crochet is beyond the scope of this article, the following abbreviations and basic stitches will be used throughout the three crafts. Please seek out resources online or from your local library to familiarize yourself with them.

BLO: Back loops only
Ch: Chain
St: Stitch
Sc: Single crochet
Sc inc: Single crochet increase
Sc dec: Single crochet decrease
Hdc: Half double crochet
Hdc dec: Half double crochet decrease
Dc: Double crochet
{ }: Repeat pattern between
Sl St: Slip stitch
Rev Sc: Reverse single crochet
FO: Fasten off

Mabon Cornucopia

A classic symbol of abundance at this time of year is the cornucopia, usually filled with the fruits of the season. The full horn of plenty symbolizes not only abundance but also generosity due to the bounty spilling out for all to partake. Generosity is the proof that we recognize the Mother's endless blessings. There is enough, and enough, and enough to share!

I recall my mother putting out the wicker horn of plenty filled with wax fruits and veggies. Imagining that still-life display sparks memories that can send me right back there. It brings feelings of joy and a sense of looking forward to the winter holidays. That mindset of "good things yet to come" is perfect for performing prosperity spells. The cornucopia will remind us that there is no shortage of the Mother's love.

Let's make a small version that can be used on an altar during spellcasting.

You will need:
Size H/8 5.00 mm crochet hook
52 yards (1 ounce) of 4-ply yarn
Stitch marker
Scissors
Yarn needle

Work in BLO in a spiral. Use a stitch marker to mark rounds.
Ch 2
Round 1. 6 Sc in 2nd Ch from hook
Round 2. 1 Sc in each St around (6)
Round 3. {Sc, Sc inc} around (9)
Round 4. 1 Sc in each St around (9)
Round 5. {Sc twice, Sc inc} around (12)
Round 6. 1 Sc in each St around (12)
Round 7. {Sc 3 times, Sc inc} around (15)
Round 8. 1 Sc in each St around (15)
Round 9. {Sc 4 times, Sc inc} around (18)
Round 10. 1 Sc in each St around (18)
Round 11. {Sc 5 times, Sc inc} around (21)
Round 12. 1 Sc in each St around (21)
Round 13. {Sc 6 times, Sc inc} around (24)
Round 14. {Sc 7 times, Sc inc} around (27)
Round 15. {Sc 8 times, Sc inc} around (30)
Round 16. 1 Sc in each St around (30)
Round 17. Sl St in next St, 1 Rev Sc around (30)
Turn the horn so that the tip is pointing away from you.
Sl St in spiral of free loops back to the beginning.
FO, leaving a long tail.
Weave the tail under Sl Sts to Rev Sc row.
Pull the work into a horn shape.
Secure, FO, and weave in the end.

Keep this little horn of plenty on your altar and place a symbol of something you would like to see multiply in your life inside. As you do so, say,

With this gift I place within, may it return to me times ten.

Get creative with your horn offerings. It doesn't always have to be money, though that is the go-to thing. Surely, a li'l pumpkin would be an appropriate offering placed in the horn.

Li'l Pumpkin

The pumpkin symbolizes abundance and prosperity. In addition to being packed full of nutrition to keep us healthy, they also are jam packed with seeds that connote potential and creativity.

When carved into a jack-o'-lantern, the pumpkin provides protection from evil and negative forces. A white pumpkin can be used to represent the Moon and is filled with Full Moon energy. Imagine Cinderella's carriage and let it take you to your heart's desire. Besides, it just wouldn't be fall without a pumpkin!

You will need:

Size F/5 3.75 mm crochet hook

52 yards (1 ounce) of 4-ply yarn in pumpkin color (Use 3-ply for a smaller pumpkin.)

3 yards of yarn in stem color

Scissors

Yarn needle

Using the pumpkin color:
Ch 13
Row 1. Hdc in 2nd Ch from hook, Hdc across, Ch 1 and turn (12)
Row 2. Hdc across, Ch 1 and turn
Row 3. In BLO Hdc across, Ch 1 and turn
Rows 4–16. Repeat rows 2 and 3, ending with a row 2

At this point you may want to embroider a face and make your lil pumpkin into a jack-o'-lantern. It's easier to create the face on a flat surface but still possible if you wait until it is stuffed. Just be sure to have the face facing out when you stitch the tube together.

Sl St first and last rows together to form a tube (12)
Make 8 Hdc dec over ends of rows, weave closed, FO
Stuff the pumpkin firmly.
Make 8 Hdc dec over opposite ends of rows, FO, leaving a very long end for sectioning. Weave the end closed.
Use the yarn needle to wrap yarn around the outside of pumpkin at BLO rows and up through the center. Pull tightly to form 8 bulges. Knot securely, FO, and weave in the end.

Using the stem color:
Pick up Sc at each Hdc dec (8).
Continue Sc in spiral until desired stem length.
Sl St end closed, FO, and weave in the end.

For the tendril:
Ch 13, 2 Sc in each chain, FO, tie ends together, and use them to tie the tendril to the pumpkin at the base of the stem.

The cornucopia with a pumpkin inside becomes a wonderful party favor for the fall feast. Include a card that wishes health and prosperity for the coming New Year—the Witch's New Year, of course. Samhain is the third and final harvest in the Wheel of the

Year and, as with the nature of circles, marks the beginning of the whole cycle starting over.

Samhain Skull

The world at large is celebrating Halloween with a vengeance, so it is easy to get in the spirit by picking up some new home décor almost anywhere. Some folks leave their Christmas lights up all year round. I'm pretty much always ready for Samhain without too much effort.

There is a serious undercurrent to all the revelry, though, for the Witch. As we move toward Samhain, the darkness grows. Our thoughts wander toward the veil as it thins, and we think about our beloved dead. It is appropriate to set up an ancestor altar with keepsakes and remembrances to those who came before. Time must be made for quiet reflection so any messages from Spirit can come through to us.

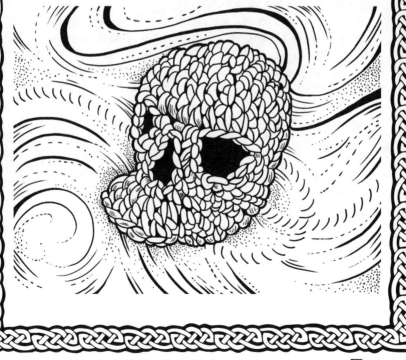

This Samhain skull was designed to act as a poppet for one who has crossed the veil. It could hold an LED light or herbs to hold sacred space on your altar. A word to the wise: no real flames, please. Crochet and fire do not mix.

You will need:
Size H/8 5.00 mm crochet hook
104 yards (2 ounces) of 4-ply yarn
Scissors
Yarn needle

Sl St in end of each round, Ch 1 to begin next round
Ch 2
Round 1. 8 Hdc in 2nd Ch from hook
Round 2. Hdc inc around (16)
Round 3. {Hdc, Hdc inc} around (24)
Round 4. {Hdc twice, Hdc inc} around (32)
Round 5–6. Hdc around (32)
Round 7. Hdc in 20 Sts, leaving remaining Sts unworked
Round 8. Ch 1, turn, Hdc in 20 Sts, Ch 4, skip 4 Sts on round 6, Sl St 4 on round 6, Ch 4, skip 4 Sts on round 6, Sl St in 1st Hdc of round 8
Round 9. Ch 1, turn, Sc in same St, Sc in 4 Chs, skip 1, Sl St in 2 Sts, skip 1, Sc in 4 Chs, Sc around
Round 10. Ch1, Sc in same St, Sc in next 2 Sts, Ch 2, skip 6, Sc around
Round 11. Sc dec, Sc 4, {Sc dec, Sc} 6 times, Sc dec
Round 12. Ch 1, Sc, Ch 1, 2 Dc in each of next 4 Sts, Ch 1, Sc around
Round 13. In BLO {Sc, Sc dec} around
Round 14. Sc dec around, FO, weave in the end

• • • ☽ • • •

The days will continue to grow shorter toward the winter solstice. Once upon a time, it would be a cold and dark race between the food supply and the weather. Nowadays that would only apply to areas that might be affected by blizzards or storms. It's good for us to think about how good most of us have it and be grateful. Gratitude begets abundance and leads us back into the light.

The Fiber Magick Wheel of the Year is a four-part series that encourages creativity at every turn. As we move through the year using each of the eight sabbats as mile markers, we will create projects that will enhance our magick and embody the essence of the season.

Stay crafty!

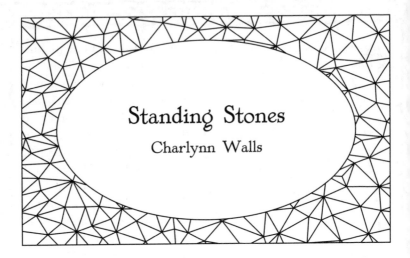

Standing Stones

Charlynn Walls

Standing stones have always evoked wonder and continue to resonate with today's Pagans. I have long been intrigued by these massive stone structures. Their purposes have long been disputed and argued about by archaeologists. Some are grave markers, and some have purposes that remain lost to time. The stones, however, are harbingers of a time long past. They have been silent sentinels that have watched the passing of cultures but continue to move forward in time.

Types of Standing Stones

When we discuss standing stones, you are probably picturing Stonehenge in your mind, and you would absolutely be correct. That henge contains monoliths that are paired and capped in concentric circles. The henges like Stonehenge and Avebury are thought to have been built for astronomical purposes. But there are many other types of standing stones that occur across the world. There are single monoliths, or menhir, that stand at attention. They can stand alone, in rows, or in a configuration that outlines the boundaries of a sacred space. The stones can come in a variety of shapes, including spherical ones. Adding to the comprehensive picture of sacred stones are also those that mark the graves of souls long passed.

Depending on the region and the culture, the stones' purposes may have been significantly different. One thing that they do have in common is that their true purposes are mostly lost to the annals of time. They do, however, show the determination and persistence of humankind. It took considerable effort to move and shape the stones into the sites we see today.

Pilgrimage Sites with Standing Stones

Stonehenge is one of the most well-known standing stone sites in the world. It is located in Salisbury, England, and has been the subject of much controversy over the years. However, each year there are those who participate in rites at the site for the winter and summer solstices.

Avebury Henge is a site that is similar to Stonehenge and not that far away from it. Also found in England, this is another site full of stone rings and is thought to have been used for religious ceremonies.

Carnac is a site that contains a massive amount of individual standing stones that are arranged in rows but not connected. The location of this site is near Carnac in France. The original intent of the stones has been lost over time, but it does give an impressive visual.

The Stone Spheres can be found in Costa Rica. While these spheres are man-made out of the surrounding volcanic rock, their provenance cannot be determined. Many of the spheres have been moved from their original locations or damaged. The largest of these stones is sixteen tons, which only adds to the mystery.

The Deer Stones are located throughout Mongolia and Siberia. They get their name from the images of deer that are carved into the stone. These monoliths are scattered throughout the landscape, and though there is speculation that they are meant to honor some of their leaders, the original intent remains a mystery.

Gochang Dolmen Site is found in South Korea. This site is known for having hundreds of burials. The burials are identified by two standing stones that are capped by a third, called *dolmen*.

Energies of Standing Stones

Engaging with standing stones is a great way to connect to the energies of the ancestors. Many of these stones are often thought to have denoted graves or gateways to the afterlife. As a result, the energy surrounding them can be used to work with those beyond the veil. The stones act like a gate or guidepost in order to anchor the individual to their reality while walking between the others.

Due to the nature of standing stones, they can also be used as a catalyst to work with them as a part of exploring the mysteries. They can be used to draw upon the power of connectivity and used in initiatory rites. Other energies present include the representation of the immovable and long-lasting power of nature. These energies can be harnessed to give your rites the longevity to bear fruit.

Standing Stone Rite: Gateway to the Ancestors

You will need:
Dish of salt
Incense
White candle
Dish of water
Container (A flowerpot or shallow bowl will work.)
Dirt or sand to fill the container
Stones (1 or many)
Toothpick

Bring together the items that you will need for the ritual prior to beginning. This ritual can be completed indoors or outdoors depending on your preference. Arrange your items in your workspace outside or on your altar indoors. You will want your items arranged so that the container, stones, and dirt or sand are in the center. Place the incense, water, salt, and candle in their corresponding quarters.

Once your space has been set up, find a comfortable place to stand or sit for the duration of the rite. You will want to ground and center yourself before beginning. Make sure that you take a cleansing breath and relax your body. Feel the stress of the day melt off you. Feel it move from the top of your head and flow down and out of your body through your feet. Take another breath and feel the connectedness of the self with the earth. As you draw breath, you also draw that energy into yourself, completing the loop.

Now that you are centered, you will want to call the quarters in order to establish your circle. You are free to expand on or create your own calls for the quarters. I start in the north per the traditions that I have personal experience with. You may feel called to start in another order, and that is also fine.

Hail to the Guardians of the North, the guardians of nourishment and totality. Grant me the strength of my ancestors as I walk this path. Hail and welcome!

Place a pinch of salt to the north.

Hail to the Guardians of the East, the guardians of communication and consciousness. Grant me the wisdom of my ancestors as I walk this path. Hail and welcome!

Light the incense and wave it to the east.

Hail to the Guardians of the South, the guardians of the primal flame and willpower. Grant me the courage of my ancestors as I walk this path. Hail and welcome!

Light the candle and hold it up to the south.

Hail to the Guardians of the West, the guardians of emotion and introspection. Grant me the intuition of my ancestors as I walk this path. Hail and welcome!

Dip your fingertips into the container of water and sprinkle a few drops to the west.

You may also choose at this time to invite the God and Goddess into your circle. You can use the pantheon you are most comfortable with. For this rite, you would want to use deities that deal with carrying messages or connecting with the spirit realm.

Lord and Lady, lend us your divine will to travel through the gateway to the spirit realm in order to hear the wisdom of the ancestors. Hail and welcome!

A LITTLE BIT OF MAGIC

Modern sites that practitioners can visit and are similar in nature to those with standing stones include Woodhenge at Cahokia Mounds, IL, and a replica of Stonehenge at Missouri S&T in Rolla, MO.

Face your altar and retrieve your stones. You will want to place them in your container temporarily so you can cleanse both that vessel and your standing stones. You can utilize one stone or several if you want to make a circular structure, depending on your preference. My preference is for many stones, so I will add several to the container for cleansing. Take the salt and sprinkle a small amount on the stones and in the container. Take the candle and move it around the container and stones. Similarly, take the incense and move the items through the smoke. Finally, sprinkle some water on the container and your standing stones. Once this is completed, you can say,

By the power of the elements, these items are cleansed. Allow them to provide a way for our consciousness to transcend.

With the items cleansed, you are now able to channel your intent into them for the ritual. Focus on them and see yourself completing a gateway beyond the veil. Allow yourself to be open to the possibilities and the messages that they will provide to you.

Now you will begin the work of constructing your standing stone mini site for you to utilize its ability to create a gateway. This can be done in a container to keep on your altar, or if you have space in your flowerbed or yard, you can make a more permanent version. For the purposes here, we will be creating a standing stone gateway in a movable container. Take your container and fill it two-thirds of the way full of either dirt or sand. I prefer to use sand so that I can keep the surface clean, and I can also use it to help with the meditative process through creating surface designs in the sand.

At each of the quarters, you are going to draw the symbol for the element near the outermost edge of the container. Starting in the north, draw the symbol for earth, which is represented by a downward facing triangle with a line parallel to the base. Next, turn

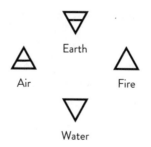

to the east and draw the symbol for air as it is represented by an upward-facing triangle with a line parallel to its base. Turning to the south, draw the representation for fire as it is represented by a triangle with the point turned upward. Finally, turn to the west and draw the symbol for water, a triangle with the point facing down.

Once the quarters and elements are represented in the sand, start placing your stones. Make sure that you are pushing them far enough into the sand that they stand up. I am placing three stones in each quarter: two upright stones with a stone topping them both. These create a door or window in each cardinal direction, which will allow the ancestors to bring their messages through. You could also place a single stone in each quarter or create a spiral of individual standing stones. You can create whatever configuration is speaking to you.

After you complete the construction of your stone site, the meditative work begins. Take a breath and focus on the stones in front of you. You can imagine yourself standing among them in your mind's eye. Since we are working with standing stone energy, focus on the northern quarter. Call out and repeat three times,

Stones guarding the Otherworld like silent sentinels, allow us passage to commune with our predecessors and make their messages comprehendible.

Hold that space between the realms and allow yourself to be open to the messages from your ancestors. Take note of any images or whispered messages that may come through. When you are ready to close the doorway, say,

Thank you for your wisdom and counsel. Return to your realm with peace and love.

Take a moment to ground yourself. This would be the time to do cakes and ales in order to help facilitate that process.

Now it is time to release the spirits and the quarters:

Lord and Lady, thank you for your divine guidance in this rite. Stay if you will, go if you must. Hail and farewell!
Guardians of the West, thank you for providing a connection to my ancestors but allowing me peace of mind during the interaction. Hail and farewell!

Guardians of the South, thank you for providing the courage to blaze the trail and speak to the ancestors. Hail and farewell!

Guardians of the East, thank you for bestowing the wisdom of my ancestors upon me. Hail and farewell!

Guardians of the North, thank you for the strength of heart to work with the ancestors in order to hear their message. Hail and farewell!

Resources

"Avebury." English Heritage. Accessed June 26, 2023. https://www.english-heritage.org.uk/visit/places/avebury/.

Cartwright, Mark. "Carnac." World History Encyclopedia. August 4, 2014. https://www.worldhistory.org/Carnac/.

Cock-Starkey, Claire. "6 of the World's Most Mysterious Standing Stones." Mental Floss. Last modified October 8, 2020. https://www.mentalfloss.com/article/91669/6-worlds-most-mysterious-standing-stones.

Encyclopaedia Britannica Online. S.v. "Stonehenge." By Mike Parker Pearson. Accessed June 21, 2023. https://www.britannica.com/topic/Stonehenge.

Misachi, John. "The Mystery of the Stone Spheres of Costa Rica." World Atlas. July 17, 2019. https://www.worldatlas.com/articles/stone-spheres-of-costa-rica-largest-ancient-stone-balls.html.

"Mongolian Deer Stones." Smithsonian Museum Conservation Institute. Accessed June 20, 2023. https://mci.si.edu/mongolian-deer-stones.

All-Weather Spirituality

Blake Octavian Blair

Practitioners on earth-based spiritual paths and practitioners of what is often termed a "nature spirituality" revere and find awe, wonder, and the Divine in the natural world. However, sometimes there is a bit of dissonance with that fact when a bit of drizzle, snow, or even a hotter-than-desired day arrives and we find the nature-loving practitioner . . . celebrating in their living room. While our homes are indeed sacred spaces, it seems that celebrating nature (especially in regard to seasonal festivals) would preferably be done outdoors in nature if at all possible. In the following pages, we'll explore precisely how we might be able to prepare ourselves to more easily work with nature, in all of its myriad conditions, so that we may celebrate in and with it, rather than apart from it, a little more often.

In order to practice an all-weather spirituality, preparedness goes a long way. It can be said that one truly does not know a place until one has been there in all weather and seasons. It is also often said that there is no such thing as bad weather, only inadequate clothing. Both of these adages come into play when practicing all-weather spirituality. In order to explore comfortably in all weather and seasons, one will need proper gear and clothing. This may initially sound daunting or of great expense; however, it need not be. I gradually gathered outdoor clothing over a few years. One nice thing is that you can acquire pieces as the seasons turn and not all at once. This gives you time to find, purchase, or make them before you need them and to take advantage of sales for the things you must buy new. You're not going to need a super insulated coat in August or September. However, you might see a sale in October before the season begins or in March as the winter is winding down. Or you might begin knitting that wool sweater for the next winter outings in the spring so as to allow yourself time for completion.

However, acquiring proper clothing and gear and knowing what you'll need for the locations and terrain you like to traverse creates a bit of a chicken and egg scenario. You can have some idea ahead of time, but you won't have a complete picture of what you'd like or need until you encounter the conditions in nature in a given location. The best thing to do is to make a cursory assessment of items you already have for each season and to make a list of locations you'd like to scout for ritual and celebratory outings. Give a go at scouting them with what you've got. You'll be making notes on each location about needs and conditions to address anyways.

Creating Your Logbook

If one wants to be prepared and able to most comfortably celebrate in all weather, it will be helpful to create a record of favored ritual locations and their conditions in various weather. Enter the all-weather spirituality logbook. This need not be elaborate and can be in a simple notebook. It can take the form of a page for each location. Make a notation of the address or simple description of the ritual site. Then, make a chart with the weather and season down the side and across the top the different categories of concern you'll want to address. Examples for the vertical axis could be sunny and dry, hot weather, rainy and damp/chilly, rainy and hot, cold and snowy/icy, and so on. Examples of considerations you might put across the horizontal axis include clothing, specialty footwear, site mobility accessibility, trail or ground conditions, and specialty logistical or ritual items.

This chart format can be used again and again for each site. Further, the logbook will be your companion in your hands-on and feet-on-the-ground explorations of the various sites. You might find an organization format that works better for you, but this suggestion should get you started. Let us use a fictional example throughout that we'll call "Badger Hill":

Description: The first category is a brief description of the site. This functionally includes things such as type of terrain to traverse, any grades, notable and natural features of the site, and the type of general site the ritual will be at (forest grove, meadow, riverbank, park pavilion, etc.). For Badger Hill, we might write, "Small grassy meadow accessed by pine straw and dirt trail with a slight steady grade uphill. Meadow surrounded by tall pines at perimeter."

Time of Visit: You'll want to make a simple notation of the time of day you visited. This will assist making detailed sense later of other notations in other categories you make. For example, if you visit at midday, and the sun overhead seems relentless and hot, the same area may be in cast shade in late afternoon. For our little visit together to Badger Hill, we might write, "Visited early afternoon, 1:30 p.m."

Season and Weather: Make it a point to note both the season and the weather at the time of your visit. Though you might be writing in a season-specific chart section, details on how early or late in a season are useful. Over time you'll get the hang of the balance between being both detailed and concise with your notations. At Badger Hill we might note, "Early summer (early June). Shaded on path hiking in, direct sun in the meadow. A heat that gradually builds in the sun. Little shade until retreat into forest from meadow."

Terrain: This of course will be affected by factors in both time of day, season, and weather. It's important to note what is under foot (gravel, dirt, pavement, grass, rocks, mud, dry sand, etc.) as well as the grade one must traverse up or down to, from, and at the site. For Badger Hill, we might notate, "Small gradual incline uphill on the short trail through the woods to the meadow. Pine straw on trail fairly dry, only very occasional avoidable rocks and tree roots across trail. Grassy flat meadow, dry."

Mobility and Accessibility: This can be an important consideration if there is a chance you will have attendees with special needs and varying mobility needs. Exceptionally steep grades may be an issue for these persons, and so can mud for anyone in an assistive device such as a wheelchair or scooter. The same issue is presented by excessive rocks or tree roots, for example. It can also be helpful to give an assessment of available parking at the site. This can be an issue even for those who don't have specific mobility issues. If there isn't enough parking for attendees, they cannot access the site! An assessment for Badger Hill could read, "Parking: room for six to eight cars parked parallel on the shoulder of road near the trailhead. Parking and trail grade may pose accessibility issues for wheelchairs or scooters, but tree roots and rocks on trail are sparse enough they would not pose mobility issues. Trail grade is mild, did not bother my knees, and is about one quarter of a mile in length. At a leisurely pace, roughly an eight-to-ten minute walk can be allotted for the trail. Meadow itself poses no mobility issues under dry conditions." You can see I made a note about how it affected my own knees, as exceptionally long steep grades can bother them. This note about myself actually helps me gauge conditions for others.

Clothing Needs: Taking into consideration previously notated information, the entry here for this visit to Badger Hill might read, "Light summer clothing is appropriate. I chose a light long-sleeve T-shirt and pants to deter any mosquitoes that might be encountered, though they weren't bad. I appreciated having my sun hat and would suggest the same for others. Footwear note: good walking shoes with a tread are helpful and suggested."

Logistical Items and Notes: List anything you need that doesn't fit into other categories or needs further mention and detailing: for example, ice cleats for winter terrain or headlamp flashlights for visibility in twilight or darkness. An entry for our visit to Badger Hill might read as follows: "Sunscreen, a sun hat, bug net for hat and bug spray would be good to pack and have on hand. Deep candle holders that shield the flame from breezes and wind advisable. A trash bag to pack out any waste after a picnic."

You are of course heartily encouraged to adapt and customize these categories and format it to your liking to suit your needs. You'll notice that you might naturally repeat certain things in overlapping categories, such as footwear you might need under clothing and terrain and then again in logistical items. I find this redundancy isn't extraneous but rather helpful in creating a full picture and assuring proper preparation and packing. Over time you will see what form of record works best for you and develop your own style and formatting. However, getting going on this informal logistical version, a ritual site grimoire of sorts, will create a valuable asset to your practice.

Now, with your all-weather spirituality logbook at hand, preferably tucked into a backpack with a few supplies, and a quick check of the weather forecast, we're off on a little adventure!

Four Seasons of Sacredness

Most of us agree that nature is sacred. Further, I think we can all agree that sacred sites can be either ancient or modern, near or far, simple or elaborate. Sure, places such as Stonehenge in England, Devils Tower in Wyoming, or Machu Picchu in Peru are sacred, but we need not forget that our local river, park, and clearing in a forest glen along a hiking trail in our hometown are also sacred sites. All of nature is sacred, including the places that are close to us, that are dear to our affections, and that we visit regularly hold a special kind of power and are worth getting to know even better. Even in urban areas, one should not overlook city parks, greenways, and other such resources. Nature and "wild spaces" are all around us.

Choose a spot you'd like to be an entry into your logbook that you think would be a good for outdoor ritual and spiritual practice. Set up a page or pages in your logbook for your scouting mission. Be sure to leave a little room to notate information on future successive visits, whether that's extra space on the page or a few blank pages for future data recording. Part of this exercise is going to entail repeat visits. Since you've already done an initial assessment of gear you already own, pack a few supplies into a backpack for your current weather, perhaps a small biodegradable offering for the land, and your logbook, and set out to scout the location.

On the surface your mission is simple: visit the site at minimum once per season over the next year. However, ideally, you'd go more than once per season and in different weather conditions. You will fill out your logbook with all the information we outlined earlier pertinent to the different categories. The deeper level to this exercise is that you are going to gain an intimate understanding of this location, seeing it in all its seasons and during different weather. You will notice the varying moods and character of the land, you'll develop a relationship with the spirits of place, and you may even notice over time that not only do you gain a familiarity with the land, its spirits, and inhabitants (ethereal and corporeal), but they gain a familiarity with you! You will have a relationship with these sites. You'll have a practical and spiritual understanding of the various sites. You will gain a sense of what type of practices the site would be conducive for, the size of group it would accommodate, the type of equipment and supplies you'd need, and the accessibility details for different needs of potential participants.

Exceptions to Every Rule

There is an old saying that there are exceptions to every rule. While we aren't laying out a set of rules here, the phrase still has value for our discussion. Yes, it would be great for us to celebrate and make magic more outside and within nature. Yes, we should all make an effort to explore our environs and seek out a variety of ritual sites outdoors and be willing to do our work in a variety of conditions and weather with appropriate preparation. But sometimes, we have to consider alternatives.

I'm pretty lucky in that I've had really good preparation for all-weather spirituality from the grove I belong to. No matter the weather, we do the eight sabbat rituals outdoors in nature. I've learned a few preparedness tricks along the way! I even performed an initiation rite at 23 degrees Fahrenheit on top of six inches of snow. However, I have extremely good winter weather gear rated for those conditions, wasn't in any danger, and endured relatively little discomfort. As I said, no bad weather, only improper clothing. However, I encourage you to stay safe. Unless you're absolutely sure you have the proper gear and the confidence that you are safe, please keep yourself healthy and out of any danger. Do not risk frostbite or heatstroke. Don't hike in conditions and terrain you aren't comfortable with. There are alternatives.

One autumn equinox, it was not drizzling but pouring rain. My grove needed to adapt to the conditions. Those who gathered put on their rain gear (and some committed to getting wet and communing with the rain) and went outside to the beach, did a joyous ritual dance and chant in the rain that lasted about seven minutes, then dashed back inside and toweled off for a potluck in a member's home. The weather wasn't avoided: the turning of the wheel was celebrated in nature—rather intensely if briefly—and then indoors for a more leisurely time of community. Such a hybrid is possible and acceptable. On rare occasions, you might only be able to celebrate indoors, and that is always preferable to no celebration at all. Always use your judgment.

In Conclusion

Here is hoping that you feel a bit more equipped next time the weather isn't picture perfect but you still want to celebrate in nature at a beloved location. Use your logbook to create an easy packing checklist so that next time it might be a little damp and misting, you put on your raincoat and appropriate footwear and go make some magic!

Air Magic

Playing Card Divination

Charlie Rainbow Wolf

There's something mysterious around the art of reading tarot cards, but did you know that you can read playing cards just as accurately? Playing cards have a long history of being used for divination as well as parlor games. They're similar to tarot in many ways. They have four suits and court cards, although playing cards have three face cards and the tarot has four. The trump cards—or tarot major arcana—are missing, but the suit cards are very much like the pip tarot cards in decks like IJJ Swiss Tarot and others.

One of the advantages of playing cards is they are readily available in many high street shops. They're inexpensive too, sometimes being found for nothing more than pocket change. Most families will have a deck of playing cards lying around somewhere, even if it's just a random souvenir from a childhood holiday.

Reading your own cards is quite the discussion among readers, and many advocate against it, but I say go ahead. Who knows you better than you know yourself? I have a deck I use only for readings, and I often use readings as writing prompts. If you keep a journal or a Book of Shadows, you might think about doing the same.

Different readers read differently, and what works for one reader might not work for you. Always follow your own truth. Use the interpretations I've provided as a guide and remember nothing is carved in stone. Do what resonates with you and not what someone else—including me—told you. If you already read tarot or oracle cards, you'll probably find reading playing cards comes quite easily, especially pertaining to the layouts.

If you're completely new to this, that's okay too. You can still learn to read playing cards very efficiently and accurately. Like any other skill, it takes a bit of time, and a bit of patience, and a bit of practice. I believe in you—so let's get started!

The Suits

Playing cards come in many different designs, from the humorous to the ornate, from the plain to the cartoonish. What they all have in common is four suits; traditionally, those suits are hearts and diamonds for the red cards and spades and clubs for the black ones. Each suit represents a different area of your life and a different element of the zodiac. Each suit consists of ten number cards and three court cards.

The odd-numbered cards can be read as "reversed" or "contrary," which means they have a right way up and a wrong way up. Look at the ace; it has a shape that can be presented both right-way up and upside down. Usually if something is inverted, it means the meaning of the card is cloudy or delayed in some way.

Because the suit of diamonds is symmetrical, it has no inverted or upright position: all the pips look the same no matter which way the card falls. In this instance, examine the surrounding cards to see how the message should be interpreted. This is something that becomes easier with experience; the more practice you get, the more you'll intuit what the cards are saying.

Hearts

It's not a surprise this suit deals with emotions and matters of the heart—including spirituality. As far as appearance goes, hearts often (but not always) indicate a person with fair skin, light hair, and pale eyes. These cards indicate areas of compassion and awareness, or someone who may be spiritual or esoteric in some way. Hearts are also associated with the season of summer, and the element of water, and the astrological signs of Cancer, Scorpio, and Pisces. The number on the cards may indicate a given number of months. It's best not to be too specific, because many factors come into play when it comes to timing.

Diamonds

The suit of diamonds deals with worth: wealth, possessions, and finances. I tend to see it as prosperity, rather than just money or possessions. This suit focuses on tradition and structure, as well as tenacity and ambition. Diamonds indicate loyalty, determination, and focus. When applied to people, this suit represents those of dark features, who are perhaps a bit stocky or robust in their build. Diamonds represent the season of winter and are associated with the element of earth and the zodiac signs of Taurus, Virgo, and

Capricorn. The number on the cards may also indicate a given number of *years*. A year is a long time, so take this as a very rough guideline.

Spades

Spades in a reading often point to conflict. This clash doesn't have to be a quarrel or physical confrontation. It might refer to a clash of ideas, or beliefs, or commitments—within your own psyche or with another person. This suit deals with mental agility, and the mind may invent a situation that isn't even there or blow something that is there out of all proportion. The physical attributes of the people spades represent are often dark, with hazel eyes and brown hair, but this is not all-inclusive. Think about personality: people of above-average intelligence, those who are witty, analytical, and perhaps a bit aloof. Spades point to the season of autumn and represent the element of air and the Sun signs of Gemini, Libra, and Aquarius. The number on the cards may indicate a given number of *days*, but remember that timing is fluid, and nothing's carved in stone.

Clubs

Clubs represent the area in life where movement is needed. This could be climbing a career ladder, improving social standing, or any other area where advancement is desired. Clubs indicate where motivation is necessary to achieve a desired outcome. Physically, they may represent those with red hair and green eyes, but again, this is just a guideline. Who has a fiery temper? Where is passion, motivation, and enthusiasm? Clubs point to these traits. They represent the season of spring and are associated with the element of fire and the astrological signs of Aries, Leo, and Sagittarius. The number on the cards may also indicate a given number of *weeks*, but things can hasten or be delayed according to circumstance.

The Numbered Cards

Aces

When playing cards, an ace can come before the two or after the king. In reading it is the same; aces indicate beginnings and endings. The natural cycle of things is for something to end so something else might begin. I usually read the ace as newness and look at the suit and surrounding cards to see how this is unfolding.

If the ace appears right-way up, then an ending is giving way to a new beginning. Should the ace appear the wrong way up, it indicates there is someone or something creating a delay or a blockage around the new beginning. It is still likely to happen; it may just take longer than had the card been upright.

Ace of Hearts: Love and happiness
Ace of Diamonds: Positive changes
Ace of Spades: Difficulties
Ace of Clubs: Money and wealth

Twos

In numerology, two indicates duality and choices, and it's the same when reading playing cards. There's a choice to be made when a two appears. The suit reveals where the indecision is lingering, or what area of life the choice is affecting. Twos cannot be inverted, because of the even number of pips.

Two of Hearts: Romantic partnership
Two of Diamonds: Business partnership
Two of Spades: Separation
Two of Clubs: Obstacles

Threes

Threes in a card reading mean things are starting to manifest. This can be positive or negative, depending on what's been going on. For example, the Three of Hearts may imply a celebration or reunion, while the Three of Spades could mean uncertainty and overthinking. The surrounding cards will give more insights.

Because of the odd number of pips, threes can be read the right way up or upside down. How many pips are facing upright, and how many are inverted? If the majority of the pips are upright, so is the card. If they're inverted, then the card is considered to be reversed. If a card is contrary, it's suggesting there's something affecting how things could unfold.

Three of Hearts: Reunion
Three of Diamonds: Legalities
Three of Spades: Relationship triangle (not necessarily romantic)
Three of Clubs: Favorable proposition

Fours

Fours point to stability. Think of the four wheels on a vehicle, the four legs of a table, or the four corners of the earth. Four can be grounding and steady, or it can be rigid and stubborn. There's no inversion for the four because the pips are two upright and two reversed. Examine the nearby cards to fine-tune the meaning of a four in a reading.

Four of Hearts: Travel
Four of Diamonds: Financial improvement
Four of Spades: Doubts
Four of Clubs: Gullibility

Fives

Fives bring both positive and negative energy to a reading. Are there three pips upright, or only two? Three pips means the card is upright and the energy is more likely to be favorable; two pips and the card is reversed and the energy is more challenging. Fives can be capricious; their essence can change without warning. This card relates to manifestation; the other cards reveal what is manifesting.

Five of Hearts: Possible jealousy
Five of Diamonds: Inception
Five of Spades: Blessings in disguise
Five of Clubs: Alliances

Sixes

Sixes are gentle, yet flighty. There's no upright or reversed meanings because of the equal number of pips, adding to their enigmatic energy. Often sixes warn something unexpected is about to happen—anything from a little windfall to a big argument! The surrounding cards provide more clues.

Six of Hearts: Unexpected favors
Six of Diamonds: Relationship issues
Six of Spades: Small improvements
Six of Clubs: Financial success

Sevens

Sevens restore balance. Because there is an odd number of pips, the card can be upright or inverted, but even upside down, sevens are usually favorable. People talk about the seventh son of the seventh son or being in seventh heaven—both alluding to positive and slightly mysterious things. More than one seven intensifies the energy, but pay attention to whether the card is upright or not. Neighboring cards always provide additional information.

Seven of Hearts: Superficiality
Seven of Diamonds: Financial quarrels resolved
Seven of Spades: Dubious advice
Seven of Clubs: Business success

Eights

When I see eights, I see just deserts. Eight takes the stability of four and the duality of two, so it's not as rigid or fixed as a four. Like the four, it's always upright. A lack of eights may indicate a need for stability or focus. Two or more eights and the energy takes on a stubborn vibe. Wherever the eight card falls, pay attention; it's neither a fleeting nor an insignificant thing.

Eight of Hearts: Unexpected gift
Eight of Diamonds: Change in situation
Eight of Spades: Temptation
Eight of Clubs: Professional jealousy

Nines

In numerology nines indicate the end of a cycle. I see it as an apex, three triangles. It's a compound number with a complex energy. Nine can be read inverted or right-way up depending on the pips. It's usually a positive card unless surrounded by challenging ones. Negatively impacted, the very thing you fear may be about to manifest. Positively influenced, then it's time to complete this phase and move onto the next.

Nine of Hearts: Opportunity (the wish card)
Nine of Diamonds: Travel
Nine of Spades: Misfortune (the nightmare card)
Nine of Clubs: Achievement

Tens

Tens are also cards of completion, but not the same type of completion indicated by aces. Ace focuses on beginnings caused by something ending; tens indicate a fulfillment, something drawing to a close. The Ten of Hearts deals with emotional gratification, while the ten of diamonds might mean financial success.

Ten of Hearts: Good luck
Ten of Diamonds: Financial gain

Ten of Spades: Stress
Ten of Clubs: Abundance

Jacks

Jacks indicate motion; they're inspiring and artistic. They are the messengers—their suit reveals what kind of message. The number of jacks indicates how important the message is. Usually the situation is under control when a jack appears, but a bit of inattention could jeopardize this stability. Pertaining to people, jacks refer to youths of any gender.

Jack of Hearts: Warm-hearted friend
Jack of Diamonds: Unreliable news
Jack of Spades: Animosity
Jack of Clubs: An admirer

Queens

Queens represent knowledge and wisdom, uniqueness and creativity. They're nurturing, and they're always upright. Queens are enigmatic, sometimes spiritual, someone who is magical and mystical and esoteric. Relating to people, queens refer to middle age and usually to women.

Queen of Hearts: Affection
Queen of Diamonds: Gossip
Queen of Spades: Dissolution
Queen of Clubs: Good advice

Kings

Kings are quite forceful, often self-contained, and they exude confidence. A lack of kings may point to a lack of self-assurance, while too many kings could point to vanity or arrogance. Concerning people, kings point to elders and usually to men.

King of Hearts: Kindness
King of Diamonds: Authority
King of Spades: Ambition
King of Clubs: Generosity

Jokers

The joker is an odd card, and it's thought to represent the Fool from the tarot. Sometimes there's one joker to a pack of cards and sometimes there are two. A few card games use the joker as a wild card, and when reading, I feel that is exactly what he represents! The joker indicates something unexpected is about to happen or is happening. Things could change direction completely when he appears. Whether it's used or not is a matter of personal preference, but I rather like this erratic little chap.

Putting It All Together

Wheee! That was a lot of information all at once, wasn't it? Putting it all together is where you develop your skill as a reader. It's at your discretion to look at the number, marry it to the correct suit, and determine what it means. For example, the Three of Hearts means something much different from the Three of Spades—they're both threes, but the suits represent entirely different energies. It might seem overwhelming at first, but with practice it will become second nature.

The frequency with which a card or suit appears is an indication of how much emphasis it carries. For example, if the reading consists mainly of diamonds, the focus is on monetary—or at least tangible—things. If the reading is dominated by hearts, it takes on an emotional or spiritual theme. An example is a career question dominated by hearts; the cards indicate there's too much emotional attachment to the situation, or perhaps this person really loves their job.

Layouts

If you're already a card reader, feel free to jump in with your favorite spread. However, if you're new to this, you might not know where to start. My go-to spread is the three-card spread. Don't let its simplicity fool you. I've found it to be very accurate indeed, and it's possibly the one I use most.

Three-Card Spread

The left-hand card reveals what happened in the past to make things the way they are here and now. The center card indicates what is dominating and influencing things at this time. The right-hand card provides a look at the potential outcome.

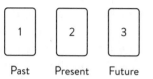

This layout can also be done with nine cards to get extra clarity:

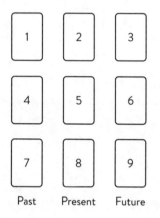

Cards 1, 4, and 7 recap what has already come to pass. Cards 2, 5, and 8 summarize how things are now. Cards 3, 6, and 9 provide insight on potential outcomes. Using multiple cards like this often provides insight into more than one conclusion. Other uses for the three-card spread might look like this:

What You Have	What You Want	How to Get It
Goals	Obstacles	Assets
Opportunity	Challenge	Outcome
Problem	Resources	Action
Unity	Division	Solution

Horseshoe Spread

I'm also partial to the horseshoe spread. It's easier than it looks and provides great insight, especially if the reading is being done to analyze a particular approach to a situation.

Card 1 reveals what happened to lead to card 2, card 3 provides a glimpse as to how that situation is viewed, and card 4 at the pinnacle reveals what is standing in the way. Card 5 looks at what is impacting things, card 6 points to the best plan of action, and the card 7 reveals what might happen.

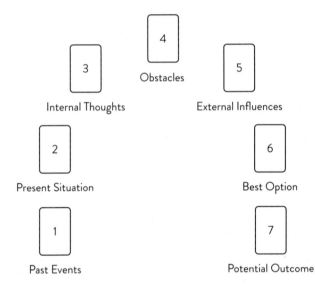

To add clarity, every card in this layout can be covered with another card, making it a fourteen-card spread, as on the next page. Analyze the meanings of both cards for each position. Sometimes an extra card is needed for further insight or clarity; don't be frightened to keep probing for the answers! If you really want to be thorough, do a three-card reading for each position, using one of the methods illustrated earlier.

Internal Thoughts

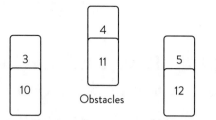

Obstacles

External Influences

Present Situation

Best Option

Past Events

Potential Outcome

Conclusion

I must stress that there really isn't a right or wrong way to do this. If you have already learned different meanings for the cards, use them. There are as many ways to read the cards as there are card readers. The cards are just a tool, and while it is possible to be a good card reader without being psychic or intuitive, it's been my experience that good readers will bond with their cards and start to create a language. The more you practice, the more it will become second nature. This is why I believe if you're serious about wanting to be a proficient reader, it's important to use the same deck, one reserved for doing readings, and practice often. Consider journaling your experiences so you can reflect back at your progress. It will grow as you grow, and very soon you'll have your own divination handbook—that's where the real magic begins!

A Deep Dive into Divination with Decans Using Tarot

Mo of Austral-Taur

Astrology and tarot are two archetypal languages frequently used for divination. Despite the cyclical nature of astrology and the randomness of tarot, these two systems can play nicely with each other! In this article, I want to explore the relationship between astrology and tarot, with a focus on the syncretism between the decans of the zodiac and the minor arcana. In doing so, I hope you can appreciate the origins of the decans, their ability to enhance your storytelling with tarot, and how they can be used to bring astrological timing into your tarot-based predictions.

Decans and Their Applications in Astrology

Tarot is not the only form of divination that gives us a capacity for storytelling. The subdivisions of the zodiacal wheel in astrology are rich with meaning and symbolism. While most people are familiar with the narratives behind each of the twelve signs of the zodiac, there are even smaller subdivisions of the zodiac that provide further nuance.

The decans of the zodiac are one of these forms of slicing up the zodiac. Decans are 10-degree divisions of the zodiacal wheel. Since there are 360 degrees, there are 36 decans. The ancient Egyptians first conceptualized the decans and associated each of them with a deity. The zodiac we know today merged the Babylonian twelve-sign division with the thirty-six divisions and diurnal rotation scheme of the Egyptians thanks to Hellenistic conquest of these regions, allowing these ideas to come together. This was transported eastward and incorporated into astrological traditions of people under Hellenic rule and those who came in contact with them. This results in a scheme that gives three decans to each of the twelve signs, making each part of the sign have its own special flavor and narrative.

Like other subdivisions of the zodiac, decans have planetary rulers and associations. There are two main schemes of decanic rulerships that can be used: Chaldean or Triplicity (see diagram below). The Chaldean scheme assigns the first and last 10 degrees of the zodiac to Mars and assigns rulers to each decan in reverse Chaldean order (which tells you about planetary speed, from slowest to fastest and repeating once you hit Saturn again). The other scheme for assigning rulerships to decans is the triplicity system, which has its origins in the Vedic astrological tradition. The first

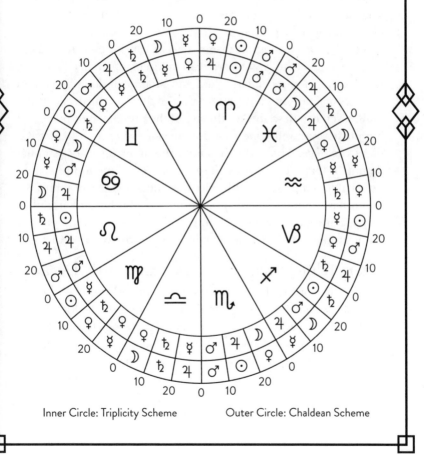

Inner Circle: Triplicity Scheme   Outer Circle: Chaldean Scheme

decan of any sign is ruled by the sign's ruling planet. The middle decan is ruled by the planetary ruler of the next sign that shares an element. The final decan is ruled by the planet ruling the last element in that sequence.

Regardless of which rulership scheme you decide to use, the decans have a wide range of uses in astrology. Decans are also referred to as "faces" due to their pictorial nature, and they have narratives or personifications associated with them as a result. True to their ancient Egyptian origins, you can invoke the deities or entities associated with them by creating talismans. Something similar emerged in the Islamicate era of astrology within the *Picatrix*, share experts Austin Coppock and T. Susan Chang. This magical text describes specific magical talismans you can use to invoke the energy of the decans for specific purposes.

Outside of astrological magic, decans can be used to add descriptive nuances to any chart you are referencing. In natal analysis, the decan of the ascendant, Sun, and Moon can describe certain features of a person's appearance or overall vibe. The decan of the midheaven can describe key themes of the profession or perceived life purpose as well. One can also consider whether a planet has dignity by face. This differs from all the other forms of essential dignity in that it describes skill sets that are unique to the planet, rather than empowerment by circumstances. Planets in their own decan have unique talents or superpowers that become useful in very specific circumstances, even when the planet is in a sign that is not supportive of its general nature, note Coppock and Chang.

Storytelling the Minor Arcana with Decans

Another use of the decans relates to the symbolism they can add to tarot. Astrology was syncretised with tarot via the Golden Dawn tradition. This early twentieth-century occultist society pulled from various spiritual and esoteric traditions to create their version of a Rosetta Stone, but for the occult, explains Chang. The beauty of tarot lies in the ability to tell a story. Most people are familiar with the two major story arcs within tarot: the progression through the major arcana and the movement through each suit in the minor

arcana. However, there are many more story arcs within the minor arcana that might be missed at first glance!

Everyone is familiar with the progression through the suits of the minor arcana. The four suits correspond to the four classical elements each associated with a domain of life: actions, resources, intellect, and relationships. However, each element has a lesson or journey that it is on. In her book *36 Secrets: A Decanic Journey through the Minor Arcana of the Tarot,* T. Susan Chang references the elemental major arcana cards and how their symbolism maps onto the lessons of each element. Her themes of the elemental journey through the minor arcana are outlined in the table below:

Suit	Element	Major Arcana	Thematic Keywords
Wands	Fire	Judgment	Hero's Journey, making of legends, self-actualization
Pentacles	Earth	The World	The struggle for embodiment, longevity, sustenance
Swords	Air	The Fool	Cultivating knowledge, pursuit of wisdom, intellectual development
Cups	Water	The Hanged Man	Liberation (*moksha*), self-sacrifice, emotional freedom and fulfillment

Therefore, the numerical sequence of the minors through their suit of choice describes different stages of that journey. Each of the three decans of the zodiac are depicted by three cards within the minor arcana sequence. The cards associated with each decan take on the qualities of the segment of the sign they are corresponding to.

Besides the element, the modality of a sign is an important quality to consider when applying astrology to tarot. Modality is a quality of a sign that tells you how it moves to perform the themes of the element it is assigned to. The three modalities are cardinal, fixed, and mutable. Cardinal signs are the initiators of their respective element. Fixed signs are the sustaining force of their respective element. Mutable signs are the transition points of each element,

before moving off to the next part of a sequence. When applying this to tarot, it reveals an interesting pattern where the two, three, and four of any suit are cardinal; the five, six, and seven of any suit are fixed; and the eight, nine, and ten of any suit are mutable! You might be wondering where the aces fit into this scheme. They represent the raw potential of each element. The progression from ace to the two describes the development of that raw potential into something more specific.

The following illustration depicts the zodiac wheel, modality, element, and the corresponding cards for the decans:

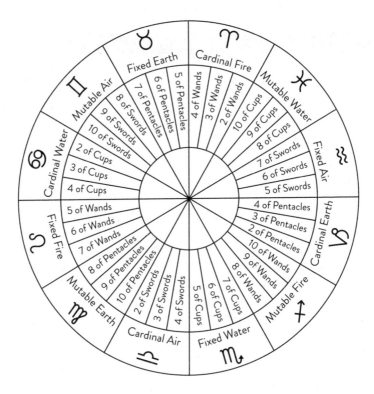

Cards That Share a Number

Thinking of the cards in zodiacal fashion allows us to play with different relationships between cards to enhance our capacity for sto-

rytelling with tarot. There are many ways we can accomplish this. The first of these is to think about cards that share a number with each other. While this might seem obvious to those experienced with tarot, thinking about the cards in terms of how they are positioned on a wheel paints a different picture. These cards share a modality but differ in element, meaning that they form the hard aspects (square and opposition) to one another on the zodiacal wheel. This is significant, as signs making hard aspects are angular relative to each other, describing critical turning points on a wheel. Each number has a key theme or meaning associated with it, and the journey through the four elements of that card describes critical periods. The card that would be in the opening square from your chosen card may represent the first challenge you experience. The card representing the opposite decan would describe a key

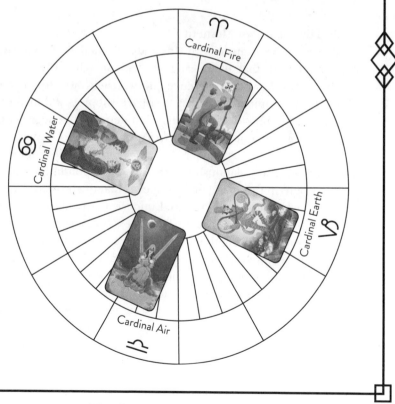

turning point or something coming to light. The card representing the closing square would be the key lesson or culmination of the themes represented by the first card in the sequence.

Let's use the twos of each suit to make our case, which is fun since they represent the most cardinal points of the zodiacal wheel. Twos are cards of choices but also of recognizing a need for change. If we start with the Two of Wands, we make our initial choice to build something from a blank slate. By the time we get to the Two of Cups, we are challenged by the recognition of an object of desire, if not something that we want to feed our energy into. However, the progression to the Two of Swords makes us aware of imbalance and the need to make objective choices that maintain equilibrium. Finally, things culminate with the Two of Pentacles, where we can choose to ride the tides of opportunity to build a firmer foundation.

Cards That Share an Element

Another thing we can do with this zodiacal framework is revisit the story of cards that are sharing an element. While these cards are obviously following a sequence and tell their own story if you follow them in numerical order, there are subplots within these narratives. The three decans of each sign describe the beginning, middle, and end of one's experience of each modality. Of each modality, the 10-degree segments in the beginning, middle, and end make perfect trine relationships with the corresponding parts of the other signs in that element. This means that the twos, fives, and eights of each suit all have a shared underlying theme since they describe the beginning of a sign. The threes, sixes, and nines also have a shared underlying theme, since they are the centerpiece of what can be achieved within a modality. Finally, the fours, sevens, and tens also share underlying meanings since they describe the conclusion of what is achieved in each modality.

Using the middle decans of the fire signs, you see key themes around the consequences of putting yourself out there. In the Three of Wands scenario, you have sent out representatives to make yourself known in hopes that people will come support you. When

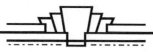

we progress to the Six of Wands situation, you see someone has successfully reaped the benefits and has people celebrating them for their successes. By the Nine of Wands scenario, we see that one has to defend the reputation that they created for themselves. You have worked too hard and come too far to risk it now.

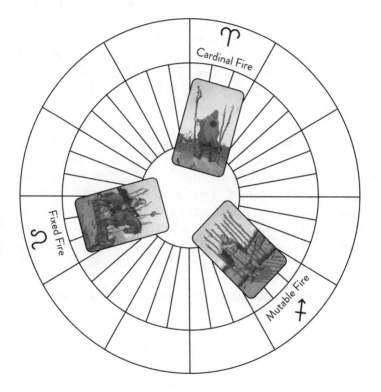

Adjacent Cards

Next, we have the story of cards that are adjacent to one another. This is going to be less relevant for the threes, sixes, and nines of every suit since they are the centerpiece of a modality they are in (see page 60). This becomes more interesting for cards at the beginning and end of a sign, since they are bordering boundaries between signs. So while the numerical sequence continues, the next number starts in a different suit. For example, on the zodiacal wheel the Ten of Wands would be sandwiched between the Nine of Wands and the Two of Pentacles, since it represents the last 10 degrees of Sagittarius. While we are familiar with the idea that the Ten of Wands marks the end of the journey through the fire suit, it takes on a slightly different meaning when you consider that it is right next to the beginning of the journey through the earth suit. The Two of Pentacles has connotations of being in flux and looking for new opportunities to plant seeds to grow. This suggests that perhaps the desire to endure difficult extremes to pursue the promise of glory elsewhere may serve the purpose of finding new places to build foundations. It provides more context for the purpose behind carrying a heavy load and going on an intense journey.

Cards That Share Planetary Influences
Finally, we can look at themes of cards sharing a planetary ruler or similar combinations of planetary influences. Though these cards might appear different at first glance, they actually have underlying similarities through the planetary combinations that exist between them. This is easier to do when using the Chaldean scheme since nearly every planet rules five decans, except Mars, who controls six decans.

Predicting with Decans and the Minor Arcana

I have often heard some people in tarot circles decry the use of tarot for making specific predictions, because there is too much room for subjectivity, which can leave room for error. However, bringing astrological symbolism into tarot can provide details that allow for more specific predictions to be made. The main context astrology provides is related to the ability to time events. Every card is associated with a sign, segment of a sign, element, or planetary energy. There are several clues you can use to get a sense of timing.

First, you want to see whether there are transits in the sky that match the astrological associations of the cards in question. For example, Mars was moving through the sign of Leo at the time I wrote this article. The Seven of Wands is the Mars in Leo card, as this is the Mars-ruled decan of that sign. If I were to draw the Seven

of Wands in a question, I would assume that something about the movement of Mars through Leo is relevant to my situation. Since my natal chart also features Mars in Leo in that particular decan, I would assume that my Mars return would be relevant to the outcome of the question.

Next, you want to see if there are multiple cards that implicate a particular sequence of the zodiac. This is also a major timing clue. For example, if I were to draw the Five, Six, and Seven of Wands within a spread, this would point me toward a need to focus on Leonine energies since these cards are associated with the decans of Leo. This could imply that an event would be taking place sometime during Leo season or some other major transit through the sign of Leo. For example, at the time of my writing this, Venus is in her pre-retrograde shadow before she will retrograde in Leo at the end of next month. If I were asking something about relationships and those cards were to pop up in my spread, it would tip me off to the fact that some of the themes I would deal with center on this transit.

Also, it is important to see if any major arcana cards confirm the energy that is being expressed through the minor arcana. This is because the majors also carry their own astrological signfications, which are more sign-, element-, or planet-based. Playing on my Leo influence example, if the Strength card were to pop up in a reading along with the Five, Six, or Seven of Wands, I would also pay attention to movements through the sign of Leo to describe turning points within a situation that someone is asking about.

Finally, the symbolism of the decans (but also the majors too) provides specifics about people that may be implicated in a situation, beyond just relying on the court cards themselves. In fact, you can use them in conjunction with court cards to describe the people who are relevant to a situation. The King of Wands in some of the astrological correspondence systems is associated with the sign of Leo, if not just a fire sign with lots of fire influence. If you are drawing the Seven of Wands along with the King of Wands, not only is this suggesting that the person you are dealing with is likely to have Leo placements, but maybe they have Mars there too. You may find that this person has a Sun in the final 10 degrees of Leo.

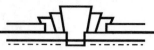

This person may also have the ascendant or Moon there as well. If Strength also appeared in the spread, this would provide additional testimony.

A Symbolic Journey

Astrology and tarot are two symbolic and divinatory languages that are extremely powerful when they are used creatively together. Applying an astrological framework can enhance your storytelling as a tarot reader and enhance your ability to make specific, timely predictions. In parallel, seeing the resonance with tarot can also make astrology function less like a mechanical clock for timing events and allow you to see it more as the unfolding of a story or symbolic journey. This can be useful in forms of astrology that rely heavily on the descriptive imagery of planets and how they relate to each other to make predictions.

References

Brennan, Chris. *Hellenistic Astrology: The Study of Fate and Fortune.* Denver, CO: Amor Fati Publications, 2020. Pages 11–36.

Coppock, Austin. "Exploring the Decans." Post-Conference Webinar at NORWAC 2020, May 24, 2020.

Chang, T. Susan. *36 Secrets: A Decanic Journey through the Minor Arcana of the Tarot.* Anima Mundi Press, 2021. Pages 3–4, 38, 118–19, 131–32, 144, 153–54, 161, 189–90, 250.

The Air Dagger

Chic and S. Tabatha Cicero

Throughout history, the practice of magic has always included a large variety of sharp and pointy things used as implements! For as long as people have been forging metal blades, they have been creating swords, spears, knives, and daggers for invoking, tracing magical figures, casting energy, and banishing. Of course the most common of these is the magic sword—legends of magical swords used by gods and heroes are plentiful the world over.

Daggers of Myth and Legend

Magical daggers are not as well known, but there are some notable exceptions. The wavy, asymmetrical *kris* dagger of Indonesia was considered to have magical powers and was used as a talisman. The three-sided *phurba* of Indo-Tibetan Buddhism was used to free evil spirits from suffering and to drive away the delusions that serve as obstacles to enlightenment. Finally, in the Welsh traditions of King

Arthur, there is the magical dagger known as *Carnwennan*, which had the power to make its bearer invisible.

A fourteenth-century grimoire called *The Key of Solomon the King* listed several such implements, including knives, a sword, a sickle, a poniard, a lance, and a dagger. However, some of these of these implements, such as sickle, poniard, and dagger, may have been later additions to the original manuscript, based upon a misreading of Latin terms.

In addition to the magic sword and the magic wand, two bladed implements prominently featured in *The Key of Solomon the King* are a pair of knives, one with a white handle and one with a black handle. The white-hilted knife was to be crafted on the day and hour of the planet Mercury and inscribed with certain characters and the Hebrew acronym *AGLA*. This knife could be used to trace all figures required in a given ritual except for the circles. The black-hilted knife was to be crafted on the day and hour of Saturn; it was also inscribed with characters and was used for threatening disobedient or malevolent spirits.

These two ritual knives from the grimoire are probably the source of the Wiccan white-handled knife, sometimes referred to as a *bolline,* used for inscribing candles and cutting herbs and cords. The black-handled *athame* is used to represent power and direct energies, especially when casting and banishing the magic circle, making the athame interchangeable with a magic sword.

The two knives of the *Key of Solomon the King* were also the origin of the Golden Dawn's two magical daggers: a simple black-hilted dagger used for the Lesser Ritual of the Pentagram and the yellow-hilted Air Dagger, inscribed with divine names and sigils associated with the element of air. It is used to invoke and dismiss the energies of that ethereal elemental.

Elemental Tools

All bladed implements can be considered weapons by design. In ritual they are often used for spiritual protection. But we can see that in Wiccan rites, the primary uses of the bolline and the athame are for creating, defining, and directing. The same is true for the Golden Dawn's Air Dagger. Along with the Earth Pentacle, the Water Cup, and the Fire Wand, the Air Dagger is one of the four traditional elemental "weapons" used in the personal ritual work of the skilled magician.

The title of "weapons" recalls a time in the ancient world when one of the primary duties of a magician was to perform *apotropaic magic,* or magic that drives away evil. But referring to the four elemental implements of the Golden Dawn as weapons fails to accurately describe how these devices are employed in our tradition and might be an unintentional remnant of a medieval worldview from an era when almost all spirits were thought to be hostile toward the magician. Because they are used to invoke and dismiss the powers of the elements, it would be better to refer to the Fire Wand, Water Cup, Earth Pentacle, and Air Dagger as Elemental Tools rather than Elemental Weapons.

The Element of Air

Some may wonder why the tarot suit of swords and the magical dagger of the magician are associated with air and not fire within the Golden Dawn tradition. The answer has to do with characteristics assigned to the elements.

The attribution of the four elements of the minor arcana of the tarot comes from nineteenth-century French occultist Éliphas Lévi. It was Lévi who equated *Vav,* the third letter of the name יהוה,

YHVH (the Tetragrammaton, or Holy "Four-Lettered Name" of the Divine), with the element of air and the Qabalistic World of *Yetzirah,* the formative, airy, astral realm and with the tarot suit of swords.

Air has the qualities of heat and moisture. It is the element of speed, communication, expression, mediation, connection, reconciliation, adaptation, abstraction, skill, dexterity, changeability, and conflict. Air rules the intellect, mental abilities, knowledge, the weather, illness,

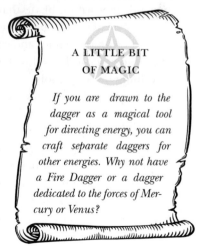

A LITTLE BIT
OF MAGIC

If you are drawn to the dagger as a magical tool for directing energy, you can craft separate daggers for other energies. Why not have a Fire Dagger or a dagger dedicated to the forces of Mercury or Venus?

the conceptual, and all gaseous physical matter. The direction corresponding to air is east. In Hebrew, air is called *Ruach*, meaning "breath" as well as "spirit."

Air represents the conscious mind, thought processes, and mental activity. One of the primary functions of the mind is to understand our environment, to analyze things and separate them into various categories for our better understating. To break down our impressions into component parts that will aid our faculty of discernment. Example: Is a certain plant good for food or is it poisonous? Whichever category you determine it to be will depend on your knowledge of plants. The mental act of separating things into categories can be compared to the cutting action of a sword slicing through the air or a knife cutting herbs.

In addition to its cutting action, the dagger can be compared to the tip of a spear, cast through the air to hit its target.

Creating Your Air Dagger

Instructions for creating a traditional Golden Dawn Air Dagger can be found in our book *Secrets of a Golden Dawn Temple*, but here we will show you how to create a more personalized Air Dagger that incorporates symbolism that you choose to include on your dagger.

Many readers will not have the ability or desire to forge a dagger blade out of metal, and there is certainly no need to do so! Simply buy a dagger with a blade that is of a size and weight that speaks to you. The blade will be fine as is. It is the hilt that will need to be adorned with the names and sigils of air. The handle or hilt of your chosen dagger will need to have a surface area large enough for inscribing these symbols.

A dagger hilt is composed of two sections, the shaft (or grip) and the crossbar, which sits against the bottom of the blade. Both sections can be painted with symbolism. If the crossbar of your chosen dagger is large enough, then painting symbols on it should be no problem. But if your dagger does not have a large crossbar, then you may have to alter the hilt to get all the symbolism to fit.

One way of enlarging the crossbar of the dagger to a more appropriate size and shape is to use oven-hardening clay. Simply mold the clay over the hilt into the desired shape and bake it in the oven following the directions for hardening the day.

Another way to enlarge the hilt is to remove the blade entirely from the old hilt and mount it on a new one. This method will only work with basic daggers that have wooden hilts and a metal stick tang (sometimes called a rat tail), not a blade with a full tang that is the size and shape of the handle itself.

The shaft of an inexpensive dagger will usually have a wooden hand grip between a brass guard crossbar and a pommel. You will need to take the hilt apart by securing the wooden shaft of the dagger in a pair of vice grips. Then take another pair of vise grips or pliers and unscrew the brass pommel until it comes off. All the parts of the handle should come off once the pommel is removed, although you may require a hammer to loosen the various parts. All that will remain is the dagger blade with a metal shank (the stick tang) attached. This entire operation should take no more than five minutes. If you are handy with woodworking (or know someone who is), you can create a new wooden hilt with a larger crossbar in the shape of a T or a cross, or even in a crescent-shape.

You may be lucky enough to find a dagger with a metal hilt that is large enough for the needed symbols. If so, simply cover the blade with masking tape or painter's tape. Use emery cloth or coarse sandpaper on the handle of the dagger to "rough up" the surface of the metal, enough to hold the primer coat of paint. Then apply a coat of good quality primer white enamel paint. Allow it to dry thoroughly. Apply two to three coats of yellow enamel paint. Remove the masking tape before the final coat is entirely dry so you don't chip the paint. When the final yellow coat is dry, apply all the Hebrew names and sigils in violet paint with a thin liner brush. Follow all directions for safety, application, and cleanup.

If you've crafted a new hilt out of oven-hardening clay or wood, then cover the blade with masking tape and use acrylic paint in primer white, yellow, and violet.

Make sure all the paint is completely dry before adding a finish coat of sealant. For wood, use a non-yellowing acrylic lacquer spray. For oven-hardening clay, brush on a finish coat of polymer clay varnish. Do your research on different brands of polymer clay finish coats, as some products might have a chemical reaction with the clay and cause the finish coat to be sticky. For either wood or clay hilts, let the finish coat dry overnight before removing the masking tape from the blade.

The following table provides a list of forces and symbols that you can apply to your Air Dagger. Choose whatever symbolism speaks to you.

Correspondences of Air	
Godname of Air	יהוה, YHVH, "Yod Heh Vav Heh," Tetragrammaton or "Four-Lettered Name"
Archangel of Air	Raphael
Angel of Air	Chassan
Ruler of Air	Aral
Zodiac Signs	Libra, Aquarius, Gemini
Tarot Cards	The Fool (with Justice, The Star, and The Lovers for the zodiac signs)
Hebrew Letters	Vav (as a group), with Lamed, Tzaddi, and Zayin for the zodiac signs
Planets	Mercury, Luna, Sol
Colors of the Signs	Libra (green), Aquarius (violet), Gemini (orange)
Angel of Air Signs	Zaltzel
Sephiroth	Kether, Tiphareth, Yesod
Deities of Air	Anu, Enlil, Vul, Adad, Nuet, Shu, Hathor, Thoth, Zeus, Hera, Hermes, Mercury, Boreas, Zephyrus, Eurus, Notus, Aeolus, Thor
Animals	Birds (especially eagles and ravens), bat, butterfly, dragonfly, monkey
Symbols	Upright triangle bisected with a line, sky, clouds, mountaintop, swirls of steam or mist, rainbow
Metals	Mercury
Woods	Acacia, almond, aspen, banyan, bodhi, maple, palm, pecan, pine, slippery elm
Gemstones	Topaz, chalcedony, aventurine, jasper, mica, pumice, sphene
Fabrics	Chiffon, voile, gauze

You are now ready to consecrate your Air Dagger, charging it with power and dedicating it to magical work.

A Simple Consecration Ritual
for Your Air Dagger

The first step in ritual preparation is to map out your sacred space. Depending on your circumstances, you may already have a room completely dedicated as a personal temple. If you don't have a temple room, it's not a problem. Clear off any table, desk, or dresser-top and cover it with a cloth in the color that best represents the element of air to you. Yellow is commonly associated with air, but you might prefer sky blue or cloud white. (Your dagger, your choice!) But if you choose yellow, you can take advantage of the Golden Dawn's system of flashing colors, or colors that produce an optical "pulsing" effect when placed next to each other. Violet is the flashing color to yellow, so place a circle of violet ribbon, twine, or cord on the center of your altar-top to enhance the energetic vibration of these complementary colors. Keep a barbecue lighter and a stick of incense on hand: scents corresponding to air include benzoin, lavender, gum mastic, sage, star anise, pine resin, lemongrass, bergamot, and marjoram. Take your pick! Place a yellow candle outside of the violet circle, on the side farthest away from you. (Use an LED candle if safety is a concern.) Place a simple folding paper hand fan outside the circle on the side closest to you. Have a yellow silk or linen cloth on hand to wrap your dagger after the ritual. Place the dagger in the center of the circle on your altar-top.

Start the ritual either sitting or standing, whichever you prefer. Then focus on your breath. Begin a sequence of slow, rhythmic breathing to shift your awareness away from the mundane and dissipate all stress and muscular tension. Inhale slowly to the count of one, then exhale slowly to the count of two. Feel a harmonious connection with the Divine.

Pause for a few moments. Next begin a technique of breath control known in yoga as *nadhi sodhana,* or "alternate nostril breathing," which uses your dominant hand to assist in breathing. Start by emptying all the air from your lungs. With your thumb, block your right nostril and inhale through the left nostril only, taking a deep belly breath. When full of air, block your left nostril with your ring finger while continuing to keep the right nostril closed for a short moment. Then release your thumb and exhale slowly and fully through your right nostril. Pause briefly, then inhale again through the right nostril. Exhale through the left nostril. Close both nostrils briefly. An inhalation and exhalation through both nostrils counts as a complete circuit of breathing. (You can combine this with the Golden Dawn's Fourfold Breath: inhaling to the count of four, holding full to the count of four, exhaling to the count of four, and remaining empty to the count of four. Complete about ten cycles of breathing. Nadhi sodhana breathing can increase the amount of oxygen taken into the body, calming the mind and boosting concentration.) Relax and let your breathing return to normal.

If you were sitting, stand in front of the altar. Light the stick of incense and take up the closed hand fan. Begin to vibrate or intone the name of power *IAO* (pronounced EE-AH-OH in slow, long syllables). This trigram is the Western equivalent to the eastern mantra *om*, and the three letters refer to a triad of Egyptian deities Isis, Apophis, and Osiris—or the cycle of life, death, and re-

birth. As you vibrate the name, visualize the figure of a triangle with its apex pointed upward toward the yellow candle. Trace the lines of this triangle clockwise directly over your dagger with the closed hand fan, starting from the top point. While tracing the first line, inhale deeply then slowly vibrate "eee." When tracing the second line intone "aahh." Trace the third line and vibrate "oohh." Trace the triangle and intone the name five times (as five is the number of Spirit). Then trace a horizontal line through the triangle, bifurcating it into top and bottom sections: △. This is the traditional Western symbol of air.

Open the hand fan and begin to fan the air over your dagger. Say:

The heaven is above and the earth is beneath. And between the Light and the Darkness, the energies vibrate. I call upon the Divine Source of All, by the Majesty of the Divine, by the Name of Power YHVH, the Archangel of Air RAPHAEL, the Angel CHASSAN, the Triad Angel ZALTZEL and the ruler ARAL, to bestow this present day and hour, and confirm their mystic and potent influence upon this Air Dagger, which I hereby dedicate to purity and occult work, and may its grasp strengthen me in the work of the Magic of Light! May it aid me in all things that require knowledge, intellect, skill, communication, expression, mediation, and healing.

Now you may dedicate your dagger to any personal deity you deem appropriate, especially one who embodies the powers of air. Imagine a halo of light pulsating around your dagger, infusing it with divine energy. When you feel ready, thank any deities, angels, or beings you have called to aid your ritual. Finally, wrap your consecrated dagger in the yellow cloth. Extinguish the candle and close the rite.

· · · ☽ · · ·

You can now use your Air Dagger to invoke or banish any of the powers and attributes of the element of air. The methods of breath control and energized visualization given here can be easily adapted for a variety of magical purposes. Call upon the forces that have gone into your dagger's creation whenever you feel the need for swift action or mental clarity. Use it to banish illness and invoke convalescence and good health. Most of all, use it to enliven your ongoing spiritual journey with the sacred Breath of Spirit!

Resources

Cicero, Chic, and Sandra Tabatha Cicero. *Secrets of a Golden Dawn Temple.* Bk. 1, *Creating Magical Tools.* Loughborough, UK: Thoth Publications, 2004.

Decker, Ronald, Thierry Depaulis, and Michael Dummett. *A Wicked Pack of Cards: The Origins of the Occult Tarot.* London: Gerald Duckworth & Co., 2002.

Farrar, Stewart. *What Witches Do: The Modern Coven Revealed.* Marlborough, UK: The Crowood Press, 2021.

Greer, John Michael. *The New Encyclopedia of the Occult.* St. Paul, MN: Llewellyn Publications, 2003.

Mathers, Samuel Liddell. *The Key of Solomon the King: Clavicula Salomonis.* Newburyport, MA: Samuel Weiser, 2016.

Treasure Mapping
Sara Mellas

Manifestation is a concept that's been gaining popularity in recent years. Though the phenomenon has existed for as long as humankind and perhaps even before then, the conscious practice of manifesting is something in which modern society has grown increasingly interested. One familiar method for manifesting facets of the energetic realm into the physical realm is to create a vision board. Perhaps you've even made one!

A vision board, also called a dream board, is a material means of working with the law of attraction. It is a collage of images and affirmations specifically chosen to represent one's goals and dreams, serving to motivate and support one in manifesting past intangibles into present and future reality.

While a vision board is a beautiful and helpful thing, those who are magically inclined may want to take the idea further through the practice of treasure mapping. A treasure map is also a collage of curated images and affirmations, but it's created with intention and ritual that make it considerably more energetically potent than a standard vision board—and resultingly more effective.

What Makes a Treasure Map Different?

Although a treasure map is fundamentally similar to a basic vision board, there are two main factors that differentiate and characterize it: timing and organization.

Timing is the defining element of a treasure map. The map must be created in the two-week period between the Aries New Moon and the following Libra Full Moon—no earlier and no later. Of course, it's perfectly fine to make a vision board at any time throughout the year, but the main intention of a treasure map is to harness the initiatory energy of Aries and the potent first lunation of the astrological new year. The exact dates and times of the New and Full Moons will vary from year to year, so it's important to always check when these lunations will occur.

This year's Aries New Moon occurs on March 29, 2025, at 6:58 a.m. EST at 9 degrees of Aries. Mercury will be retrograde at 0 degrees of Aries, giving us an opportunity to revisit and revise any relatively new ideas for things we'd like to initiate or ways of thinking about certain matters in our lives. Venus will also be retrograde at 28 degrees of Pisces, making it nearly conjunct Mercury and Neptune at 29 degrees of Pisces. This is a beautiful energy for reassessing our values and realigning with our soul's desire and purpose. With Mars at 22 degrees of Cancer and Neptune at the very last degree of the zodiac, our intuition will be intensely heightened, providing insight on how to best act on the realization of our dreams. What's more, the North Node of fate will be positioned at 26 degrees of Pisces at the time of the New Moon, less than 2 degrees away from Saturn at 24 degrees of Pisces, which is nearing an exact sextile to Uranus at 24 degrees of Taurus. This is an opportunity to use the lessons we've learned in the past several years to break free of self-imposed limitations, allowing ourselves to move forward into our destiny, embracing the karmic responsibilities of our souls. Last, Mars will have just moved past a square to Chiron at 22 degrees of Aries, encouraging us to bravely heal from any losses, hurts, and insecurities, and integrate them to our advantage in the forthcoming chapters of our lives.

Organization is another critical component of creating a treasure map. There are many different ways you can choose to organize your map depending on what resonates with you personally. The purpose of all organizational approaches is to create a map that reflects a comprehensive vision for one's life and doesn't overemphasize or neglect any area of existence.

Creating Your Treasure Map

Before you even begin your treasure map, a bit of preparation in the weeks leading up to the Aries New Moon will greatly support the process. Through the month of March, take inventory of your life—your home, your habits and thoughts, your work, your finances, and your relationships. If you come across anything that causes "clutter"—whether it's physical clutter, negativity, anxiety, or any other kind of energetic blockage—get rid of it! Recycle or donate the items in your home that no longer serve a purpose, then thoroughly clean and organize your space. This effort is as essential as it is worthwhile.

As you evaluate the other areas of your life, reflect on what is adding value to your experience and what is detracting from it. If anything can be reasonably let go of or changed, take the steps necessary to do so. For that which cannot be simply discarded like clutter in a closet, use the awareness of its existence to inform how you'd like your life to look and feel differently going forward. This insight will be valuable to what you choose to depict on your treasure map. In addition to images, you'll only need a few basic items to create a treasure map:

Supplies

1 large foam-core board or posterboard (White provides a simple
   blank canvas, but if you feel drawn to a certain color, go for it!)
Printer paper and color ink (if printing images from online)
Scissors
Craft glue
Marker or pen

Images

Imagery is the primary element of a treasure map. It should be chosen with intention and care, as it's a powerful representation of what you'll attract into your life and how you'll spend your energy in the coming year. It's great to meditate on what imagery you might like to put on your map in the weeks leading up to the Aries New Moon, but it's very important to wait to source and select photos until *after the New Moon has occurred.* The first lunation of the astrological new year is a very powerful energy that will affect what images you feel drawn to—often ones you may not have expected just a few days prior! Remember, in 2025, the Aries New Moon will occur on March 29 at 6:58 a.m. EST.

There are two ways you can source imagery for your treasure map:

1. Browse the internet for images that catch your eye. You can use a basic Google search, Pinterest, or a photo-forward social media site like Instagram or Tumblr. For convenience, save or screenshot these images to your computer, then arrange them in a Word or Pages document. This way, you can adjust each photo to the size you'd like and save paper. Then, simply print the pages and cut out the individual images.
2. Look for images in magazines. For our modern purposes, this can be more time-consuming and less fruitful, especially for actively sourced images. But if you prefer to stay off the computer and are resourceful, cutting your photos out of magazine pages is a fine option.

Approach your imagery search as follows:

Actively Sourced Imagery

Begin with searching for images that are specific to your larger goals for the year. For example, if you'd like to plant a flower garden in your backyard, choose a photo of your ideal garden in full bloom. If you've been wanting to travel to a specific destination, find a photo of the place that catches your eye. If some of your dreams aren't as physical or specific, such as "getting a promotion" or "meeting new people," look for images that represent how you imagine your life will look and feel once those dreams become reality—perhaps a photo of a large office or a candid group of people smiling.

Receptively Sourced Imagery

While you're searching for specific images to represent your goals and wishes, you may find you feel drawn to certain photos that have seemingly nothing to do with what you're seeking. Pay attention to these photos. If you notice yourself lingering over a picture of a ladybug for no apparent reason, or if you come across a photo of the Rocky Mountains that inspires positive feelings within you, recognize it as an indication that the image belongs on your treasure map. In fact, once you've sourced all your "active" images, it's worthwhile to spend some time passively browsing, noting if anything captures your attention. The universe has a unique way

of knowing what we need before we know it ourselves, and these signs tend to come through when we we're open to receiving them.

A Photo of You

Your treasure map must include a photograph of you! It can be a portrait, a selfie, or a candid, as long as you are the only person in it and you like the photo. It's perfectly okay to take a new picture specifically for your map, or you can use one that was taken within the last few years. The more confident in yourself you felt at the time the photo was taken, the better.

Words

Words are totally optional to include on your treasure map, but they make a powerful addition. In the space between images, you may choose to write single words that resonate with you, scripture, spells, or affirmations. For all affirmations, be sure to phrase them in the present tense, beginning with "I am" instead of "I will" or "I want."

Organization

Organizing the images on your treasure map is important, but how you choose to do so is up to you! As mentioned earlier, the intent is to ensure you're looking at your aspirations holistically; this isn't to say you need an equal number of images across all "categories" or shouldn't emphasize a certain area in accordance with your goals, but it's helpful for maintaining balance and perspective. Here are two suggestions to get you started on choosing your images and organizing them:

Astrological Houses

Most forms of Western astrology divide the 360-degree astrological chart into twelve sections, each of which corresponds to different areas of life and is associated with a specific zodiac sign and planetary ruler. You may choose to arrange your map linearly, starting with the first house at the top and creating a row of images for each house, or in a circle like the horoscope, grouping the first house images at the center-left and working counterclockwise through the rest.

First House: Physical appearance, the self, experience of the world

Second House: Personal finances and income, possessions, self-worth

Third House: Communication, siblings and close friends, commutes and short trips

Fourth House: Home, immediate family, ancestry

Fifth House: Creative passions, children, recreation, romance

Sixth House: Routines, health, occupations, service, pets

Seventh House: One-on-one relationships: marriages, business partnerships, clients

Eighth House: Transformation, taxes, loans, inheritance, sex, death, the occult

Ninth House: Higher education, religion, foreign cultures and long-distance travel, publishing

Tenth House: Career, reputation, legacy, contribution to society

Eleventh House: Community, large groups, humanitarianism, technology and innovation, hopes and dreams

Twelfth House: Spiritually and connection to the Divine, intuition, the subconscious

The Bagua

Originating in China, the bagua are used in Taoist cosmology and are integral to most feng shui practices. There are many versions, but the essence of the bagua is eight symbols representing the fundamental principles of existence, each corresponding to a color, element, and direction. It's ideal to arrange your imagery in accordance with the directions, beginning with health at the center of your map, then working around it.

Direction	Colors	Element	Correspondences
Center	Yellow, orange, brown	Earth	Health
South	Red	Fire	Fame, reputation
Southwest	Pink	Earth	Love, partnerships
West	White	Metal	Children, fulfillment
Northwest	Gray	Metal	Allies and supporters, travel
North	Black	Water	Career, life path
Northeast	Dark blue	Earth	Knowledge, personal growth
East	Teal	Wood	Family, new beginnings
Southeast	Purple	Wood	Wealth, abundance

Ritual and Creation

Once you've gathered all your images and supplies, it's time to put everything together! This process must be done in the two-week window between the Aries New Moon (March 29, 2025 at 6:58 a.m.) and the Libra Full Moon (April 12, 2025 at 8:22 p.m. EST).

How you ritualize the creation of your map is wholly up to you and your personal practices. You may choose to work alone or alongside a group of friends. You might say a prayer or incantation beforehand, set up a small altar, call in your guides, or play music while you work. Or you may do nothing beyond taking a few deep breaths to

get started. What's important is that you feel grounded and present throughout the process; setting an intention, whether silently or audibly, before you create your map is helpful and recommended.

Start with the photo of you. Position it in whichever area of the board pertains to the self—either in the center, the top, or center-left, depending on how you've decided to organize your map. Proceed by positioning the loose photos on the board according to the divisions within your choice of organization to get an idea for spacing and how you'd like to arrange them. Once you're satisfied, glue each photo in place.

Take a pen and add whatever words, phrases, and affirmations you feel called to write in the spaces between photos. Last, sign the bottom right corner of the map to seal your intention.

After you stand back and admire your work, put it on display! It's very important that you put your map in an unobstructed place where you'll see it daily, like in an office or bedroom. You may even choose to take a photo of the map and set it as your computer or phone screensaver as well!

Finding Treasure

Once your treasure map is created, the only thing more for you to do is be open to the opportunities, changes, and manifestations that will unfold in your life over the coming year. After the Libra Full Moon on April 12, your map is considered complete, and it's imperative to resist adding any images or phrases to it. Trust that the universe guided you to select the images you did, at the time you did, for a reason.

On the rare occurrence when you need to remove an image from the map, you may do so at the Cancer New Moon (June 25 at 6:32 a.m. EST). Feeling this need is very unlikely, and should only be done if your safety or well-being has been compromised. For example, if you'd added a photo of a significant other to your map and you parted ways under unfavorable circumstances, by all means, remove their photo from your map. But, do not remove any images simply because your goals have taken a different shape over a few months or if you believe an opportunity "deadline" had passed—things will often show up in our lives in ways that differ from our original expectations!

As with all manifestation practices, treasure mapping is about finding a balance of putting action behind your intentions and being patient and receptive to what the universe has to offer. Sometimes, blessings may seemingly fall into our laps, but usually, it's up to us to meet the universe halfway with our willingness and diligence. Above all, continue to exercise gratitude, openness, and compassion.

In the weeks following the Libra Full Moon, you may find you feel newly inspired or emboldened to take steps toward reaching your goals. Synchronicities may appear in your day-to-day life that catch your attention, or unanticipated invitations may come in. Pay close attention, as it's not unusual to see signs both big and small that can be traced back to the imagery on your map. For instance, one year, I receptively sourced an image of a fox, for reasons unbeknownst to me at the time. Not only did my favorite song I discovered that year include the word *fox* in the title, but I also got hired for a job by an individual whose last name was Fox.

The Aries New Moon energy you'll work with to create your treasure map unfolds to various potencies in late June to early July, mid-October, and mid to late January of 2026, so you'll likely see certain developments and manifestations of your intentions around these times. However, divine timing never fails to surprise and delight, and it can lead us to find treasure we didn't even realize we were seeking, at times we hadn't realized we were seeking it. Trust that there is a plan for you—one that's better than you can imagine. Your treasure map will guide you through it, leading you to uncover gold all along the way.

Magic of the Spoken Word

Mhara Starling

Words have power!" was a lesson drilled into me by my late mentor. From my very beginnings as a Witch, I understood that the spoken word was a powerful tool within magical practice. The right words, chosen with purpose or drawn forth via divine inspiration and uttered with passion and power can alter reality.

Nothing exemplifies just how powerful the spoken word is more than our obsession as humans with stories. We are a storytelling species; our reality is experienced via narrative. Our parents and grandparents recited fairy tales and nursery rhymes to us in our youth, and scattered within these fantastical tales are morals, lessons, and warnings we carry with us throughout our lives. It is often stories that inspire us to choose the paths we walk. On a personal level, I do not think I would be a Witch today if it were not for those enchanting legends concerning magicians, witches, faeries, and the magic of the landscape that I grew up hearing.

Having grown up in Wales—a Celtic nation known for its rich tapestry of legends and folktales—poetry, prose, and song have always been an incredibly important aspect of my cultural upbringing. Even in Wales's national anthem we uplift the importance of word weavers, as we describe our nation as *gwlad beirdd a chantorion enwogion o fri* (a land of poets and singers, those of great stature). It is no wonder, in my eyes, why the spoken word, theatricality, poetry, and song play such a significant role in my magic.

The magical quality of words was always known in my little corner of the world. The Welsh language itself, my native tongue, evolved from the ancient Brythonic language as a common language for poets to compose their poetry in. The ancient bards and poets of this Celtic land were, in their own way, magicians. Their words could make or break kings, change people's perspectives, and fire the spirit of warriors prior to battles. Their words held

power, and their mastery of their art was respected by even the great kings of the past.

Within this specifically Welsh cultural context, our bardic tradition always held an enchanted quality. The bards often sang of a force known as *Awen* (pronounced *ah-when*), a force of divine poetic inspiration. It was Awen that gave their words a quality that went beyond the mundane. Many modern-day Pagans are likely familiar with the concept of Awen, as it has become a central concept within many traditions of Druidry and Witchcraft today. It is unmistakeably a force loaded with magic, and it is a force we tap into daily.

According to the bards of old, Awen originates with the Divine. The Divine form Awen in the Otherworld, where it then seeps into our world. As it enters into our world, like a gentle breeze or a flowing river, we then breathe it in, and within us it takes shape. Finally, as we create art, whether it be in the form of a song, a poem, a dance, a book, a painting, or anything creative, we birth the Awen into the world for all to be witness to.

A force formed by divine power in the mystical Celtic Otherworld, which flows into our world and into our very bodies, so that we may birth something powerful, evocative, and transformative—no one could ever convince me that this isn't an inherently magical concept. We feel the Awen when we are inspired on a deeply visceral level. When our breath is taken away by a glorious view or when inspiration seems to strike like a bolt of lightning, that is Awen.

Drawing Forth the Awen

Though it was believed that Awen could come to us at any moment, it was also very much common belief that one could summon the Awen via magical means. Numerous folktales state that certain magical places, if visited at certain times in the year, could grant those who stayed overnight with either madness or poetic inspiration. These places were usually ancient burial mounds or rugged mountaintops. Liminal places and liminal times. It was usually during the solstices that one would venture to these places in order to become either inspired or to lose one's mind.

As an artist and creative myself, I developed my own methods of summoning the Awen at times when it is needed. When writer's block or burnout hits, it is these methods I turn to. The exercise that follows is one simple and accessible example of these methods I have developed.

Perform this exercise at a liminal time: dusk or dawn, midnight or midday. I also find that it is incredibly effective if carried out just before going to sleep. If you are the type of person who prefers to practice magic outdoors, take yourself to a liminal space, such as a crossroad or stile, the edge of a forest or body of water, or a graveyard. When I conduct this exercise, I often drink mugwort tea beforehand and burn an incense blend containing herbs associated with opening up the ways between our world and the Otherworld. This is not essential to the exercise, but feel free to ritualize this as much as you would like.

I then sit in a comfortable position and close my eyes. I rock my body gently back and forth, and recite the following incantation:

Othered forces of the deep
The ebb and flow of below
Come in dreams as I do sleep
Unbind my mind, let it flow
Inspiration, come to me
Like a river may it stream
Let it be so I may see
All that I could wish to dream

Upon reciting this incantation, intone the word *Awena* (pronounced *ah-when-ah*) over and over again. This word is the verb of Awen, so while Awen means divine inspiration, Awena is a verb that means to divinely inspire. By intoning this word, singing it, you are asking the spirits of the Otherworld to imbue you with poetic gift, divine inspiration. Sing the word over and over, as many times as feels right. Then, wait. Inspiration should follow; give it time. Do not stress about it—just allow it to flow through you.

Narrative Charms

Beyond the bardic tradition, imbued with its enchanted belief in *Awen*, the magical traditions of the land I grew up in were also filled to the brim with the underpinning belief that narrative and the spoken word hold great power. The practice of *Swyngyfaredd*, which I translate to mean "the art of enchantment," was a folk magic practice that involved the practitioner aiding the community via their magical skills. One notable skill of the *Swynydd* (the practitioner of Swyngyfaredd) was the ability to *Swyno,* or "charm."

While today, when someone says the word *charm,* we often think of lucky charms, objects that one carries to draw forth good luck or protection, historically charms were empowered, magical words.

These words were often spoken aloud or written on a piece of paper and carried in the pocket or stuffed into walls and floorboards. Certain charms were said to have the power to avert evil, protect the home or the self, or even heal illnesses.

One folk belief in Wales was that for nine generations, the descendants of those who had eaten the flesh of the eagle had the power to charm away the shingles. This was known as *Swyno'r Ryri* ("charming the shingles"). These charmers would spit on the afflicted areas of their clients, before reciting the following charm:

Yr Eryr Eryres
Mi a'th ddanfonais
Dros naw môr a thros naw mynydd
A thro snaw erw o dir anghelfydd
Lle na chyfartho ci, ac na frefo fuwch
Ac na ddelo yr eryr byth yn uwch

Male eagle, female eagle
I send you by my breath,
Over nine seas, and nine mountains
And over nine acres of unprofitable land
Where no dog shall bark, and no cow shall low
And where no eagle shall higher rise

While the belief surrounding being able to charm away the shingles had very specific lore about how one became such a charmer, charming in general was predominately a generational skill. It was taught from one family member to the next. The first woman to have been accused of Witchcraft in Wales, Gwen ferch Ellis, claimed to have learned to charm via her sister.

Certain elements of charming still exist in certain parts of Wales, where we see superstitious practices, such as saying this upon seeing a lone magpie:

Piogen wen, piogen ddu
Lwc i mi a lwc i ti

White magpie, black magpie
Luck to me and luck to you

The speaker then spits onto the floor. This practice is said to avert bad luck that solitary magpies are considered omens of.

Within charms, the power was predominately believed to come from the words themselves as well as from the practitioner utilizing them. Interestingly, many traditional charms are essentially stories being recited. The practice of charms holding a narrative quality to them is not unique to Wales. We see it in charms across the world and even have a word for charms of this quality that carry a mythic narrative within them: *historiola*.

One example from my cultural background is a charm known as the "little creed." This is a Christian protection charm folks would recite that drew upon the power of God and the Virgin Mary. But the charm itself is essentially a story of someone walking up a mountain and seeing God and Mary beaming with joy, and then a strange gray man appears and shrouds them in a veil of protection. While it is a Christian charm, I cannot help but see an essence of the bardic tradition and of powerful word magic being utilized in it.

Crafting Your Own Narrative Charm

Charms, in my opinion, are incredibly easy to create. While I do not believe they can merely be a jumble of words put together without any thought (the words must be divinely inspired and empowered), it is still simple and effective to write our own charms. For example, here is a charm I wrote that calls upon Braint, a local river goddess in my tradition who is known for her ability to heal. The charm itself is written in a format that includes rhymes, because the rhythm of the rhymes awakens a sense of magic within me.

I walked to the river and placed my feet into the stream
The goddess saw me sitting there as though lost within a dream
She noticed I was poorly, with very little to say
And so she sent a healing current to wash the illness away
And then we sang a merry song here at the river's edge

I walked to the river & placed
my feet into the stream
The goddess saw me sitting there
as though lost within a dream
She noticed I was poorly with very
little to say.
And so she sent a healing current
to wash the illness away
And then we sang a mer
here at the river's edge
In celebration of daffodil
birds & the bramble hedge
Braint, goddess of the r
may your waters wash all
ails me away.

In celebration of the daffodils, the birds, and the bramble hedge
Oh Braint, goddess of the river, may your waters wash all that ails me
away

The idea is simple: write a short narrative that encapsulates a concept such as healing or protection. Perhaps include a line or two in reverence to the deities you work with in your practice, dedicating the charm to their name and empowering it with both your own power and theirs. And then, tell the story. Breathe the narrative to life. Is that not what every spell is at heart, telling a tale in such a profound way that it becomes reality?

Finding the Power in the Spoken Word

In addition to being brought up within a culture obsessed with poetry, story, and song, I also have a background as a performer. As an actor, the power of words is deeply apparent to me. The theater is a place of power, where we transport people from the mundane trivialities of every day to fantastical worlds beyond their very imagination.

There is a magic in performance, as the ancient bards would likely agree. After all, many Celtic myths and legends originated in an oral tradition, where these legends were not bound to ink and paper but were performed with passion. When it comes to modern Witchcraft, I believe we often forget to truly embrace this magical quality found in words and in performance. Far too often have I attended a public ritual where the incantations were awkwardly read off a piece of paper, rather than truly embodied and delivered with power. Ritual is but the original version of theater in my eyes, and the more we embody the material we are working with, the more power there is to our ritualistic and magical work.

Take some time to learn a chant or incantation deeply. Learn to recite it without having to look at a piece of paper. The incantation or chant could be one you have written yourself, or it could be one you heard elsewhere and love. I personally love to work with material from my cultural background—poems, songs, and stories my people have recited for generations. When we speak with words that are culturally relevant and important to us, we are essentially doing ancestor work. We are speaking with the voices of the dead. When we recite something old, those words have been recited before by those who came before us. By breathing them to life once more, we are waking up a continuum that stretches back into the mists of time, while also adding our own unique flare to them. And that, to me, is magical indeed.

However, finding our own words is also incredibly powerful. Drawing forth from the wellspring of inspiration to birth something that is entirely our own is an act of pure magic, an act that echoes the search for Awen. Whatever you decide, whether it be to recite something old, tried, and tested, or you experiment and create something new, get to know the words intimately. Play with them. Play with the way you recite them. Sing them. Do whatever it is you can to connect to those words as deeply as you can. Then, the magic can begin, for once you have done this, you can embody the material in a profound manner, and when you next recite them, whether it be during a magical working, a ritual, or something more low key, you will truly feel how much magic there is to the relationship you have with those words.

Our lips and our voices can be shrines to the gods we devote ourselves to. There is no better offering for the gods, our ancestors, or our spirit allies in my eyes than a carefully crafted song, story, poem, incantation, or chant. We are all natural storytellers; it is who we are. Find the words that bring you power and rejoice in them.

Evolving Our Soul through Sabian Symbols

Majorie Gatson

Sabian Symbols are an astrological tool that can be used to perceive future events and describe the energy of the times. Astrology reveals to us what is coming ahead of time and helps us interpret cycles that are unfolding in the collective consciousness. I will be analyzing the major astrological events for 2025 and how Sabian Symbols can be used as insight into our evolution.

A Brief History of Sabian Symbols

One hundred years ago in 1925, renowned astrologer Marc Edmund Jones created a set of intuitive symbols with accomplished clairvoyant and psychic medium Elise Wheeler. Jones desired to create a set of symbols that would help his astrology students better understand the degrees of the zodiac. Wheeler was one of his spiritually gifted students, and together they set out to create symbols for each of the 360 degrees of the zodiac.

In just one afternoon, Jones and Wheeler came together to create the Sabian Symbols rather spontaneously. To form the symbols,

Jones had 360 small blank index cards with each minuscule zodiac degree written in the corner. Jones shuffled the cards and at random flashed them at Wheeler, asking her what she saw when shown each card. Without either of them knowing the zodiac sign or degree written in the corner, Jones would quickly write down what Wheeler envisioned using her clairvoyant abilities.

The Sabian Symbols are not to be confused with glyph symbols. What Jones and Wheeler unveiled were a series of symbolic images or scenes constructed into phrases that can be read as premonitions. The Sabian Symbols reflect many different interpretations and potentialities of each zodiac degree. Each day of the zodiac has a Sabian Symbol. When using Sabian Symbols, you always round up the degree of an astrological transit or event to find the symbol. For example, my degree on the day I was born is 6°33' of Aries. This would be the Sabian Symbol for 7° Aries.

Jones published the Sabian Symbols and his interpretations of his findings. Many years later, the Sabian Symbols were reintroduced with a new perspective by well-known astrologer Dane Rudhyar. Rudhyar was friends with Jones and had the privilege of seeing the original written Sabian Symbols right before Jones's passing. Rudhyar's book *An Astrological Mandala: The Cycle of Transformations and Its 360 Symbolic Phases* is one of the most profound pieces of literature on the Sabian Symbols today and what I will be referencing to interpret important Sabian Symbols for 2025.

Sabian Symbols are also deeply connected to the psychology of astrology that was popularized by Carl Jung. The collective unconscious is a theory Jung developed that connected archetypes and our shared conscious experiences. Astrology ties into psychology, for we are all experiencing the same astrological events collectively, but we have our own personal experience of these events as well. When understanding how an astrological event or transit will affect the collective consciousness, you have to have an understanding of astrology and what each zodiac sign and planet represents. We also need to be aware of social and political events going on in the world as well. This knowledge is what is needed to analyze the Sabian Symbols.

Sabian Symbols provide us with the intuitive language of how astrological events will manifest, what to expect, and what to do about them. It is a glimpse into the future that can give us a better sense of awareness to help us prepare for personal and global transformations. Interpretation of the symbols should be holistic and connect with the cosmic and social cycles in our modern life. Each phrase integrates our consciousness, the occult, and different archetypes the same way divination does. The Sabian Symbols are a century old, but their meaning still holds relevance today.

Sabian Symbols of 2025

To begin decoding the astrological energy for the Sabian Symbols of 2025, I would like to start with the Moon's nodes and the eclipses of the year. I will then cover the Sabian Symbols of Jupiter entering Cancer, Saturn in Pisces, Neptune entering Aries, and Uranus entering Gemini.

Eclipses are a time of intense and powerful manifestation. We should think of eclipses as a portal opening or a portal closing when it pertains to certain themes or events in our lives. The six months in between each eclipse season is a moment in our lives when we are creating and finalizing visions and scenarios we have manifested when the new portal opened.

Each solar and lunar eclipse is aligned with a zodiac sign that is reflective of the Moon's nodes. The North Node and South Node are invisible points on the Moon. The North Node represents the unforeseen future we are collectively and individually embracing. It is similar to Jupiter, for it is a point of strength and opportunity in our lives. In contrast, the South Node is the past we are leaving behind. The South Node has a connection to Saturn, for it is where we go inward to reflect upon our weaknesses and vulnerabilities. The Moon's nodes move backward through the zodiac wheel and spend about eighteen and half months in two zodiac signs that are in opposition. This balance of duality allows us to search deeper within our psyche to continue toward forward progress in our lives and remain present in this transformation. The Moon's nodes in 2025 will be in Aries, Pisces, and Virgo, which result in all the lunar and solar eclipses being in these signs as well. Here are the Sabian Symbols of the first set of eclipses in 2025 and the themes we are to experience. As I interpret each Sabian Symbol, I will also be referencing Dane Rudhyar's key terms for each symbol.

March 14 Total Lunar Eclipse

The first total lunar eclipse is on March 14, 2025, and will be in Virgo at 23°57'. The Sabian Symbol for 24° Virgo is "Mary and her little lamb." Rudhyar's keynote is "To keep a vibrant and pure simplicity at the core of one's being as one meets the many tests of existence" (Rudhyar 165–66). My interpretation of this Sabian Symbol means society will have a more positive outlook of the future, but there will be many new challenges to come. In times of change, all we can hold on to is the trust that things will be better than they were before. This optimism keeps humanity going as we strive to create a new normal and redefine what security means. Now that Pluto has finished its dance in Capricorn and will remain in Aquarius until 2043, humanity is naive about what this new astrological era will bring. The United States will also be going through its

Pluto return for the first time in 250 years, so this will mean much revolutionary upheaval politically and within society. Aquarius is the sign of the future, and we have to envision something different from what we have experienced before. There will be many fresh new ideas coming, especially with the advances in technology, which also falls under Aquarius's rulership. We can create a new and better world, but it will require us to be soft and optimistic and to trust that we can invent a new sense of stability within our lives.

Neptune Enters Aries

The next major transit that happens in 2025 is Neptune entering Aries on March 30. Saturn will also be entering Aries on May 25 and will be sharing the first degree of Aries with Neptune. The Sabian Symbol for the first degree of Aries is "A woman just risen from the sea. A seal is embracing her." Rudhyar's keynote is "Emergence of new forms and of the potentiality of consciousness" (Rudhyar 49–51). I think it is really profound that there is a woman rising from the sea, not a man, which can be the obvious expectation when we are referencing the masculine sign of Aries. I also find this Sabian Symbol aligning with the feminine message of tarot. The first human archetype we encounter on the Fool's journey in tarot is the feminine High Priestess and next is the Empress. It is not until later that we encounter masculine energy with the Emperor and the Hierophant providing its council. The first degree of Aries and the first few major arcana cards in tarot begin the Fool's new journey with a female perspective and intuited awareness.

The woman rising from the sea is embraced by a seal—this is where the first glimpse of duality between feminine and masculine creation takes place. You can also connect this Sabian Symbol as the woman being the end of the zodiac in Pisces, and the seal is Aries waiting to begin a new cycle. Notice the action for the seal is "embracing," not harming or acting with malice toward the woman. By 2025 in society, hopefully more men in positions of power will start to see women as equals and not second-class citizens. There is hope that men will join the feminist movement to fight for our bodily autonomy and equal rights. We have to find balance between the sexes in order to survive the next few decades, especially with the rapid rise of AI. The divine feminine is facing a new reality and is fighting back against the oppression of the past. Also, hopefully more women will be in more positions of political power to preserve our rights for equality, and we will have more men as allies toward the feminist revolution.

March 29 Partial Solar Eclipse

On March 29, 2025, we will have a partial solar eclipse at 9°00' of Aries. The Sabian Symbol is "A crystal gazer." Rudhyar's keynote is "The development of an inner realization of organic wholeness" (Rudhyar 56). New seeds of life are visioned through clairvoyant abilities. In 2025, we will be starting from scratch. A new beginning and zodiac cycle in Aries is transforming us to be more inventive and assertive so we can take charge of our lives in a new way. Broke is the beginning. Having new visions and being brave enough to take charge and test them out is the pure essence of Aries. We must learn to trust our imagination and intuition to help us create a new world. Aries is the first sign of the zodiac and portrays the duality of the pioneering ram as well as the naivety of the baby lamb. The quest is about to begin, but first it must be envisioned. After the dramatic shift and change of late-stage capitalism beginning to collapse in 2023 and 2024, renewal, new beginnings, and curiosity will lead us to cultivate a new societal existence.

However, with Aries being Mars ruled, this energy will not be subtle. It will be a full-on war and may be an unpredictable and messy one too. The Aries tarot card ruler is the Emperor. With new authority and control emerging, so will anarchy and disorder. Neptune will also be nearing Aries at this time and rules the imagination and illusions. We must do our best to not be lead by a disillusioned leader, political party, or system or get lost in our own abyss. Radical change starts with being intuitive, and there is a reason why in the Fool's voyage, the mysticism of the feminine High Priestess is being consulted first before action is taken into reality with the Emperor.

Jupiter Enters Cancer

On June 9, Jupiter enters Cancer at 1°. The Sabian Symbol is "On a ship the sailors lower an old flag and raise a new one." Rudhyar's

keynote is "A radical change of the allegiance exteriorized in a symbolical act: a point of no return" (Rudhyar 110–11). Rudhyar describes this Sabian Symbol as a moment of crisis and a sharp turning point. We are reorienting our values as a society and maybe even leadership as well. New ambitions and assimilating new ideas birthed with the emergence of cardinal energy will result in much systemic change. There is no going back to the ways things once were. Jupiter will expand the crisis we are in but will give us a larger worldview of what we can create from the ashes of the old world. Cancer rules the Mother, intuition, emotional intelligence, and the past. We are faced with the duality of yin and yang, feminine and masculine energy, and how we want to embody it energetically and through physical autonomy. The LGBTQIA+ and nonbinary spectrum community will continue to challenge and shift gender expression and identity. A new world is being created, with marginalized groups at the forefront of this revolution, raising a new flag.

Uranus Enters Gemini

Another major transit in 2025 that will change society for the next seven years is Uranus entering Gemini on July 7. Uranus is the planet of individualization, innovation, chaos, and breaking free from convention. Gemini is the sign of communication and curiosity. This promotes activity such as local travel and the use of social networks. The Sabian Symbol for the first degree of Gemini is "A glass-bottomed boat reveals undersea wonders." Rudhyar's keynote is "The revelation of unconscious energies and submerged psychic structures" (Rudhyar 89). The metaphor of a glass-bottomed boat, reveals to us that there is more to our unconscious that remains unexplored. We have to remain curious and open in order to find answers to our questions. Saturn is in Pisces, and this transit will result in new aquatic discoveries and breakthroughs. Only about 20 percent of the ocean has been explored, so with Saturn in Pisces, new oceanic discoveries will emerge. However, many tragedies and mysteries will result in this exploration as well. Collectively, we will be looking deeper into the unknown. There is much glitter beneath the surface, but we have to be introspective and curious enough to discover it.

September 7 Total Lunar Eclipse

The second and last set of eclipses for 2025 fall into the signs of Pisces and Virgo. The total lunar eclipse in Pisces is at 15°23'. The Sabian Symbol for 16° Pisces is "In the quest of his study a creative individual experiences a flow of inspiration." Rudhyar's keynote is "Reliance upon one's inner source of inspiration or guidance" (Rudhyar 278–79). Pisces is the mystic and the magician. It is magic. To find our magic, we must rest and live a fantasy within our imagination. Creative and intuitive people need to sit around and do nothing. As the mind relaxes, inspiration finds us. The world is shifting toward a more spiritual narrative, and the metaphysical is becoming more valued in mainstream society. People are searching for something more, a deeper connection within themselves and

Spirit. To find this connection, we need to concentrate and seek solitude in the quietness of our inner world. A renewed sense of faith in ourselves results in having gratitude for the cosmic divinity around us and the guidance, protection, and faith it provides.

September 21 Partial Solar Eclipse

The last partial solar eclipse of the year is on September 21 in Virgo at 29°05'. The Sabian Symbol for 30° Virgo is "Totally intent upon completing an immediate task, a man is deaf to any allurement." Rudhyar's keynote is "The total concentration required for reaching any spiritual goal" (Rudhyar 169). What is being created must not be disturbed in its installment process. There could be a bit of hardheadedness as we individually and collectively write new laws, ethos, and rules for ourselves and society. It is time to create from our imagination to manifest a new world vision. However, as the inception of a new world is being birthed, we may wrestle to not repeat old structures and dogmas of the past. Distraction can come in many ways, shapes, and forms with the intent to deter us from maintaining a certain direction toward a more progressive and creative future. Now more than ever, we will have to fight to stay focused on the goals at hand for chaos, and opposition will be working hard to disrupt the end result. With our undeterred devotion to the task, we will thank ourselves later for avoiding temptation so we can complete what we set out to accomplish.

Saturn Direct in Pisces

The last Sabian Symbol I want to explore is Saturn at 25°09' Pisces when it goes direct on November 28, after being retrograde in Aries. The Sabian Symbol for 26° Pisces is "Watching the very thin moon crescent appearing at sunset, different people realize that the time has come to go ahead with their different projects." Rudhyar's keynote is "A keen appreciation of the value of individualized responses to any challenge of life" (Rudhyar 285–86). Saturn is the planet of grief and reality. A new reality is approaching that will result in a more liberated and enlightened society. The year 2025 will be a time when we can expect expansion, despite the population displaying reluctance. People's modus operandi is to hold on to their own individual beliefs and values. Old ways die hard. We cannot expect people to conform, especially when conformity jeopardizes what we're used to. As Rudhyar states, "In a society that glorifies individualism, everyone should therefore accept this fact and not try to compel other individuals to conform to a single pattern of response" (Rudhyar 168–69). There is grief in letting go of outdated paradigms, but what is being created will give us more to look forward to.

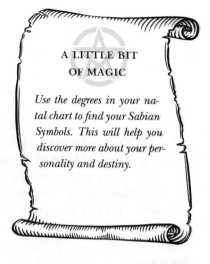

A LITTLE BIT OF MAGIC

Use the degrees in your natal chart to find your Sabian Symbols. This will help you discover more about your personality and destiny.

In 2025, something new is being born despite how juvenile and aggressive it may start. The future will not start slow. With the quick advances in technology, oceanic discovery, and a renowned sense of inner awareness to our individualistic needs and values, we can no longer be controlled by the dying patriarchal capitalist ethos of a bygone era—we have to invent new systems and structures. For something new to be embraced, we need solidarity in a community that has a new vision. Sabian Symbols mirror the future energy of our world, and their insight can help us better understand the times we are in and where we are headed. Sabian Symbols carry their own duality, but if we allow ourselves to be open to exploring all potentialities of our conscious reality, that is where true evolutionary growth can take place in our world.

A Sabian Symbol Tarot Spread

Find the Sabian Symbol of your Sun Sign to use this tarot spread. Consult a reference book like Rudhyar's or an online resource such as Lisa Hill's sabiansymbols.com/symbols and locate the corresponding Sabian Symbol for the sign and degree shown in your birth chart. Feel free to pull oracle and astrology cards alongside tarot when using on this spread.

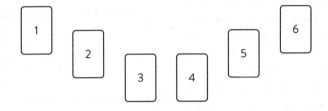

Card 1: What is the magic of my Sabian Symbol?

Card 2: What inspiration can my Sabian Symbol provide?

Card 3: What are the challenges my Sabian Symbol represents?

Card 4: How can my Sabian Symbol help my spiritual evolution?

Card 5: What hidden talents does my Sabian Symbol reveal?

Card 6: How can my Sabian Symbol help me achieve my destiny?

Resource

Rudhyar, Dane. *An Astrological Mandala: The Cycle of Transformations and Its 360 Symbolic Phases.* New York: Random House, 1973.

2025 Almanac

The Date

The date is used in numerological calculations that govern magical rites. Below is a calendar for 2025.

JANUARY

			1	2	3	4
5	6	7	8	9	10	11
12	13	14	15	16	17	18
19	20	21	22	23	24	25
26	27	28	29	30	31	

FEBRUARY

						1
2	3	4	5	6	7	8
9	10	11	12	13	14	15
16	17	18	19	20	21	22
23	24	25	26	27	28	

MARCH

						1
2	3	4	5	6	7	8
9	10	11	12	13	14	15
16	17	18	19	20	21	22
23	24	25	26	27	28	29
30	31					

APRIL

		1	2	3	4	5
6	7	8	9	10	11	12
13	14	15	16	17	18	19
20	21	22	23	24	25	26
27	28	29	30			

MAY

				1	2	3
4	5	6	7	8	9	10
11	12	13	14	15	16	17
18	19	20	21	22	23	24
25	26	27	28	29	30	31

JUNE

1	2	3	4	5	6	7
8	9	10	11	12	13	14
15	16	17	18	19	20	21
22	23	24	25	26	27	28
29	30					

JULY

		1	2	3	4	5
6	7	8	9	10	11	12
13	14	15	16	17	18	19
20	21	22	23	24	25	26
27	28	29	30	31		

AUGUST

					1	2
3	4	5	6	7	8	9
10	11	12	13	14	15	16
17	18	19	20	21	22	23
24	25	26	27	28	29	30
31						

SEPTEMBER

	1	2	3	4	5	6
7	8	9	10	11	12	13
14	15	16	17	18	19	20
21	22	23	24	25	26	27
28	29	30				

OCTOBER

			1	2	3	4
5	6	7	8	9	10	11
12	13	14	15	16	17	18
19	20	21	22	23	24	25
26	27	28	29	30	31	

NOVEMBER

						1
2	3	4	5	6	7	8
9	10	11	12	13	14	15
16	17	18	19	20	21	22
23	24	25	26	27	28	29
30						

DECEMBER

	1	2	3	4	5	6
7	8	9	10	11	12	13
14	15	16	17	18	19	20
21	22	23	24	25	26	27
28	29	30	31			

The Day

Each day is ruled by a planet that possesses specific magical influences:

SUNDAY (SUN): Healing, spirituality, success, strength, and protection.

MONDAY (MOON): Peace, sleep, healing, compassion, friends, psychic awareness, purification, and fertility.

TUESDAY (MARS): Passion, sex, courage, aggression, and protection.

WEDNESDAY (MERCURY): The conscious mind, study, travel, divination, and wisdom.

THURSDAY (JUPITER): Expansion, money, prosperity, and generosity.

FRIDAY (VENUS): Love, friendship, reconciliation, and beauty.

SATURDAY (SATURN): Longevity, exorcism, endings, homes, and houses.

The Lunar Phase

The lunar phase is important in determining the best times for magic.

THE WAXING MOON (from the New Moon to the Full) is the ideal time for magic to draw things toward you.

THE FULL MOON is the time of greatest power.

THE WANING MOON (from the Full Moon to the New) is a time for study, meditation, and little magical work (except magic designed to banish harmful energies).

The Moon's Sign

The Moon continuously "moves" through the zodiac, from Aries to Pisces. Each sign possesses its own significance.

ARIES: Good for starting things, but lacks staying power. Things occur rapidly, but quickly pass. People tend to be argumentative and assertive.

TAURUS: Things begun now last the longest, tend to increase in value, and become hard to alter. Brings out appreciation for beauty and sensory experience.

GEMINI: Things begun now are easily changed by outside influence. Time for shortcuts, communication, games, and fun.

CANCER: Stimulates emotional rapport between people. Pinpoints need, supports growth and nurturance. Tends to domestic concerns.

LEO: Draws emphasis to the self, central ideas, or institutions, away from connections with others and other emotional needs. People tend to be melodramatic.

VIRGO: Favors accomplishment of details and commands from higher up. Focuses on health, hygiene, and daily schedules.

LIBRA: Favors cooperation, social activities, beautification of surroundings, balance, and partnership.

SCORPIO: Increases awareness of psychic power. Precipitates psychic crises and ends connections thoroughly. People tend to brood and become secretive.

SAGITTARIUS: Encourages flights of imagination and confidence. This is an adventurous, philosophical, and athletic Moon sign. Favors expansion and growth.

CAPRICORN: Develops strong structure. Focus on traditions, responsibilities, and obligations. A good time to set boundaries and rules.

AQUARIUS: Rebellious energy. Time to break habits and make abrupt changes. Personal freedom and individuality is the focus.

PISCES: The focus is on dreaming, nostalgia, intuition, and psychic impressions. A good time for spiritual or philanthropic activities.

Color and Incense of the Day

The color and incense for the day are based on information from *Personal Alchemy* by Amber Wolfe and relate to the planet that rules each day. This information can be taken into consideration along with other factors when planning works of magic or when blending magic into mundane life. See page 264 for a list of color correspondences. Please note that the incense selections listed are not hard and fast. If you cannot find or do not like the incense listed for the day, choose a similar scent that appeals to you.

Holidays and Festivals

Holidays and festivals of many cultures, nations, and spiritual practices are listed throughout the year. The exact dates of many ancient festivals are difficult to determine; prevailing data has been used.

Time Zones

The times and dates of all astrological phenomena in this almanac are based on **Eastern Standard Time (EST)**. If you live outside of the Eastern time zone, you will need to make the following adjustments:

PACIFIC STANDARD TIME: Subtract three hours.

MOUNTAIN STANDARD TIME: Subtract two hours.

CENTRAL STANDARD TIME: Subtract one hour.

ALASKA: Subtract four hours.

HAWAII: Subtract five hours.

DAYLIGHT SAVING TIME (ALL ZONES): Add one hour.

Daylight Saving Time begins at 2 am on March 9, 2025, and ends at 2 am on November 2, 2025.

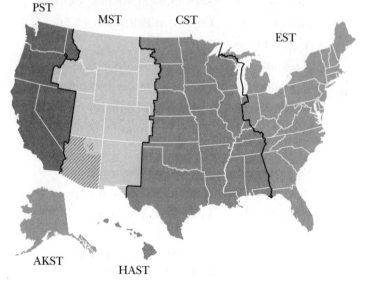

Please refer to a world time zone resource for time adjustments for locations outside the United States.

2025 Sabbats
and Full Moons

January 13	Cancer Full Moon 5:27 pm
February 2	Imbolc
February 12	Leo Full Moon 8:53 am
March 14	Virgo Full Moon 2:55 am
March 20	Ostara (Spring Equinox)
April 12	Libra Full Moon 8:22 pm
May 1	Beltane
May 12	Scorpio Full Moon 12:56 pm
June 11	Sagittarius Full Moon 3:44 am
June 20	Midsummer (Summer Solstice)
July 10	Capricorn Full Moon 4:37 pm
August 1	Lammas
August 9	Aquarius Full Moon 3:55 am
September 7	Pisces Full Moon 2:09 pm
September 22	Mabon (Fall Equinox)
October 6	Aries Full Moon 11:48 pm
October 31	Samhain
November 5	Taurus Full Moon 8:19 am
December 4	Gemini Full Moon 6:14 pm
December 21	Yule (Winter Solstice)

All times are Eastern Standard Time (EST)
or Eastern Daylight Time (EDT)

2025 Sabbats in the Southern Hemisphere

Because Earth's Northern and Southern Hemispheres experience opposite seasons at any given time, the season-based sabbats listed on the previous page and in this almanac section are not correct for those residing south of the equator. Listed here are the Southern Hemisphere sabbat dates for 2025:

February 2	Lammas
March 20	Mabon (Fall Equinox)
May 1	Samhain
June 20	Yule (Winter Solstice)
August 1	Imbolc
September 22	Ostara (Spring Equinox)
November 1	Beltane
December 21	Midsummer (Summer Solstice)

2025 Solar and Lunar Eclipses

Lunar eclipse	March 14	23° ♍ 57'
Solar eclipse	March 29	9° ♈ 00'
Lunar eclipse	September 7	15° ♓ 23'
Solar eclipse	September 21	29° ♍ 05'

Two- and three-dimensional maps of the visibility range of an eclipse can often be found online leading up to the event. Even if it's not visible in your area, you can still draw on the energy of this astrological phenomenon.

2025 Energetic Forecast
Charlie Rainbow Wolf

Welcome to 2025! This is a busy year in the stars! The overall vibe is one of change, as three of the heavyweight outer planets are switching signs. Pluto is settling himself into Aquarius. Neptune leaves Pisces and enters Aries; he hasn't visited there since the mid-1800s. Uranus will dip his toe into Gemini for the first time since the end of the Great Depression. These are slow-moving planets, and their impact is going to be subtle but long-lasting.

Neptune and Pluto will be in and out of sextile this year. They've been dancing together on and off for well over 100 years, as they're both slow-moving planets, and Pluto's orbit is erratic. The harmonious aspect of these two inspires imagination. What will they create? The trend in AI developments is interesting, to say the least! Pluto is the planet of destruction and rebirth, but hopefully Neptune's sensitivity and desire for peace will help to turn things around in a positive way. These planets reach an exact sextile in 2026, but the approach will be felt throughout this year. Expect to see an increase in creativity, spiritual matters, metaphysics, and philosophical pursuits—and perhaps a few temper tantrums too.

Uranus enters Gemini on July 7 but then slips back into Taurus on November 7, before he finally permanently enters Gemini next year. This could bring some uncertainty; whenever there are Uranus-Gemini transits, there are usually shifts when it comes to borders and territories. Uranus in Gemini makes a strong statement, and while that isn't firmly established 2026, we'll get a taste of what may come this year.

There are four eclipses this year; a total lunar eclipse on March 14, a partial solar eclipse on March 29, a total lunar eclipse on September 7, and a partial solar eclipse on September 21. The latter is the most important as it happens at a very impactful degree. Pay attention to what you are doing during the duration of this eclipse,

especially to your mindset, for it will set the tone of things until the next solar eclipse in eleven months.

This year begins with Mars retrograde in Leo, potentially making it hard to get those resolutions off the ground. Mars and Leo are both fiery; Mars is the planet of movement and action, and when it is retrograde, then movement and action become delayed and frustrated. It leaves its backward journey and stations direct in February.

Not long after Mars sorts itself, Venus starts her retrograde journey. Venus rules both relationships and finances, and it's best not to make any hard and fast plans or sign any contacts when she's retrograde. She begins her backward dance in March and stations direct in April.

Mercury turns retrograde three times this year: in March, in July, and in November. Mercury gets a lot of bad rap when he turns retro, but this is actually a good time for reviewing, revising, rethinking, redoing—any of those *re-* words! This is also a good time to reflect how things are unfolding and revisit plans to see how they might be improved. Mercury goes retrograde so often that we've gotten quite used to it and learned how to navigate it fairly well.

The heavier planets all make their annual retrograde trip this year too. I've mentioned the big ones—Pluto, Neptune, and Uranus—but Saturn and Jupiter will take part too. Every planet is retrograde this year at some point! For more details on how this is going to affect you, check out *Llewellyn's 2025 Astrological Pocket Planner*.

Numerologically, the universal number for 2025 is 9. The number 9 is linked to endings—not necessarily expiration, but rather bringing things to a conclusion and tidying up loose ends, ready to start anew. This is a good year to release things that have been weighing you down. Let go of outmoded ideas, clear clutter in your environment, release beliefs that no longer work for you, and let toxic relationships fall by the wayside. Anything that is carried into next year is likely to stay with you for the next nine-year cycle, and that would be unwelcome baggage.

It's the Lunar New Year on January 29, when the year of the Wood Snake arrives. This is a good year for giving up bad habits and leaving anything unwanted behind—very much in harmony with this year's numerology. The traits of the Wood Snake are intelligence, organization, order, and refinement.

The tarot card for the year is the Hermit. The Hermit uses introspection to examine his own psyche for the answers he's seeking. This also resonates with the numerology of this year because often the Hermit will appear as one cycle closes and another one opens.

January

Energetically, January 1 is a reset of a new day, a new month, a new year, and a new energetic cycle. Everything seems to resonate with an energy of determination and hope for what's yet to come. January's universal month number is 10, the number of completion and beginnings. It makes sense: all the holiday festivities are over, and

now it is time for knuckling down to business. The tarot card for this month is the Wheel of Fortune, echoing the changes the New Year brings. The Sun leaves Capricorn and enters Aquarius on the 19th, perhaps bringing a bit of a rebellious streak with it, especially as it's making a conjunction to Pluto on the 21st! This energy will be magnified when Mercury enters Aquarius on the 27th. The end of the month is a good time to purge. The Moon is waxing as we start the year—favorable for new plans and projects. The Full Moon in Cancer on the 13th is advantageous for emotional or relationship issues to come out into the open. The New Moon in Aquarius on the 29th marks the beginning of the Lunar Year of the Snake and is an excellent time to work on manifesting what you desire.

February

February opens with the celebration of Imbolc, a Pagan festival that marks the first signs of spring. The universal month number is 11. In numerology, this is a master number representing leadership, charisma, and inspiration. The first eleven days of this month are a particularly good time to make progress on plans and projects. The tarot card for this month is the Justice card, bringing in a need for balance and fairness. The Sun is in Aquarius until the 18th. This adds determination, but there could be some friction around the 8th or the 9th with Mercury aspecting Mars as it conjuncts the Sun. The Full Moon in Leo on the 12th is good for socializing, but there's tension from the dissipating Mercury aspects, and Mars remains retrograde until the 23rd. The month ends with a New Moon in Pisces on the 27th, a good time for reflection and introspection.

March

Daylight Saving Time starts March 9 at 2:00 a.m.—one of my favorite times for ritual. The lost hour when the clocks jump forward creates an opportune time for banishing anything you want to purge from your life. Do the spellwork at 2:00, then put your

clock forward and let the lost hour consume what you've released. March's universal month number 3. It's a warm and social number, but be mindful not to overindulge or overdo things. March's tarot card is the Hanged Man, asking you what sacrifices you are willing to make to achieve your goals. The Sun is in Pisces until the 20th, when it enters Aries and marks the spring equinox.

Mercury is in the shadow period for the upcoming retrograde, which starts 15 March in Aries. Expect delays and frustrations during this time, as Mercury retrograde will impede Aries's fiery energy. Take time to review plans and projects rather than acting on them. Venus retrograde—also in Aries—commences on the 1st. This might add complexity and irritations to anything concerning relationships and financial matters. It's best not to make any life-changing commitments at this time. There's a Full Moon in Virgo 14th. This is the date of a full lunar eclipse too, ideal for releasing any emotional baggage or toxic relationships—especially those that are standing in your way of being organized and feeling complete. The partial solar eclipse on the 29th could accentuate the frustrations created by the retrogrades, especially as Neptune leaves its home in Pisces and makes its first sojourn into Aries since the mid-1800s on the 30th.

April

The first of April is often called April Fools' Day, but with Neptune easing his way into Aries while Venus and Mercury are retrograde, I see nothing foolish here! April's universal month number is 4, a number of balance and security, but there could also be some rigidity involved and a lot of unnoticed behind-the-scenes activity. The tarot card is the Death card, but this has more to do with transformation than physical death. The Sun is in Aries and moves into Taurus on the 19th, grounding the energy for Easter Sunday on the 20th. The month gets off to a mediocre start, because even though the overall energy is one of activity and movement, Mercury retrograde does not end until the 7th, the same day Venus ret-

rograde conjuncts Saturn. Setbacks and misunderstandings could arise when it comes to relationships and financial matters until the 24th, when Venus—which stations direct on the 12th—kisses Saturn again in her forward movement. The Full Moon in Libra on the 12th adds energy to the exasperations of the retrograde mess. By the New Moon in Taurus on the 27th, things should be settling down, ready to start afresh.

May

May Day is a time for celebrating fertility and rebirth in many traditions. May's universal month number is 5: gregarious, uplifting, and one that brings changes, even if they're only fleeting. The tarot card is Temperance, a reminder of the need for prudence during the Venus-Neptune conjunction on the 2nd and the Sun-Uranus conjunction on the 17th. Pluto stations retrograde on the 4th, but he stays in Aquarius, so there might not be any big disruptions there. The Sun then enters Gemini on the 20th. Mercury enters its ruling sign of Gemini, then makes quick aspects to Saturn, Neptune, and Pluto between the 25th and the 27th—the last 10 days of May could get inconveniently busy. The Full Moon is in Scorpio on the 12th, highlighting passionate encounters of all kinds, and the New Moon closes the month with some reflective and introverted energies on the 26th.

June

June starts quite quietly, although anything not dealt with immediately could fester from the time Mercury makes a conjunction in Cancer with Jupiter on the 10th until the planet of communication and travel enters Leo on the 26th. The universal month number is 6, which brings a bit of harmony and stability to the month. The tarot card for June is the Devil, but this has less to do with demons and more to do with what baggage you're still carrying and what is inhibiting you from moving ahead. Jupiter enters Cancer—a cardinal water sign—on the 9th, and the Sun follows it at Midsummer on the

20th. The Full Moon in Sagittarius on the 11th brings a humanitarian and feel-good factor to any Midsummer celebrations, while the New Moon in Cancer finishes the month on quite a reserved and potentially moody note.

July

July sees Uranus enter Gemini for the first time since 1949. Gemini and Uranus are both impulsive and unreserved—and because of Uranus's slow and somewhat erratic orbit, this is just a taste of things to come. Venus begins to move into a square with Mars starting on the 21st, which could create friction—and then there's a Mercury retrograde to deal with. It turns in Leo on the 18th, creating potential drama until it stations direct next month. Other retrogrades include Neptune in Aries from the 4th and Saturn in Aries from the 13th. The retrograde conjunction in a fire sign may lead to additional frustrations and delays. The Sun enters Leo on the 22nd and soon makes a trine with both Saturn and Neptune; discipline may be needed to avoid overload. The universal month number is 7: esoteric and inquisitive and unpredictable. The Tower is this month's tarot card, and both the universal number and the Tower—with its sudden and sometimes destructive potential—seem to reflect what Uranus is bringing. The Full Moon in Capricorn on the 10th may struggle to ground this energy. The New Moon in Leo on the 24th may lead to frustrations and discord.

August

Mercury retrograde is still in full swing at the start of this month, along with Saturn and Neptune. The latter two are hanging around a while, and they open the month with adverse aspects to Venus, which—coupled with her negative alignment with Pluto—could briefly impact finances and relationships. Mercury stations direct in Leo on the 11th, although the shadow period lasts until the 25th. Given all these factors, most of the month may be a bit com-

plicated. The universal month number is 8, which brings either an anchor or a shackle, depending on the situation. The tarot card is the Star, bringing the message that things are hopeful, even when they seem problematic. The Sun enters Virgo on the 22nd, and it's a good time to seek out Virgo's practical and orderly nature. The Full Moon in Aquarius on the 9th might bring arguments or discord, so exercise patience. The New Moon in Virgo on the 23rd starts to bring some easier energies to the close of the month.

September

The month opens with more discord as Saturn enters Pisces again and Mercury makes fleeting and awkward aspects to Saturn, Neptune, Uranus, and Pluto. Uranus stations retrograde in Gemini on the 6th; pay attention to what has transpired the last couple of months because it's very likely more of that will happen next year. Venus enters Virgo on the 19th, followed by the Sun entering Libra

on the 22nd, which marks the autumn equinox. Relationships of all kinds may start to become a bit more stable. The universal month number is 9, the number of bringing things to a close. The tarot card is the Moon, appropriate with the eclipses this month! The total lunar eclipse is in Pisces on the 7th and brings an energy that is surreal and dreamy—perhaps even surreptitious. A partial solar eclipse occurs on the 21st in Virgo, looking for balance and order.

October

After the eclipses and the retrogrades of the last few weeks, October starts fairly quiet, but a Venus-Neptune opposition mid-month could bring some nebulousness to relationships and financial matters. Pluto stations direct on the 13th but stays in Aquarius, and Neptune re-enters Pisces on the 22nd, right before the Sun enters Scorpio on the 22nd. Spiritual or psychological matters may become more noticeable. The universal month number is 1, the number of new beginnings. The tarot card is the Magician, who reminds you that you have everything at hand to create what you want—but there's a difference between movement and action! The Full Moon in Aries on the 6th adds an urgency to things, while the New Moon in Libra on the 21st brings a sense of balance. The month closes with Halloween and All Hallows' Eve and an opportunity to reflect on how the year is unfolding.

November

The 1st and 2nd of November are All Saints' Day and All Souls' Day, respectively, and mark the start of the Old New Year. Daylight Saving Time ends at 2:00 a.m. on the 2nd, and the combination makes this a wonderful time for magic. Do the ritual, then put the clocks back and repeat the ceremony with a different outcome. Uranus pops back into Taurus on the 7th, where he'll stay until next spring. If you want a glimpse of what lies ahead, review the last 4 months. Mercury is slowing and will station retrograde on the

9th in Sagittarius, which could create some challenges in communications and travel plans. The retrograde ends in Scorpio on the 29th—just long enough to create some interesting discussions over the Thanksgiving dinner table on the 27th! Jupiter will join the retrograde parade, stationing in Gemini on the 11th, potentially slowing plans and projects down but also giving you pause to review and revise them. The Sun moves into Sagittarius on the 21st, and this is reflected in the bustle of holiday preparations for so many people. The universal month number is master number 11 again, so look back to February for patterns that may repeat. The tarot card is the High Priestess, adding wisdom and knowledge to the month. The Full Moon in Taurus on the 5th brings a bit of social stability (it's needed with all those retrogrades), while the New Moon in Scorpio on the 20th creates a bit of mystery around plans and ideas.

December

As we close the year, Jupiter, Uranus, and Neptune are still retrograde, with Neptune direct on the 10th, still at home in Pisces. The heavier planets won't mess quite so much up as the inner planets do when they're retrograde, but their restrained influence is there all the same. Mercury is also direct but still in his shadow until the 17th, which could create misunderstandings or miscommunications. Mars enters Capricorn on the 15th, and the Sun follows on the 21st, the night of the winter solstice. This is a good time for balancing what has happened in this year with your goals and desires for 2026. The universal month number is 3, which could bring some very intense emotions around the holiday festivities. The tarot card is once again the Hanged Man; what sacrifices did you make this year? What more are you willing to sacrifice to realize your ambitions next year? A Full Moon in Gemini on the 4th echoes Sagittarius's outgoing energy, while the New Moon on the 19th in Sagittarius may well be looking for a bit of a respite from all the holiday socializing!

January

1	**Wednesday**	
	New Year's Day • Kwanzaa ends	Moon Sign: Capricorn
	Waxing Moon	Moon enters Aquarius 5:50 am
	Moon phase: First Quarter	Incense: Marjoram
	Color: Brown	

2	**Thursday**	
	Hanukkah ends	Moon Sign: Aquarius
	Waxing Moon	Incense: Clove
	Moon phase: First Quarter	
	Color: Purple	

3	**Friday**	
	St. Genevieve's Day	Moon Sign: Aquarius
	Waxing Moon	Moon enters Pisces 10:21 am
	Moon phase: First Quarter	Incense: Violet
	Color: Rose	

4	**Saturday**	
	Kamakura Workers' Festival (Japanese)	Moon Sign: Pisces
	Waxing Moon	Incense: Magnolia
	Moon phase: First Quarter	
	Color: Black	

5	**Sunday**	
	Bird Day	Moon Sign: Pisces
	Waxing Moon	Moon enters Aries 2:01 pm
	Moon phase: First Quarter	Incense: Hyacinth
	Color: Yellow	

◑	**Monday**	
	Epiphany	Moon Sign: Aries
	Waxing Moon	Incense: Hyssop
	Second Quarter 6:56 pm	
	Color: Silver	

7	**Tuesday**	
	Tricolor Day (Italian)	Moon Sign: Aries
	Waxing Moon	Moon enters Taurus 5:11 pm
	Moon phase: Second Quarter	Incense: Ylang-ylang
	Color: White	

January

---

8 Wednesday
Midwives' Day (Bulgarian)
Waxing Moon
Moon phase: Second Quarter
Color: Topaz

Moon Sign: Taurus
Incense: Honeysuckle

---

9 Thursday
Feast of the Black Nazarene (Filipino)
Waxing Moon
Moon phase: Second Quarter
Color: Crimson

Moon Sign: Taurus
Moon enters Gemini 8:07 pm
Incense: Apricot

---

10 Friday
Feast of St. Leonie Aviat
Waxing Moon
Moon phase: Second Quarter
Color: Pink

Moon Sign: Gemini
Incense: Mint

---

11 Saturday
Carmentalia (Roman)
Waxing Moon
Moon phase: Second Quarter
Color: Brown

Moon Sign: Gemini
Moon enters Cancer 11:24 pm
Incense: Sage

---

12 Sunday
Revolution Day (Tanzanian)
Waxing Moon
Moon phase: Second Quarter
Color: Gold

Moon Sign: Cancer
Incense: Almond

---

13 Monday
Twentieth Day (Norwegian)
Waxing Moon
Full Moon 5:27 pm
Color: White

Moon Sign: Cancer
Incense: Rosemary

---

14 Tuesday
Feast of the Ass (French)
Waning Moon
Moon phase: Third Quarter
Color: Black

Moon Sign: Cancer
Moon enters Leo 4:12 am
Incense: Geranium

January

15 Wednesday
Korean Alphabet Day
Waning Moon
Moon phase: Third Quarter
Color: Yellow

Moon Sign: Leo
Incense: Lilac

16 Thursday
Teachers' Day (Thai)
Waning Moon
Moon phase: Third Quarter
Color: Green

Moon Sign: Leo
Moon enters Virgo 11:46 am
Incense: Nutmeg

17 Friday
St. Anthony's Day (Mexican)
Waning Moon
Moon phase: Third Quarter
Color: White

Moon Sign: Virgo
Incense: Thyme

18 Saturday
Feast of St. Athanasius
Waning Moon
Moon phase: Third Quarter
Color: Indigo

Moon Sign: Virgo
Moon enters Libra 10:33 pm
Incense: Sandalwood

19 Sunday
Edgar Allan Poe's birthday
Waning Moon
Moon phase: Third Quarter
Color: Orange

Moon Sign: Libra
Incense: Frankincense
Sun enters Aquarius 3:00 pm

20 Monday
Martin Luther King Jr. Day • Inauguration Day
Waning Moon
Moon phase: Third Quarter
Color: Ivory

Moon Sign: Libra
Incense: Lily

◗ Tuesday
St. Agnes's Day
Waning Moon
Fourth Quarter 3:31 pm
Color: Gray

Moon Sign: Libra
Moon enters Scorpio 11:20 am
Incense: Bayberry

January

22 Wednesday
St. Vincent's Day (French)
Waning Moon
Moon phase: Fourth Quarter
Color: Brown

Moon Sign: Scorpio
Incense: Lavender

23 Thursday
Feast of St. Ildefonsus
Waning Moon
Moon phase: Fourth Quarter
Color: Purple

Moon Sign: Scorpio
Moon enters Sagittarius 11:29 pm
Incense: Myrrh

24 Friday
Alasitas Fair (Bolivian)
Waning Moon
Moon phase: Fourth Quarter
Color: Coral

Moon Sign: Sagittarius
Incense: Vanilla

25 Saturday
Burns Night (Scottish)
Waning Moon
Moon phase: Fourth Quarter
Color: Blue

Moon Sign: Sagittarius
Incense: Pine

26 Sunday
Australia Day • Maha Shivaratri (Hindu)
Waning Moon
Moon phase: Fourth Quarter
Color: Amber

Moon Sign: Sagittarius
Moon enters Capricorn 8:43 am
Incense: Heliotrope

27 Monday
Holocaust Remembrance Day • Vogel Gryff (Swiss)
Waning Moon
Moon phase: Fourth Quarter
Color: Lavender

Moon Sign: Capricorn
Incense: Neroli

28 Tuesday
Up Helly Aa (Scottish)
Waning Moon
Moon phase: Fourth Quarter
Color: Maroon

Moon Sign: Capricorn
Moon enters Aquarius 2:31 pm
Incense: Ginger

January

☽ Wednesday
Lunar New Year (Snake)
Waning Moon
New Moon 7:36 am
Color: White

Moon Sign: Aquarius
Incense: Bay laurel

30 Thursday
Martyrs' Day (Indian)
Waxing Moon
Moon phase: First Quarter
Color: Turquoise

Moon Sign: Aquarius
Moon enters Pisces 5:52 pm
Incense: Jasmine

31 Friday
Independence Day (Nauru)
Waxing Moon
Moon phase: First Quarter
Color: Pink

Moon Sign: Pisces
Incense: Rose

January Correspondences

Stones: Garnet, moonstone
Animals: Snow goose, owl, bear, wolf
Flowers: Carnation, snowdrop
Deities: Baba Yaga, Enki, Hekate, Loki, Saturn
Zodiac: Capricorn

February Correspondences

Stones: Amethyst, obsidian
Animals: Otter, white cow, snake
Flowers: Violet, primrose
Deities: Brigid, Ea, Ishtar, Isis, Juno, Nut
Zodiac: Aquarius

February

1	**Saturday**	
	St. Brigid's Day (Irish)	Moon Sign: Pisces
	Waxing Moon	Moon enters Aries 8:10 pm
	Moon phase: First Quarter	Incense: Patchouli
	Color: Gray	

2	**Sunday**	
	Imbolc • Groundhog Day	Moon Sign: Aries
	Waxing Moon	Incense: Marigold
	Moon phase: First Quarter	
	Color: Orange	

3	**Monday**	
	St. Blaise's Day	Moon Sign: Aries
	Waxing Moon	Moon enters Taurus 10:53 pm
	Moon phase: First Quarter	Incense: Narcissus
	Color: Ivory	

4	**Tuesday**	
	Independence Day (Sri Lankan)	Moon Sign: Taurus
	Waxing Moon	Incense: Basil
	Moon phase: First Quarter	
	Color: Scarlet	

5	**Wednesday**	
	Constitution Day (Mexican)	Moon Sign: Taurus
	Waxing Moon	Incense: Lilac
	Second Quarter 3:02 am	
	Color: Yellow	

6	**Thursday**	
	Bob Marley's birthday (Jamaican)	Moon Sign: Taurus
	Waxing Moon	Moon enters Gemini 1:44 am
	Moon phase: Second Quarter	Incense: Carnation
	Color: White	

7	**Friday**	
	Feast of St. Richard the Pilgrim	Moon Sign: Gemini
	Waxing Moon	Incense: Orchid
	Moon phase: Second Quarter	
	Color: Purple	

February

8 Saturday
Prešeren Day (Slovenian)
Waxing Moon
Moon phase: Second Quarter
Color: Blue

Moon Sign: Gemini
Moon enters Cancer 6:04 am
Incense: Rue

9 Sunday
St. Maron's Day (Lebanese)
Waxing Moon
Moon phase: Second Quarter
Color: Gold

Moon Sign: Cancer
Incense: Eucalyptus

10 Monday
Feast of St. Scholastica
Waxing Moon
Moon phase: Second Quarter
Color: Gray

Moon Sign: Cancer
Moon enters Leo 12:01 pm
Incense: Lily

11 Tuesday
National Foundation Day (Japanese)
Waxing Moon
Moon phase: Second Quarter
Color: Red

Moon Sign: Leo
Incense: Cedar

☻ Wednesday
Lantern Festival (Chinese)
Waxing Moon
Full Moon 8:53 am
Color: Brown

Moon Sign: Leo
Moon enters Virgo 8:07 pm
Incense: Marjoram

13 Thursday
Parentalia (Roman)
Waning Moon
Moon phase: Third Quarter
Color: Purple

Moon Sign: Virgo
Incense: Balsam

14 Friday
Valentine's Day
Waning Moon
Moon phase: Third Quarter
Color: Coral

Moon Sign: Virgo
Incense: Cypress

February

15 Saturday

Susan B. Anthony Day
Waning Moon
Moon phase: Third Quarter
Color: Indigo

Moon Sign: Virgo
Moon enters Libra 6:45 am
Incense: Magnolia

16 Sunday

Nichiren's birthday
Waning Moon
Moon phase: Third Quarter
Color: Amber

Moon Sign: Libra
Incense: Frankincense

17 Monday

Presidents' Day
Waning Moon
Moon phase: Third Quarter
Color: Silver

Moon Sign: Libra
Moon enters Scorpio 7:19 pm
Incense: Rosemary

18 Tuesday

St. Bernadette's Third Vision
Waning Moon
Moon phase: Third Quarter
Color: Black

Moon Sign: Scorpio
Sun enters Pisces 5:07 am
Incense: Bayberry

19 Wednesday

Flag Day (Turkmenian)
Waning Moon
Moon phase: Third Quarter
Color: White

Moon Sign: Scorpio
Incense: Bay laurel

◖ Thursday

World Day of Social Justice
Waning Moon
Fourth Quarter 12:33 pm
Color: Green

Moon Sign: Scorpio
Moon enters Sagittarius 7:55 am
Incense: Mulberry

21 Friday

Feralia (Roman)
Waning Moon
Moon phase: Fourth Quarter
Color: Pink

Moon Sign: Sagittarius
Incense: Yarrow

February

22 Saturday
Caristia (Roman)
Waning Moon
Moon phase: Fourth Quarter
Color: Brown

Moon Sign: Sagittarius
Moon enters Capricorn 6:09 pm
Incense: Ivy

23 Sunday
Mashramani Festival (Guyanan)
Waning Moon
Moon phase: Fourth Quarter
Color: Yellow

Moon Sign: Capricorn
Incense: Almond

24 Monday
Regifugium (Roman)
Waning Moon
Moon phase: Fourth Quarter
Color: White

Moon Sign: Capricorn
Incense: Clary sage

25 Tuesday
St. Walburga's Day (German)
Waning Moon
Moon phase: Fourth Quarter
Color: Gray

Moon Sign: Capricorn
Moon enters Aquarius 12:40 am
Incense: Cinnamon

26 Wednesday
Zamboanga Day (Filipino)
Waning Moon
Moon phase: Fourth Quarter
Color: Topaz

Moon Sign: Aquarius
Incense: Lavender

Thursday
Independence Day (Dominican)
Waning Moon
New Moon 7:45 pm
Color: Crimson

Moon Sign: Aquarius
Moon enters Pisces 3:46 am
Incense: Myrrh

28 Friday
Ramadan begins at sundown
Waxing Moon
Moon phase: First Quarter
Color: Rose

Moon Sign: Pisces
Incense: Violet

March

1 Saturday
Matronalia (Roman)
Waxing Moon
Moon phase: First Quarter
Color: Black

Moon Sign: Pisces
Moon enters Aries 4:52 am
Incense: Sandalwood

2 Sunday
Dr. Seuss's birthday
Waxing Moon
Moon phase: First Quarter
Color: Gold

Moon Sign: Aries
Incense: Heliotrope

3 Monday
Doll Festival (Japanese)
Waxing Moon
Moon phase: First Quarter
Color: Lavender

Moon Sign: Aries
Moon enters Taurus 5:37 am
Incense: Hyssop

4 Tuesday
Mardi Gras (Fat Tuesday)
Waxing Moon
Moon phase: First Quarter
Color: Maroon

Moon Sign: Taurus
Incense: Ylang-ylang

5 Wednesday
Ash Wednesday
Waxing Moon
Moon phase: First Quarter
Color: Yellow

Moon Sign: Taurus
Moon enters Gemini 7:29 am
Incense: Honeysuckle

6 Thursday
Alamo Day (Texan)
Waxing Moon
Second Quarter 11:32 am
Color: Turquoise

Moon Sign: Gemini
Incense: Jasmine

7 Friday
Vejovis Festival (Roman)
Waxing Moon
Moon phase: Second Quarter
Color: White

Moon Sign: Gemini
Moon enters Cancer 11:29 am
Incense: Alder

8 Saturday

International Women's Day
Waxing Moon
Moon phase: Second Quarter
Color: Indigo

Moon Sign: Cancer
Incense: Patchouli

---

9 Sunday

Teachers' Day (Lebanese)
Waxing Moon
Moon phase: Second Quarter
Color: Yellow

Moon Sign: Cancer
Moon enters Leo 6:59 pm
Incense: Juniper
Daylight Saving Time begins at 2 am

---

10 Monday

Tibet Uprising Day
Waxing Moon
Moon phase: Second Quarter
Color: Gray

Moon Sign: Leo
Incense: Clary sage

---

11 Tuesday

Johnny Appleseed Day
Waxing Moon
Moon phase: Second Quarter
Color: White

Moon Sign: Leo
Incense: Ginger

---

12 Wednesday

Girl Scouts' birthday
Waxing Moon
Moon phase: Second Quarter
Color: Topaz

Moon Sign: Leo
Moon enters Virgo 3:56 am
Incense: Lilac

---

13 Thursday

Purim begins at sundown
Waxing Moon
Moon phase: Second Quarter
Color: Purple

Moon Sign: Virgo
Incense: Clove

☺ Friday

Pi Day • Holi begins at sundown (Hindu)
Waxing Moon
Full Moon 2:55 am
Color: Pink

Moon Sign: Virgo
Moon enters Libra 2:59 pm
Incense: Mint

March

15 **Saturday**
Fertility Festival (Japanese)
Waning Moon
Moon phase: Third Quarter
Color: Blue

Moon Sign: Libra
Incense: Sage
Mercury retrograde until Apr. 7

---

16 **Sunday**
St. Urho's Day (Finnish-American)
Waning Moon
Moon phase: Third Quarter
Color: Amber

Moon Sign: Libra
Incense: Marigold

---

17 **Monday**
St. Patrick's Day
Waning Moon
Moon phase: Third Quarter
Color: Ivory

Moon Sign: Libra
Moon enters Scorpio 3:30 am
Incense: Narcissus

---

18 **Tuesday**
Sheila's Day (Irish)
Waning Moon
Moon phase: Third Quarter
Color: Red

Moon Sign: Scorpio
Incense: Geranium

---

19 **Wednesday**
Minna Canth's birthday (Finnish)
Waning Moon
Moon phase: Third Quarter
Color: Brown

Moon Sign: Scorpio
Moon enters Sagittarius 4:17 pm
Incense: Bay laurel

---

20 **Thursday**
Ostara • Spring Equinox
Waning Moon
Moon phase: Third Quarter
Color: White

Moon Sign: Sagittarius
Sun enters Aries 5:01 am
Incense: Nutmeg

---

21 **Friday**
Harmony Day (Australian)
Waning Moon
Moon phase: Third Quarter
Color: Coral

Moon Sign: Sagittarius
Incense: Vanilla

March

◑ Saturday
World Water Day   Moon Sign: Sagittarius
Waning Moon   Moon enters Capricorn 3:29 am
Fourth Quarter 7:29 am   Incense: Ivy
Color: Gray

---

23 Sunday
Pakistan Day   Moon Sign: Capricorn
Waning Moon   Incense: Almond
Moon phase: Fourth Quarter
Color: Orange

---

24 Monday
Day of Blood (Roman)   Moon Sign: Capricorn
Waning Moon   Moon enters Aquarius 11:25 am
Moon phase: Fourth Quarter   Incense: Lily
Color: Silver

---

25 Tuesday
Tolkien Reading Day   Moon Sign: Aquarius
Waning Moon   Incense: Cinnamon
Moon phase: Fourth Quarter
Color: Black

---

26 Wednesday
Prince Kuhio Day (Hawaiian)   Moon Sign: Aquarius
Waning Moon   Moon enters Pisces 3:31 pm
Moon phase: Fourth Quarter   Incense: Honeysuckle
Color: White

---

27 Thursday
World Theatre Day   Moon Sign: Pisces
Waning Moon   Incense: Apricot
Moon phase: Fourth Quarter
Color: Green

---

28 Friday
Weed Appreciation Day   Moon Sign: Pisces
Waning Moon   Moon enters Aries 4:36 pm
Moon phase: Fourth Quarter   Incense: Orchid
Color: Purple

March

♓

♑ **Saturday**
Feast of St. Eustace of Luxeuil
Waning Moon
New Moon 6:58 am
Color: Brown

Moon Sign: Aries
Incense: Pine

See page 77 for an Aries New Moon ritual.

30 **Sunday**
Eid al-Fitr begins at sundown (Ramadan ends)
Waxing Moon
Moon phase: First Quarter
Color: Gold

Moon Sign: Aries
Moon enters Taurus 4:16 pm
Incense: Marigold

31 **Monday**
César Chávez Day
Waxing Moon
Moon phase: First Quarter
Color: Lavender

Moon Sign: Taurus
Incense: Neroli

March Correspondences

Stones: Aquamarine, jade, bloodstone, jasper
Animals: Cougar, whale, rabbit, frog
Flowers: Daffodil, narcissus
Deities: Diana, Kwan Yin, Poseidon, Sedna, Yemaya
Zodiac: Pisces

April

1 Tuesday

All Fools' Day • April Fools' Day
Waxing Moon
Moon phase: First Quarter
Color: Scarlet

Moon Sign: Taurus
Moon enters Gemini 4:26 pm
Incense: Cedar

2 Wednesday

The Battle of Flowers (French)
Waxing Moon
Moon phase: First Quarter
Color: Topaz

Moon Sign: Gemini
Incense: Lavender

3 Thursday

Feast of St. Mary of Egypt
Waxing Moon
Moon phase: First Quarter
Color: Turquoise

Moon Sign: Gemini
Moon enters Cancer 6:50 pm
Incense: Carnation

◐ Friday

Tomb-Sweeping Day (Chinese)
Waxing Moon
Second Quarter 10:15 pm
Color: Rose

Moon Sign: Cancer
Incense: Thyme

5 Saturday

Children's Day (Palestinian)
Waxing Moon
Moon phase: Second Quarter
Color: Blue

Moon Sign: Cancer
Incense: Patchouli

6 Sunday

Tartan Day
Waxing Moon
Moon phase: Second Quarter
Color: Orange

Moon Sign: Cancer
Moon enters Leo 12:34 am
Incense: Hyacinth

7 Monday

Motherhood and Beauty Day (Armenian)
Waxing Moon
Moon phase: Second Quarter
Color: White

Moon Sign: Leo
Incense: Rosemary
Mercury direct

April

8 Tuesday
Hana Matsuri (Japanese)
Waxing Moon
Moon phase: Second Quarter
Color: Red

Moon Sign: Leo
Moon enters Virgo 9:40 am
Incense: Basil

9 Wednesday
Valor Day (Filipino)
Waxing Moon
Moon phase: Second Quarter
Color: Brown

Moon Sign: Virgo
Incense: Lilac

10 Thursday
Siblings Day
Waxing Moon
Moon phase: Second Quarter
Color: Crimson

Moon Sign: Virgo
Moon enters Libra 9:12 pm
Incense: Balsam

11 Friday
Juan Santamaría Day (Costa Rican)
Waxing Moon
Moon phase: Second Quarter
Color: Coral

Moon Sign: Libra
Incense: Cypress

☻ Saturday
Passover begins at sundown
Waxing Moon
Full Moon 8:22 pm
Color: Gray

Moon Sign: Libra
Incense: Magnolia

13 Sunday
Palm Sunday
Waning Moon
Moon phase: Third Quarter
Color: Yellow

Moon Sign: Libra
Moon enters Scorpio 9:54 am
Incense: Eucalyptus

14 Monday
Black Day (South Korean)
Waning Moon
Moon phase: Third Quarter
Color: Silver

Moon Sign: Scorpio
Incense: Hyssop

April

15 Tuesday
Fordicidia (Roman)
Waning Moon
Moon phase: Third Quarter
Color: Maroon

Moon Sign: Scorpio
Moon enters Sagittarius 10:37 pm
Incense: Ginger

16 Wednesday
World Voice Day
Waning Moon
Moon phase: Third Quarter
Color: White

Moon Sign: Sagittarius
Incense: Bay laurel

17 Thursday
Yayoi Matsuri (Japanese)
Waning Moon
Moon phase: Third Quarter
Color: Purple

Moon Sign: Sagittarius
Incense: Clove

18 Friday
Good Friday • Orthodox Good Friday
Waning Moon
Moon phase: Third Quarter
Color: Pink

Moon Sign: Sagittarius
Moon enters Capricorn 10:12 am
Incense: Yarrow

19 Saturday
Primrose Day (British)
Waning Moon
Moon phase: Third Quarter
Color: Indigo

Moon Sign: Capricorn
Sun enters Taurus 3:56 pm
Incense: Rue

◑ Sunday
Easter • Orthodox Easter • Passover ends
Waning Moon
Fourth Quarter 9:36 pm
Color: Amber

Moon Sign: Capricorn
Moon enters Aquarius 7:22 pm
Incense: Frankincense

21 Monday
Sechseläuten (Swiss)
Waning Moon
Moon phase: Fourth Quarter
Color: Gray

Moon Sign: Aquarius
Incense: Neroli

April

22 Tuesday

Earth Day
Waning Moon
Moon phase: Fourth Quarter
Color: Black

Moon Sign: Aquarius
Incense: Bayberry

23 Wednesday

St. George's Day (English)
Waning Moon
Moon phase: Fourth Quarter
Color: Yellow

Moon Sign: Aquarius
Moon enters Pisces 1:07 am
Incense: Marjoram

24 Thursday

St. Mark's Eve
Waning Moon
Moon phase: Fourth Quarter
Color: Green

Moon Sign: Pisces
Incense: Mulberry

25 Friday

Arbor Day
Waning Moon
Moon phase: Fourth Quarter
Color: White

Moon Sign: Pisces
Moon enters Aries 3:24 am
Incense: Violet

26 Saturday

Chernobyl Remembrance Day (Belarusian)
Waning Moon
Moon phase: Fourth Quarter
Color: Brown

Moon Sign: Aries
Incense: Sandalwood

☽ Sunday

Freedom Day (South African)
Waning Moon
New Moon 3:31 pm
Color: Yellow

Moon Sign: Aries
Moon enters Taurus 3:17 am
Incense: Juniper

28 Monday

Floralia (Roman)
Waxing Moon
Moon phase: First Quarter
Color: Ivory

Moon Sign: Taurus
Incense: Lily

April

29 **Tuesday**
Showa Day (Japanese)
Waxing Moon
Moon phase: First Quarter
Color: Red

Moon Sign: Taurus
Moon enters Gemini 2:34 am
Incense: Ylang-ylang

30 **Wednesday**
Walpurgis Night • May Eve
Waxing Moon
Moon phase: First Quarter
Color: Brown

Moon Sign: Gemini
Incense: Honeysuckle

April Correspondences

Stones: Beryl, diamond, moonstone
Animals: Falcon, hawk, goat, sheep
Flowers: Sweet pea, daisy
Deities: Ares, Macha, the Morrigan, Ra
Zodiac: Aries

May

1 | **Thursday**
Beltane • May Day
Waxing Moon
Moon phase: First Quarter
Color: Crimson

Moon Sign: Gemini
Moon enters Cancer 3:23 am
Incense: Myrrh

---

2 | **Friday**
National Education Day (Indonesian)
Waxing Moon
Moon phase: First Quarter
Color: Pink

Moon Sign: Cancer
Incense: Thyme

---

3 | **Saturday**
Roodmas
Waxing Moon
Moon phase: First Quarter
Color: Black

Moon Sign: Cancer
Moon enters Leo 7:29 am
Incense: Sage

◐ | **Sunday**
Star Wars Day
Waxing Moon
Second Quater 9:52 am
Color: Gold

Moon Sign: Leo
Incense: Almond

---

5 | **Monday**
Cinco de Mayo
Waxing Moon
Moon phase: Second Quarter
Color: Lavender

Moon Sign: Leo
Moon enters Virgo 3:40 pm
Incense: Narcissus

---

6 | **Tuesday**
Martyrs' Day (Lebanese and Syrian)
Waxing Moon
Moon phase: Second Quarter
Color: Scarlet

Moon Sign: Virgo
Incense: Cinnamon

---

7 | **Wednesday**
Pilgrimage of St. Nicholas (Italian)
Waxing Moon
Moon phase: Second Quarter
Color: Yellow

Moon Sign: Virgo
Incense: Lilac

May

8 Thursday
White Lotus Day (Theosophical)
Waxing Moon
Moon phase: Second Quarter
Color: White

Moon Sign: Virgo
Moon enters Libra 3:06 am
Incense: Jasmine

9 Friday
Lemuria (Roman)
Waxing Moon
Moon phase: Second Quarter
Color: Rose

Moon Sign: Libra
Incense: Vanilla

10 Saturday
Independence Day (Romanian)
Waxing Moon
Moon phase: Second Quarter
Color: Blue

Moon Sign: Libra
Moon enters Scorpio 3:58 pm
Incense: Magnolia

11 Sunday
Mother's Day
Waxing Moon
Moon phase: Second Quarter
Color: Amber

Moon Sign: Scorpio
Incense: Hyacinth

Monday
Florence Nightingale's birthday
Waxing Moon
Full Moon 12:56 pm
Color: Gray

Moon Sign: Scorpio
Incense: Clary sage

13 Tuesday
Pilgrimage to Fátima (Portuguese)
Waning Moon
Moon phase: Third Quarter
Color: Maroon

Moon Sign: Scorpio
Moon enters Sagittarius 4:35 am
Incense: Cedar

14 Wednesday
Carabao Festival (Spanish)
Waning Moon
Moon phase: Third Quarter
Color: Topaz

Moon Sign: Sagittarius
Incense: Bay laurel

May

15 Thursday
Festival of St. Dymphna (Belgian)
Waning Moon
Moon phase: Third Quarter
Color: Green

Moon Sign: Sagittarius
Moon enters Capricorn 5:38 pm
Incense: Balsam

16 Friday
St. Honoratus's Day
Waning Moon
Moon phase: Third Quarter
Color: Purple

Moon Sign: Capricorn
Incense: Rose

17 Saturday
Norwegian Constitution Day
Waning Moon
Moon phase: Third Quarter
Color: Indigo

Moon Sign: Capricorn
Incense: Ivy

18 Sunday
Battle of Las Piedras Day (Uruguayan)
Waning Moon
Moon phase: Third Quarter
Color: Orange

Moon Sign: Capricorn
Moon enters Aquarius 1:29 am
Incense: Almond

19 Monday
Victoria Day (Canadian)
Waning Moon
Moon phase: Third Quarter
Color: White

Moon Sign: Aquarius
Incense: Neroli

☽ Tuesday
Feast of St. Aurea of Ostia
Waning Moon
Fourth Quarter 7:59 am
Color: Gray

Moon Sign: Aquarius
Sun enters Gemini 2:55 pm
Moon enters Pisces 8:28 am
Incense: Basil

21 Wednesday
Navy Day (Chilean)
Waning Moon
Moon phase: Fourth Quarter
Color: Brown

Moon Sign: Pisces
Incense: Lavender

May

22 Thursday

Harvey Milk Day (Californian)
Waning Moon
Moon phase: Fourth Quarter
Color: Crimson

Moon Sign: Pisces
Moon enters Aries 12:26 pm
Incense: Nutmeg

23 Friday

Tubilustrium (Roman)
Waning Moon
Moon phase: Fourth Quarter
Color: Coral

Moon Sign: Aries
Incense: Violet

24 Saturday

Education and Culture Day (Bulgarian)
Waning Moon
Moon phase: Fourth Quarter
Color: Gray

Moon Sign: Aries
Moon enters Taurus 1:38 pm
Incense: Sandalwood

25 Sunday

Missing Children's Day
Waning Moon
Moon phase: Fourth Quarter
Color: Yellow

Moon Sign: Taurus
Incense: Marigold

Monday

Memorial Day
Waning Moon
New Moon 11:02 pm
Color: Silver

Moon Sign: Taurus
Moon enters Gemini 1:21 pm
Incense: Rosemary

27 Tuesday

Feast of St. Bede the Venerable
Waxing Moon
Moon phase: First Quarter
Color: Red

Moon Sign: Gemini
Incense: Ginger

28 Wednesday

St. Germain's Day
Waxing Moon
Moon phase: First Quarter
Color: White

Moon Sign: Gemini
Moon enters Cancer 1:33 pm
Incense: Honeysuckle

May

♊

29 **Thursday**
Oak Apple Day (English)
Waxing Moon
Moon phase: First Quarter
Color: Green

Moon Sign: Cancer
Incense: Carnation

30 **Friday**
Canary Islands Day
Waxing Moon
Moon phase: First Quarter
Color: Rose

Moon Sign: Cancer
Moon enters Leo 4:17 pm
Incense: Orchid

31 **Saturday**
Visitation of Mary
Waxing Moon
Moon phase: First Quarter
Color: Blue

Moon Sign: Leo
Incense: Patchouli

May Correspondences

Stones: Agate, emerald, carnelian
Animals: Beaver, cow, elk
Flower: Lily of the valley
Deities: Aphrodite, Dionysus, Gaia, Horus, Osiris
Zodiac: Taurus

June

1 **Sunday**
Shavuot begins at sundown
Waxing Moon
Moon phase: First Quarter
Color: Gold

Moon Sign: Leo
Moon enters Virgo 11:00 pm
Incense: Frankincense

2 **Monday**
Republic Day (Italian)
Waxing Moon
Second Quarter 11:41 pm
Color: Ivory

Moon Sign: Virgo
Incense: Narcissus

3 **Tuesday**
Feast of St. Clotilde
Waxing Moon
Moon phase: Second Quarter
Color: White

Moon Sign: Virgo
Incense: Bayberry

4 **Wednesday**
Flag Day (Estonian)
Waxing Moon
Moon phase: Second Quarter
Color: Yellow

Moon Sign: Virgo
Moon enters Libra 9:38 am
Incense: Geranium

5 **Thursday**
Constitution Day (Danish)
Waxing Moon
Moon phase: Second Quarter
Color: Purple

Moon Sign: Libra
Incense: Mulberry

6 **Friday**
National Day of Sweden
Waxing Moon
Moon phase: Second Quarter
Color: Pink

Moon Sign: Libra
Moon enters Scorpio 10:23 pm
Incense: Cypress

7 **Saturday**
Vestalia begins (ends June 15; Roman)
Waxing Moon
Moon phase: Second Quarter
Color: Black

Moon Sign: Scorpio
Incense: Pine

June

8 Sunday
World Oceans Day
Waxing Moon
Moon phase: Second Quarter
Color: Yellow

Moon Sign: Scorpio
Incense: Eucalyptus

9 Monday
Heroes' Day (Ugandan)
Waxing Moon
Moon phase: Second Quarter
Color: Lavender

Moon Sign: Scorpio
Moon enters Sagittarius 10:56 am
Incense: Lily

10 Tuesday
Portugal Day
Waxing Moon
Moon phase: Second Quarter
Color: Maroon

Moon Sign: Sagittarius
Incense: Ylang-ylang

Wednesday
Kamehameha Day (Hawaiian)
Waxing Moon
Full Moon 3:44 am
Color: Brown

Moon Sign: Sagittarius
Moon enters Capricorn 9:55 pm
Incense: Bay laurel

12 Thursday
Independence Day (Filipino)
Waning Moon
Moon phase: Third Quarter
Color: Turquoise

Moon Sign: Capricorn
Incense: Apricot

13 Friday
St. Anthony of Padua's Day
Waning Moon
Moon phase: Third Quarter
Color: Coral

Moon Sign: Capricorn
Incense: Mint

14 Saturday
Flag Day
Waning Moon
Moon phase: Third Quarter
Color: Blue

Moon Sign: Capricorn
Moon enters Aquarius 7:00 am
Incense: Sage

June

15 Sunday
Father's Day
Waning Moon
Moon phase: Third Quarter
Color: Amber

Moon Sign: Aquarius
Incense: Heliotrope

16 Monday
Bloomsday (Irish)
Waning Moon
Moon phase: Third Quarter
Color: Silver

Moon Sign: Aquarius
Moon enters Pisces 2:09 pm
Incense: Hyssop

17 Tuesday
Bunker Hill Day (Massachusetts)
Waning Moon
Moon phase: Third Quarter
Color: Scarlet

Moon Sign: Pisces
Incense: Geranium

◑ Wednesday
Waterloo Day (British)
Waning Moon
Fourth Quarter 3:19 pm
Color: Topaz

Moon Sign: Pisces
Moon enters Aries 7:08 pm
Incense: Marjoram

19 Thursday
Juneteenth
Waning Moon
Moon phase: Fourth Quarter
Color: Crimson

Moon Sign: Aries
Incense: Jasmine

20 Friday
Litha • Summer Solstice
Waning Moon
Moon phase: Fourth Quarter
Color: White

Moon Sign: Aries
Sun enters Cancer 10:42 pm
Moon enters Taurus 9:53 pm
Incense: Vanilla

21 Saturday
National Day (Greenlandic)
Waning Moon
Moon phase: Fourth Quarter
Color: Indigo

Moon Sign: Taurus
Incense: Magolia

June

22 Sunday
Teachers' Day (El Salvadoran)
Waning Moon
Moon phase: Fourth Quarter
Color: Orange

Moon Sign: Taurus
Moon enters Gemini 10:57 pm
Incense: Juniper

23 Monday
St. John's Eve
Waning Moon
Moon phase: Fourth Quarter
Color: Gray

Moon Sign: Gemini
Incense: Neroli

24 Tuesday
St. John's Day
Waning Moon
Moon phase: Fourth Quarter
Color: Black

Moon Sign: Gemini
Moon enters Cancer 11:44 pm
Incense: Cedar

☽ Wednesday
Fiesta de Santa Orosia (Spanish)
Waning Moon
New Moon 6:32 am
Color: Brown

Moon Sign: Cancer
Incense: Lavender

26 Thursday
Islamic New Year begins at sundown
Waxing Moon
Moon phase: First Quarter
Color: Turquoise

Moon Sign: Cancer
Incense: Nutmeg

27 Friday
Seven Sleepers' Day (German)
Waxing Moon
Moon phase: First Quarter
Color: Rose

Moon Sign: Cancer
Moon enters Leo 2:05 am
Incense: Yarrow

28 Saturday
Stonewall Riots Anniversary
Waxing Moon
Moon phase: First Quarter
Color: Gray

Moon Sign: Leo
Incense: Rue

June

29 Sunday

Haro Wine Battle (Spanish)
Waxing Moon
Moon phase: First Quarter
Color: Gold

Moon Sign: Leo
Moon enters Virgo 7:44 am
Incense: Marigold

30 Monday

The Burning of the Three Firs (French)
Waxing Moon
Moon phase: First Quarter
Color: Silver

Moon Sign: Virgo
Incense: Rosemary

June Correspondences

Stones: Pearl, chalcedony, alexandrite
Animals: Deer, eagle, fox
Flower: Rose
Deities: Artemis, Cerridwen, Hermes, Odin
Zodiac: Gemini

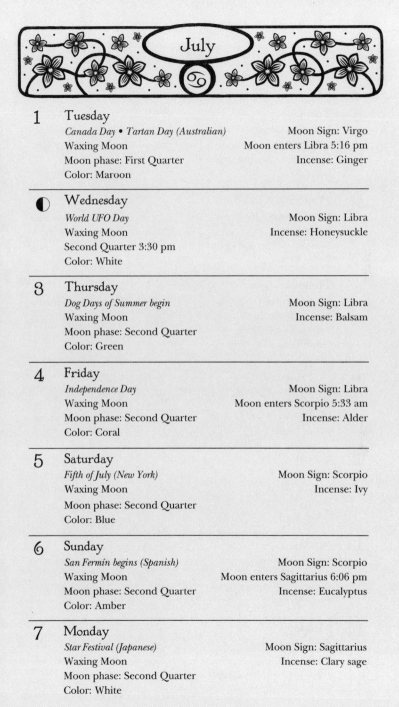

July

1 Tuesday
Canada Day • Tartan Day (Australian)
Waxing Moon
Moon phase: First Quarter
Color: Maroon

Moon Sign: Virgo
Moon enters Libra 5:16 pm
Incense: Ginger

2 Wednesday
World UFO Day
Waxing Moon
Second Quarter 3:30 pm
Color: White

Moon Sign: Libra
Incense: Honeysuckle

3 Thursday
Dog Days of Summer begin
Waxing Moon
Moon phase: Second Quarter
Color: Green

Moon Sign: Libra
Incense: Balsam

4 Friday
Independence Day
Waxing Moon
Moon phase: Second Quarter
Color: Coral

Moon Sign: Libra
Moon enters Scorpio 5:33 am
Incense: Alder

5 Saturday
Fifth of July (New York)
Waxing Moon
Moon phase: Second Quarter
Color: Blue

Moon Sign: Scorpio
Incense: Ivy

6 Sunday
San Fermín begins (Spanish)
Waxing Moon
Moon phase: Second Quarter
Color: Amber

Moon Sign: Scorpio
Moon enters Sagittarius 6:06 pm
Incense: Eucalyptus

7 Monday
Star Festival (Japanese)
Waxing Moon
Moon phase: Second Quarter
Color: White

Moon Sign: Sagittarius
Incense: Clary sage

July

8 Tuesday
Feast of St. Sunniva
Waxing Moon
Moon phase: Second Quarter
Color: Red

Moon Sign: Sagittarius
Incense: Basil

9 Wednesday
Battle of Sempach Day (Swiss)
Waxing Moon
Moon phase: Second Quarter
Color: Yellow

Moon Sign: Sagittarius
Moon enters Capricorn 4:55 am
Incense: Lilic

☺ Thursday
Nicola Tesla Day
Waxing Moon
Full Moon 4:37 pm
Color: Turquoise

Moon Sign: Capricorn
Incense: Myrrh

11 Friday
Mongolian Naadam Festival (ends July 13)
Waning Moon
Moon phase: Third Quarter
Color: Purple

Moon Sign: Capricorn
Moon enters Aquarius 1:21 pm
Incense: Thyme

12 Saturday
Malala Day
Waning Moon
Moon phase: Third Quarter
Color: Black

Moon Sign: Aquarius
Incense: Patchouli

13 Sunday
Feast of St. Mildrith
Waning Moon
Moon phase: Third Quarter
Color: Yellow

Moon Sign: Aquarius
Moon enters Pisces 7:45 pm
Incense: Almond

14 Monday
Bastille Day (French)
Waning Moon
Moon phase: Third Quarter
Color: Ivory

Moon Sign: Pisces
Incense: Lily

July

15 Tuesday

St. Swithin's Day
Waning Moon
Moon phase: Third Quarter
Color: Gray

Moon Sign: Pisces
Incense: Cinnamon

16 Wednesday

Fiesta de la Tirana (Chilean)
Waning Moon
Moon phase: Third Quarter
Color: Brown

Moon Sign: Pisces
Moon enters Aries 12:32 am
Incense: Lavender

Thursday

Gion Festival first Yamaboko parade
Waning Moon
Fourth Quarter 8:38 pm
Color: White

Moon Sign: Aries
Incense: Clove

18 Friday

Nelson Mandela International Day
Waning Moon
Moon phase: Fourth Quarter
Color: Pink

Moon Sign: Aries
Moon enters Taurus 3:59 am
Incense: Violet
Mercury retrograde until Aug. 11

19 Saturday

Flitch Day (English)
Waning Moon
Moon phase: Fourth Quarter
Color: Blue

Moon Sign: Taurus
Incense: Sage

20 Sunday

Binding of Wreaths (Lithuanian)
Waning Moon
Moon phase: Fourth Quarter
Color: Gold

Moon Sign: Taurus
Moon enters Gemini 6:22 am
Incense: Juniper

21 Monday

National Day (Belgian)
Waning Moon
Moon phase: Fourth Quarter
Color: Lavender

Moon Sign: Gemini
Incense: Hyssop

July

22 Tuesday

St. Mary Magdalene's Day
Waning Moon
Moon phase: Fourth Quarter
Color: Scarlet

Moon Sign: Gemini
Sun enters Leo 9:29 am
Moon enters Cancer 8:26 am
Incense: Geranium

23 Wednesday

Mysteries of St. Cristina (Italian)
Waning Moon
Moon phase: Fourth Quarter
Color: Topaz

Moon Sign: Cancer
Incense: Bay laurel

Thursday

Gion Festival second Yamaboko parade (Japanese)
Waning Moon
New Moon 3:11 pm
Color: Green

Moon Sign: Cancer
Moon enters Leo 11:28 am
Incense: Carnation

25 Friday

Illapa Festival (Incan)
Waxing Moon
Moon phase: First Quarter
Color: Rose

Moon Sign: Leo
Incense: Vanilla

26 Saturday

St. Anne's Day
Waxing Moon
Moon phase: First Quarter
Color: Indigo

Moon Sign: Leo
Moon enters Virgo 4:55 pm
Incense: Sandalwood

27 Sunday

Sleepyhead Day (Finnish)
Waxing Moon
Moon phase: First Quarter
Color: Amber

Moon Sign: Virgo
Incense: Frankincense

28 Monday

Independence Day (Peruvian)
Waxing Moon
Moon phase: First Quarter
Color: Silver

Moon Sign: Virgo
Incense: Rosemary

July

29 Tuesday

St. Olaf Festival (Faroese)
Waxing Moon
Moon phase: First Quarter
Color: White

Moon Sign: Virgo
Moon enters Libra 1:43 am
Incense: Ylang-ylang

30 Wednesday

Micman Festival of St. Ann
Waxing Moon
Moon phase: First Quarter
Color: Yellow

Moon Sign: Libra
Incense: Lilac

31 Thursday

Feast of St. Ignatius
Waxing Moon
Moon phase: First Quarter
Color: Purple

Moon Sign: Libra
Moon enters Scorpio 1:25 pm
Incense: Apricot

July Correspondences

Stones: Turquoise, ruby
Animals: Dog, loon, woodpecker, salmon
Flowers: Larkspur, water lily
Deities: Danu, Demeter, Luna, Mercury, Parvati
Zodiac: Cancer

Friday
Lammas
Waxing Moon
Second Quarter 8:41 am
Color: Pink

Moon Sign: Scorpio
Incense: Thyme

2 **Saturday**
Porcingula (Pecos)
Waxing Moon
Moon phase: Second Quarter
Color: Gray

Moon Sign: Scorpio
Incense: Rue

3 **Sunday**
Flag Day (Venezuelan)
Waxing Moon
Moon phase: Second Quarter
Color: Yellow

Moon Sign: Scorpio
Moon enters Sagittarius 2:00 am
Incense: Marigold

4 **Monday**
Constitution Day (Cook Islands)
Waxing Moon
Moon phase: Second Quarter
Color: Gray

Moon Sign: Sagittarius
Incense: Neroli

5 **Tuesday**
Carnival of Bogotá
Waxing Moon
Moon phase: Second Quarter
Color: Red

Moon Sign: Sagittarius
Moon enters Capricorn 1:04 pm
Incense: Basil

6 **Wednesday**
Hiroshima Peace Memorial Ceremony
Waxing Moon
Moon phase: Second Quarter
Color: Brown

Moon Sign: Capricorn
Incense: Marjoram

7 **Thursday**
Republic Day (Ivorian)
Waxing Moon
Moon phase: Second Quarter
Color: Turquoise

Moon Sign: Capricorn
Moon enters Aquarius 9:18 pm
Incense: Jasmine

August

8 Friday
Farmers' Day (Tanzanian)
Waxing Moon
Moon phase: Second Quarter
Color: Coral

Moon Sign: Aquarius
Incense: Rose

Saturday
Nagasaki Peace Memorial Ceremony
Waxing Moon
Full Moon 3:55 am
Color: Blue

Moon Sign: Aquarius
Incense: Magnolia

10 Sunday
Puck Fair (ends Aug. 12; Irish)
Waning Moon
Moon phase: Third Quarter
Color: Orange

Moon Sign: Aquarius
Moon enters Pisces 2:50 am
Incense: Frankincense

11 Monday
Mountain Day (Japanese)
Waning Moon
Moon phase: Third Quarter
Color: Ivory

Moon Sign: Pisces
Incense: Clary sage
Mercury direct

12 Tuesday
World Elephant Day
Waning Moon
Moon phase: Third Quarter
Color: Scarlet

Moon Sign: Pisces
Moon enters Aries 6:33 am
Incense: Cedar

13 Wednesday
Women's Day (Tunisian)
Waning Moon
Moon phase: Third Quarter
Color: White

Moon Sign: Aries
Incense: Lavender

14 Thursday
Independence Day (Pakistani)
Waning Moon
Moon phase: Third Quarter
Color: Crimson

Moon Sign: Aries
Moon enters Taurus 9:22 am
Incense: Clove

August

15 Friday
Bon Festival (Japanese)
Waning Moon
Moon phase: Third Quarter
Color: Rose

Moon Sign: Taurus
Incense: Mint

Saturday
Xicolatada (French)
Waning Moon
Fourth Quarter 1:12 am
Color: Brown

Moon Sign: Taurus
Moon enters Gemini 12:01 pm
Incense: Ivy

17 Sunday
Black Cat Appreciation Day
Waning Moon
Moon phase: Fourth Quarter
Color: Gold

Moon Sign: Gemini
Incense: Hyacinth

18 Monday
St. Helen's Day
Waning Moon
Moon phase: Fourth Quarter
Color: White

Moon Sign: Gemini
Moon enters Cancer 3:05 pm
Incense: Hyssop

19 Tuesday
Vinalia Rustica (Roman)
Waning Moon
Moon phase: Fourth Quarter
Color: Black

Moon Sign: Cancer
Incense: Geranium

20 Wednesday
St. Stephen's Day (Hungarian)
Waning Moon
Moon phase: Fourth Quarter
Color: Yellow

Moon Sign: Cancer
Moon enters Leo 7:17 pm
Incense: Honeysuckle

21 Thursday
Consualia (Roman)
Waning Moon
Moon phase: Fourth Quarter
Color: Green

Moon Sign: Leo
Incense: Myrrh

August

22 Friday

Feast of the Queenship of Mary (English)
Waning Moon
Moon phase: Fourth Quarter
Color: Purple

Moon Sign: Leo
Sun enters Virgo 4:34 pm
Incense: Cypress

Saturday

National Day (Romanian)
Waning Moon
New Moon 2:07 am
Color: Indigo

Moon Sign: Leo
Moon enters Virgo 1:24 am
Incense: Pine

24 Sunday

St. Bartholomew's Day
Waxing Moon
Moon phase: First Quarter
Color: Yellow

Moon Sign: Virgo
Incense: Heliotrope

25 Monday

Liberation of Paris
Waxing Moon
Moon phase: First Quarter
Color: Silver

Moon Sign: Virgo
Moon enters Libra 10:08 am
Incense: Narcissus

26 Tuesday

Heroes' Day (Namibian)
Waxing Moon
Moon phase: First Quarter
Color: Maroon

Moon Sign: Libra
Incense: Ginger

27 Wednesday

Independence Day (Moldovan)
Waxing Moon
Moon phase: First Quarter
Color: Brown

Moon Sign: Libra
Moon enters Scorpio 9:27 pm
Incense: Lilac

28 Thursday

St. Augustine's Day
Waxing Moon
Moon phase: First Quarter
Color: Turquoise

Moon Sign: Scorpio
Incense: Mulberry

August

29 Friday

Qixi Festival (Chinese)
Waxing Moon
Moon phase: First Quarter
Color: Coral

Moon Sign: Scorpio
Incense: Yarrow

30 Saturday

St. Rose of Lima Day (Peruvian)
Waxing Moon
Moon phase: First Quarter
Color: Blue

Moon Sign: Scorpio
Moon enters Sagittarius 10:04 am
Incense: Rue

Sunday

La Tomatina (Valencian)
Waxing Moon
Second Quarter 2:25 am
Color: Orange

Moon Sign: Sagittarius
Incense: Juniper

❖

August Correspondences

Stones: Peridot, carnelian
Animals: Crow, owl, sturgeon
Flowers: Gladiolus, poppy
Deities: Amaterasu, Helios, Sekhmet, Ra
Zodiac: Leo

September

1 **Monday**
Labor Day • Labour Day (Canadian)
Waxing Moon
Moon phase: Second Quarter
Color: Ivory

Moon Sign: Sagittarius
Moon enters Capricorn 9:45 pm
Incense: Rosemary

2 **Tuesday**
St. Mammes's Day
Waxing Moon
Moon phase: Second Quarter
Color: Red

Moon Sign: Capricorn
Incense: Cinnamon

3 **Wednesday**
National Feast of San Marino
Waxing Moon
Moon phase: Second Quarter
Color: Topaz

Moon Sign: Capricorn
Incense: Bay laurel

4 **Thursday**
Feast of St. Rosalia
Waxing Moon
Moon phase: Second Quarter
Color: Green

Moon Sign: Capricorn
Moon enters Aquarius 6:32 am
Incense: Carnation

5 **Friday**
International Day of Charity
Waxing Moon
Moon phase: Second Quarter
Color: Rose

Moon Sign: Aquarius
Incense: Thyme

6 **Saturday**
Ghost Festival (Chinese)
Waxing Moon
Moon phase: Second Quarter
Color: Gray

Moon Sign: Aquarius
Moon enters Pisces 11:54 am
Incense: Sage

Sunday
Grandparents' Day
Waxing Moon
Full Moon 2:09 pm
Color: Gold

Moon Sign: Pisces
Incense: Almond

September

8 Monday
International Literacy Day
Waning Moon
Moon phase: Third Quarter
Color: Lavender

Moon Sign: Pisces
Moon enters Aries 2:37 pm
Incense: Lily

9 Tuesday
Remembrance for Herman the Cheruscan (Asatru)
Waning Moon
Moon phase: Third Quarter
Color: Scarlet

Moon Sign: Aries
Incense: Basil

10 Wednesday
National Day (Belizean)
Waning Moon
Moon phase: Third Quarter
Color: Brown

Moon Sign: Aries
Moon enters Taurus 4:03 pm
Incense: Lavender

11 Thursday
Patriot Day
Waning Moon
Moon phase: Third Quarter
Color: Crimson

Moon Sign: Taurus
Incense: Jasmine

12 Friday
Mindfulness Day
Waning Moon
Moon phase: Third Quarter
Color: White

Moon Sign: Taurus
Moon enters Gemini 5:38 pm
Incense: Mint

13 Saturday
The Gods' Banquet
Waning Moon
Moon phase: Third Quarter
Color: Indigo

Moon Sign: Gemini
Incense: Sandalwood

Sunday
Holy Cross Day
Waning Moon
Fourth Quarter 6:33 am
Color: Amber

Moon Sign: Gemini
Moon enters Cancer 8:30 pm
Incense: Eucalyptus

September

15 Monday
International Day of Democracy
Waning Moon
Moon phase: Fourth Quarter
Color: Silver

Moon Sign: Cancer
Incense: Neroli

16 Tuesday
Independence Day (Mexican)
Waning Moon
Moon phase: Fourth Quarter
Color: Gray

Moon Sign: Cancer
Incense: Ylang-ylang

17 Wednesday
Teacher's Day (Honduran)
Waning Moon
Moon phase: Fourth Quarter
Color: White

Moon Sign: Cancer
Moon enters Leo 1:20 am
Incense: Honeysuckle

18 Thursday
World Water Monitoring Day
Waning Moon
Moon phase: Fourth Quarter
Color: Purple

Moon Sign: Leo
Incense: Clove

19 Friday
Feast of San Gennaro
Waning Moon
Moon phase: Fourth Quarter
Color: Pink

Moon Sign: Leo
Moon enters Virgo 8:23 am
Incense: Orchid

20 Saturday
St. Eustace's Day
Waning Moon
Moon phase: Fourth Quarter
Color: Black

Moon Sign: Virgo
Incense: Ivy

Sunday
UN International Day of Peace
Waning Moon
New Moon 3:54 pm
Color: Yellow

Moon Sign: Virgo
Moon enters Libra 5:41 pm
Incense: Juniper

September

22 Monday

Mabon • Fall Equinox • Rosh Hashanah begins at sundown Moon Sign: Libra
Waxing Moon   Sun enters Libra 2:19 pm
Moon phase: First Quarter   Incense: Clary sage
Color: White

23 Tuesday

Feast of St. Padre Pio   Moon Sign: Libra
Waxing Moon   Incense: Bayberry
Moon phase: First Quarter
Color: Maroon

24 Wednesday

Schwenkenfelder Thanksgiving (German-American)   Moon Sign: Libra
Waxing Moon   Moon enters Scorpio 5:00 am
Moon phase: First Quarter   Incense: Marjoram
Color: Brown

25 Thursday

Doll Memorial Service (Japanese)   Moon Sign: Scorpio
Waxing Moon   Incense: Nutmeg
Moon phase: First Quarter
Color: Turquoise

26 Friday

Feast of Santa Justina (Mexican)   Moon Sign: Scorpio
Waxing Moon   Moon enters Sagittarius 5:37 pm
Moon phase: First Quarter   Incense: Rose
Color: Rose

27 Saturday

Meskel (Ethiopian and Eritrean)   Moon Sign: Sagittarius
Waxing Moon   Incense: Magnolia
Moon phase: First Quarter
Color: Blue

28 Sunday

Confucius's birthday   Moon Sign: Sagittarius
Waxing Moon   Incense: Frankincense
Moon phase: First Quarter
Color: Gold

September

Monday

Michaelmas
Waxing Moon
Second Quarter 7:54 pm
Color: Gray

Moon Sign: Sagittarius
Moon enters Capricorn 5:55 am
Incense: Hyssop

---

30 Tuesday

St. Jerome's Day
Waxing Moon
Moon phase: Second Quarter
Color: Red

Moon Sign: Capricorn
Incense: Basil

September Correspondences

Stones: Sapphire, sardonyx, zircon
Animals: Bear, stag, fox
Flowers: Aster, morning glory
Deities: Frigg, Hestia, Persephone, Odin
Zodiac: Virgo

October

♎

1 Wednesday

Yom Kippur begins at sundown
Waxing Moon
Moon phase: Second Quarter
Color: Yellow

Moon Sign: Capricorn
Moon enters Aquarius 3:52 pm
Incense: Bay laurel

2 Thursday

Gandhi's birthday
Waxing Moon
Moon phase: Second Quarter
Color: White

Moon Sign: Aquarius
Incense: Jasmine

3 Friday

German Unity Day
Waxing Moon
Moon phase: Second Quarter
Color: Coral

Moon Sign: Aquarius
Moon enters Pisces 10:07 pm
Incense: Yarrow

4 Saturday

St. Francis's Day
Waxing Moon
Moon phase: Second Quarter
Color: Brown

Moon Sign: Pisces
Incense: Pine

5 Sunday

Republic Day (Portuguese)
Waxing Moon
Moon phase: Second Quarter
Color: Orange

Moon Sign: Pisces
Incense: Heliotrope

☺ Monday

Sukkot begins at sundown
Waxing Moon
Full Moon 11:48 pm
Color: White

Moon Sign: Pisces
Moon enters Aries 12:48 am
Incense: Narcissus

7 Tuesday

Nagasaki Kunchi Festival (ends Oct. 9)
Waning Moon
Moon phase: Third Quarter
Color: Black

Moon Sign: Aries
Incense: Geranium

October

8   Wednesday
Arbor Day (Namibian)
Waning Moon
Moon phase: Third Quarter
Color: Topaz

Moon Sign: Aries
Moon enters Taurus 1:12 am
Incense: Lilac

9   Thursday
Leif Erikson Day
Waning Moon
Moon phase: Third Quarter
Color: Green

Moon Sign: Taurus
Incense: Balsam

10   Friday
Finnish Literature Day
Waning Moon
Moon phase: Third Quarter
Color: Purple

Moon Sign: Taurus
Moon enters Gemini 1:12 am
Incense: Thyme

11   Saturday
Meditrinalia (Roman)
Waning Moon
Moon phase: Third Quarter
Color: Indigo

Moon Sign: Gemini
Incense: Patchouli

12   Sunday
National Festival of Spain
Waning Moon
Moon phase: Third Quarter
Color: Yellow

Moon Sign: Gemini
Moon enters Cancer 2:37 am
Incense: Marigold

◑   Monday
Sukkot ends • Indigenous Peoples' Day
Waning Moon
Fourth Quarter 2:13 pm
Color: Silver

Moon Sign: Cancer
Incense: Rosemary

14   Tuesday
National Education Day (Polish)
Waning Moon
Moon phase: Fourth Quarter
Color: Red

Moon Sign: Cancer
Moon enters Leo 6:47 am
Incense: Cinnamon

October

15 Wednesday
The October Horse (Roman)
Waning Moon
Moon phase: Fourth Quarter
Color: Brown

Moon Sign: Leo
Incense: Lavender

16 Thursday
The Lion Serman (British)
Waning Moon
Moon phase: Fourth Quarter
Color: Turquoise

Moon Sign: Leo
Moon enters Virgo 2:06 pm
Incense: Apricot

17 Friday
Dessalines Day (Haitian)
Waning Moon
Moon phase: Fourth Quarter
Color: Rose

Moon Sign: Virgo
Incense: Violet

18 Saturday
Feast of St. Luke
Waning Moon
Moon phase: Fourth Quarter
Color: Blue

Moon Sign: Virgo
Incense: Sage

19 Sunday
Mother Teresa Day (Albanian)
Waning Moon
Moon phase: Fourth Quarter
Color: Amber

Moon Sign: Virgo
Moon enters Libra 12:01 am
Incense: Eucalyptus

20 Monday
Feast of St. Acca
Waning Moon
Moon phase: Fourth Quarter
Color: Lavender

Moon Sign: Libra
Incense: Lily

☽ Tuesday
Apple Day (United Kingdom)
Waning Moon
New Moon 8:25 am
Color: Scarlet

Moon Sign: Libra
Moon enters Scorpio 11:42 am
Incense: Ylang-ylang

October

22 Wednesday
Jidai Festival (Japanese)
Waxing Moon
Moon phase: First Quarter
Color: White

Moon Sign: Scorpio
Sun enters Scorpio 11:51 pm
Incense: Marjoram

23 Thursday
Revolution Day (Hungarian)
Waxing Moon
Moon phase: First Quarter
Color: Crimson

Moon Sign: Scorpio
Incense: Myrrh

24 Friday
United Nations Day
Waxing Moon
Moon phase: First Quarter
Color: Pink

Moon Sign: Scorpio
Moon enters Sagittarius 12:19 am
Incense: Alder

25 Saturday
St. Crispin's Day
Waxing Moon
Moon phase: First Quarter
Color: Indigo

Moon Sign: Sagittarius
Incense: Ivy

26 Sunday
Death of Alfred the Great
Waxing Moon
Moon phase: First Quarter
Color: Orange

Moon Sign: Sagittarius
Moon enters Capricorn 12:53 pm
Incense: Hyacinth

27 Monday
Feast of St. Abbán
Waxing Moon
Moon phase: First Quarter
Color: Ivory

Moon Sign: Capricorn
Incense: Clary sage

28 Tuesday
Ohi Day (Greek)
Waxing Moon
Moon phase: First Quarter
Color: White

Moon Sign: Capricorn
Moon enters Aquarius 11:55 pm
Incense: Ginger

October

☽ Wednesday
Double Ninth Festival (Chinese)
Waxing Moon
Second Quarter 12:21 pm
Color: Brown

Moon Sign: Aquarius
Incense: Honeysuckle

---

30 Thursday
John Adams's birthday
Waxing Moon
Moon phase: Second Quarter
Color: Purple

Moon Sign: Aquarius
Incense: Mulberry

---

31 Friday
Halloween • Samhain
Waxing Moon
Moon phase: Second Quarter
Color: Rose

Moon Sign: Aquarius
Moon enters Pisces 7:46 am
Incense: Violet

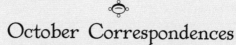

October Correspondences

Stones: Opal, tourmaline
Animals: Bat, rat, crow, raven, dove
Flower: Calendula
Deities: Athena, Cernunnos, Hephaestus,
Shiva, Venus
Zodiac: Libra

November ♏

1 Saturday
All Saints' Day • Día de los Muertos
Waxing Moon
Moon phase: Second Quarter
Color: Black

Moon Sign: Pisces
Incense: Rue

---

2 Sunday
All Souls' Day
Waxing Moon
Moon phase: Second Quarter
Color: Yellow

Moon Sign: Pisces
Moon enters Aries 10:39 am
Incense: Frankincense
Daylight Saving Time ends at 2 am

---

3 Monday
Culture Day (Japanese)
Waxing Moon
Moon phase: Second Quarter
Color: Silver

Moon Sign: Aries
Incense: Neroli

---

4 Tuesday
Election Day (US)
Waxing Moon
Moon phase: Second Quarter
Color: Maroon

Moon Sign: Aries
Moon enters Taurus 11:16 am
Incense: Cedar

☺ Wednesday
Loy Krathong Lantern Festival (Thai)
Waxing Moon
Full Moon 8:19 am
Color: Topaz

Moon Sign: Taurus
Incense: Lilac

---

6 Thursday
St. Leonard's Ride (German)
Waning Moon
Moon phase: Third Quarter
Color: Turquoise

Moon Sign: Taurus
Moon enters Gemini 10:20 am
Incense: Jasmine

---

7 Friday
Feast of St. Willibrord
Waning Moon
Moon phase: Third Quarter
Color: Coral

Moon Sign: Gemini
Incense: Mint

November

8 **Saturday**
World Urbanism Day
Waning Moon
Moon phase: Third Quarter
Color: Blue

Moon Sign: Gemini
Moon enters Cancer 10:06 pm
Incense: Pine

9 **Sunday**
Fateful Day (German)
Waning Moon
Moon phase: Third Quarter
Color: Gold

Moon Sign: Cancer
Incense: Almond
Mercury retrograde until Nov. 29

10 **Monday**
Martin Luther's Birthday
Waning Moon
Moon phase: Third Quarter
Color: Gray

Moon Sign: Cancer
Moon enters Leo 12:34 pm
Incense: Hyssop

11 **Tuesday**
Veterans Day • Remembrance Day (Canadian)
Waning Moon
Moon phase: Third Quarter
Color: Black

Moon Sign: Leo
Incense: Cinnamon

12 **Wednesday**
Feast Day of San Diego (Tesuque Puebloan)
Waning Moon
Fourth Quarter 12:28 am
Color: Yellow

Moon Sign: Leo
Moon enters Virgo 6:52 pm
Incense: Marjoram

13 **Thursday**
Festival of Jupiter
Waning Moon
Moon phase: Fourth Quarter
Color: Crimson

Moon Sign: Virgo
Incense: Apricot

14 **Friday**
Feast of St. Lawrence O'Toole
Waning Moon
Moon phase: Fourth Quarter
Color: Purple

Moon Sign: Virgo
Incense: Vanilla

November ♏

15 Saturday
King's Feast (Belgian)
Waning Moon
Moon phase: Fourth Quarter
Color: Gray

Moon Sign: Virgo
Moon enters Libra 4:44 am
Incense: Sandalwood

16 Sunday
St. Margaret of Scotland's Day
Waning Moon
Moon phase: Fourth Quarter
Color: Orange

Moon Sign: Libra
Incense: Eucalyptus

17 Monday
Queen Elizabeth's Accession Day
Waning Moon
Moon phase: Fourth Quarter
Color: White

Moon Sign: Libra
Moon enters Scorpio 4:44 pm
Incense: Narcissus

18 Tuesday
Independence Day (Moroccan)
Waning Moon
Moon phase: Fourth Quarter
Color: Red

Moon Sign: Scorpio
Incense: Basil

19 Wednesday
Garifuna Settlement Day (Belizean)
Waning Moon
Moon phase: Fourth Quarter
Color: Brown

Moon Sign: Scorpio
Incense: Honeysuckle

☽ Thursday
Revolution Day (Mexican)
Waning Moon
New Moon 1:47 am
Color: Green

Moon Sign: Scorpio
Moon enters Sagittarius 5:26 am
Incense: Clove

21 Friday
Native American Heritage Day
Waxing Moon
Moon phase: First Quarter
Color: Rose

Moon Sign: Sagittarius
Sun enters Sagittarius 8:36 pm
Incense: Thyme

November

22 Saturday
National Adoption Day
Waxing Moon
Moon phase: First Quarter
Color: Indigo

Moon Sign: Sagittarius
Moon enters Capricorn 5:53 pm
Incense: Patchouli

---

23 Sunday
Labor Thanksgiving (Japanese)
Waxing Moon
Moon phase: First Quarter
Color: Gold

Moon Sign: Capricorn
Incense: Heliotrope

---

24 Monday
Evolution Day
Waxing Moon
Moon phase: First Quarter
Color: Lavender

Moon Sign: Capricorn
Incense: Rosemary

---

25 Tuesday
Feast of St. Catherine of Alexandria
Waxing Moon
Moon phase: First Quarter
Color: Scarlet

Moon Sign: Capricorn
Moon enters Aquarius 5:16 am
Incense: Ginger

---

26 Wednesday
Constitution Day (Indian)
Waxing Moon
Moon phase: First Quarter
Color: Topaz

Moon Sign: Aquarius
Incense: Lavender

---

27 Thursday
Thanksgiving Day (US)
Waxing Moon
Moon phase: First Quarter
Color: Turquoise

Moon Sign: Aquarius
Moon enters Pisces 2:24 pm
Incense: Nutmeg

◐ **Friday**
Republic Day (Chadian)
Waxing Moon
Second Quarter 1:59 am
Color: Pink

Moon Sign: Pisces
Incense: Yarrow

November

29 Saturday

William Tubman's birthday (Liberian)
Waxing Moon
Moon phase: Second Quarter
Color: Blue

Moon Sign: Pisces
Moon enters Aries 8:07 pm
Incense: Magnolia
Mercury direct

30 Sunday

St. Andrew's Day (Scottish)
Waxing Moon
Moon phase: Second Quarter
Color: Amber

Moon Sign: Aries
Incense: Marigold

November Correspondences

Stones: Citrine, cat's eye, topaz
Animals: Snake, eel, goose, raccoon
Flower: Chrysanthemum
Deities: Anubis, Inanna, Kali, Pluto
Zodiac: Scorpio

December

1 Monday
Feast for Death of Aleister Crowley (Thelemic)
Waxing Moon
Moon phase: Second Quarter
Color: Gray

Moon Sign: Aries
Moon enters Taurus 10:13 pm
Incense: Neroli

---

2 Tuesday
Republic Day (Laotian)
Waxing Moon
Moon phase: Second Quarter
Color: Maroon

Moon Sign: Taurus
Incense: Bayberry

---

3 Wednesday
St. Francis Xavier's Day
Waxing Moon
Moon phase: Second Quarter
Color: Brown

Moon Sign: Taurus
Moon enters Gemini 9:48 pm
Incense: Bay laurel

☻ Thursday
Feasts of Shango and St. Barbara
Waxing Moon
Full Moon 6:14 pm
Color: Purple

Moon Sign: Gemini
Incense: Balsam

---

5 Friday
Krampus Night (European)
Waning Moon
Moon phase: Third Quarter
Color: White

Moon Sign: Gemini
Moon enters Cancer 8:54 pm
Incense: Rose

---

6 Saturday
St. Nicholas's Day
Waning Moon
Moon phase: Third Quarter
Color: Black

Moon Sign: Cancer
Incense: Sage

---

7 Sunday
Burning the Devil (Guatemalan)
Waning Moon
Moon phase: Third Quarter
Color: Gold

Moon Sign: Cancer
Moon enters Leo 9:48 pm
Incense: Hyacinth

December

8 Monday
Feast of the Immaculate Conception
Waning Moon
Moon phase: Third Quarter
Color: Ivory

Moon Sign: Leo
Incense: Hyssop

9 Tuesday
Anna's Day (Swedish)
Waning Moon
Moon phase: Third Quarter
Color: Red

Moon Sign: Leo
Incense: Geranium

10 Wednesday
Alfred Nobel Day
Waning Moon
Moon phase: Third Quarter
Color: White

Moon Sign: Leo
Moon enters Virgo 2:20 am
Incense: Lilac

◑ Wednesday
Pilgrimage at Tortugas
Waning Moon
Fourth Quarter 3:52 pm
Color: Green

Moon Sign: Virgo
Incense: Carnation

12 Friday
Fiesta of Our Lady of Guadalupe (Mexican)
Waning Moon
Moon phase: Fourth Quarter
Color: Rose

Moon Sign: Virgo
Moon enters Libra 11:04 am
Incense: Orchid

13 Saturday
St. Lucy's Day (Scandinavian and Italian)
Waning Moon
Moon phase: Fourth Quarter
Color: Blue

Moon Sign: Libra
Incense: Ivy

14 Sunday
Hanukkah begins at sundown
Waning Moon
Moon phase: Fourth Quarter
Color: Yellow

Moon Sign: Libra
Moon enters Scorpio 10:51 pm
Incense: Frankincense

December

15 Monday

Consualia (Roman)
Waning Moon
Moon phase: Fourth Quarter
Color: Silver

Moon Sign: Scorpio
Incense: Lily

16 Tuesday

Las Posadas begin (end Dec. 24)
Waning Moon
Moon phase: Fourth Quarter
Color: Gray

Moon Sign: Scorpio
Incense: Cedar

17 Wednesday

Saturnalia (Roman)
Waning Moon
Moon phase: Fourth Quarter
Color: Topaz

Moon Sign: Scorpio
Moon enters Sagittarius 11:38 am
Incense: Marjoram

18 Thursday

Feast of the Virgin of Solitude
Waning Moon
Moon phase: Fourth Quarter
Color: Turquoise

Moon Sign: Sagittarius
Incense: Myrrh

Friday

Opalia (Roman)
Waning Moon
New Moon 8:43 pm
Color: Pink

Moon Sign: Sagittarius
Moon enters Capricorn 11:53 pm
Incense: Cypress

20 Saturday

Feast of St. Dominic of Silos
Waxing Moon
Moon phase: First Quarter
Color: Indigo

Moon Sign: Capricorn
Incense: Pine

21 Sunday

Yule • Winter Solstice
Waxing Moon
Moon phase: First Quarter
Color: Orange

Moon Sign: Capricorn
Sun enters Capricorn 10:03 am
Incense: Juniper

December ♑

22 Sunday
Hanukkah ends
Waxing Moon
Moon phase: First Quarter
Color: Ivory

Moon Sign: Capricorn
Moon enters Aquarius 10:52 am
Incense: Clary sage

23 Tuesday
Larentalia (Roman)
Waxing Moon
Moon phase: First Quarter
Color: Scarlet

Moon Sign: Aquarius
Incense: Ginger

24 Wednesday
Christmas Eve
Waxing Moon
Moon phase: First Quarter
Color: Brown

Moon Sign: Aquarius
Moon enters Pisces 8:09 pm
Incense: Lavender

25 Thursday
Christmas Day
Waxing Moon
Moon phase: First Quarter
Color: Crimson

Moon Sign: Pisces
Incense: Jasmine

26 Friday
Kwanzaa begins (ends 1/1) • Boxing Day
Waxing Moon
Moon phase: First Quarter
Color: Coral

Moon Sign: Pisces
Incense: Mint

Saturday
St. Stephen's Day
Waxing Moon
Second Quarter 2:10 pm
Color: Gray

Moon Sign: Pisces
Moon enters Aries 3:02 am
Incense: Patchouli

28 Sunday
Feast of the Holy Innocents
Waxing Moon
Moon phase: Second Quarter
Color: Amber

Moon Sign: Aries
Incense: Almond

December

29 Monday

Feast of St. Thomas à Becket
Waxing Moon
Moon phase: Second Quarter
Color: White

Moon Sign: Aries
Moon enters Taurus 6:57 am
Incense: Rosemary

30 Tuesday

Republic Day (Madagascan)
Waxing Moon
Moon phase: Second Quarter
Color: Red

Moon Sign: Taurus
Incense: Cinnamon

31 Wednesday

New Year's Eve
Waxing Moon
Moon phase: Second Quarter
Color: Yellow

Moon Sign: Taurus
Moon enters Gemini 8:13 am
Incense: Honeysuckle

December Correspondences

Stones: Turquoise, onyx, bloodstone, blue topaz
Animals: Elk, horse, stag, reindeer
Flowers: Narcissus
Deities: Artemis, Jupiter, Rhiannon, Thor
Zodiac: Sagittarius

Fire Magic

Ozark Faery Curses

Brandon Weston

Faery faith could be considered a foundational tradition in the Ozark Mountains. It has crossed the line dividing the *tradition-alists* and the more modern *neotraditionalists* and is one of the few areas where both groups agree. Ozarkers inherited their beliefs about faeries from both European and Indigenous sources. As with many of our traditions, this is a cultural amalgam. This mixture is exemplified with a specific type of Ozark faery group called the *Little People*. These are the most common faeries to be discussed by Ozarkers. Because of their popularity, they are often credited for almost all faery curses. For this reason, we will be focusing on the Little People alone within this article.

I can't stress enough about how belief in the Little People has shaped (and is still shaping) Ozark traditions. Many Ozarkers won't even say the name *Little People* lest they risk them showing up on their doorstep. Rural farmers often still leave portions of their crops for the Little People to ensure good harvests the following year. There are still strict taboos against destroying natural land features, especially waterways and springs. Stories of the Little People still abound today, even though most people will preface such tales with phrases like, "I'm not superstitious, but . . ." Among all the beliefs I've examined, belief in the Little People is one of the few to span across so many different divides. Young and old, churchgoers and non-believers, urban and rural—almost all Ozarkers have some story about the Little People and their involvement in human affairs.

The Little People

While the definition of faery is still widely debated, the Little People themselves have a much more developed image among Ozarkers. Physically, the Little People are closer to Cherokee descriptions of the ᏴᎾ ᏦᎤᏓᎢᎢ (*yvwi tsunsdii*), or "little people," as they are still called in English. They are described in both Indigenous and Ozark accounts as being exactly like human beings except smaller, more magical, and invisible unless they choose to be seen. They are said to have their own cities, language, religion, stories, jobs, and so on. They often even dress like humans do. It's highly likely that much of this lore was inherited as a mixture of beliefs from across many different Indigenous nations in the Southeast.

The personalities of the Ozark Little People are much closer to those of the pan-European faery-type beings. The Ozark Little People are fierce protectors of nature. I have a theory that belief in the Little People was once so strong among old Ozarker settlers because their need to protect the natural world around them was so strong. If your family relied on a natural spring for drinking water, then protecting that spring became top priority. Tales about the Little People punishing humans who tamper with natural water sources with deadly curses then became a way of protecting such vital resources.

Sources of Magic and Woe

By and large, Ozarkers will say that if you're kind, the Little People will also be kind, and if you're cruel, their cruelty toward you will be endless. In many stories, the Little People aid humankind in one way or another: for example, leading lost humans back out of the woods in exchange for some food or entertainment. Healers and magical practitioners often credit the Little People as the source of their power. This was once taboo in the old Ozarks, where working with spirit entities was considered Witchcraft and therefore condemned by the conservative culture. For this reason, many old healers would work with angel guides, often bearing a striking resemblance to the Little People. While working with faeries was condemned, using angels as a source of divine power was just personal piety and often overlooked by the community.

We should never assume we know anything about the personalities and actions of the Little People. Never enter any deals with faery beings without fully knowing what you're willing to give and what is expected of you. The Little People are skilled legalists, so maintaining detailed contracts is a must. Not all interactions with the Little People are so personal, however. In most cases, Ozarkers approach the Little People with the utmost respect and from a great distance—the greater the better. Here's my list of useful rules:

- Respecting the land is the easiest way to respect the Little People.
- Don't promise anything you aren't willing to deliver.
- Don't be ungenerous. A little given with a good heart is worth more than a lot given with a disingenuous intention.
- You never have to make any deals if you don't want to.
- The Little People love regularity—work on a schedule if you're going to work at all.
- Always include the Little People in festivities held in your home by leaving out some of the food you're offering to your family or friends. The Little People hate being left out of the fun.

A Rainbow of Curses

If you're able to adhere to these basic rules, you will always have positive interactions with the Otherworld. If not, you might unfortunately suffer from one of the many curses that are credited to the Little People. In fact, remedies for such curses account for a great deal of the herbal and magical cures in the Ozark healer's arsenal. These rainbow curses, as I like to call them, are sourced in ancient taboos surrounding things like hunting practices, honoring the land, and honoring the sources of well-being in life, like fire and food. Many of the remedies for these curses include ritual actions that realign the individual back to the equilibrium of nature. Con-

fessing what was done, for example, is a simple yet powerful way of realigning a cursed individual back to a state of harmony with these unseen forces. It should be noted that the symptoms associated with these curses are defined by their strangeness, suddenness, and intensity. Having a cold doesn't mean you have the "water curse." Having a sudden and intense cold right after doing some disrespectful action at a body of water might, though.

Red: Blood Curse

The blood curse is sourced from disrespecting animal-kind. Such actions can include hunting for sport—an activity traditionally discouraged by old Ozarkers. This means killing an animal and then leaving behind the meat: for example, killing a deer only for its antlers. Disrespectful actions also include not giving thanks for the food that is provided by the animal. Appeasing the Little People after a hunt might be as simple as leaving behind food and drink offerings. One informant told me his family always left the major organs of the kill behind in an organized pile as a way of propitiating the Little People and the spirit of the animal itself.

Symptoms

- "Blood sickness"—high/low blood pressure, digestion issues
- Wasting disease
- Redness or rashes on skin with no apparent cause
- Red, burning eyes
- "Boiling blood"—intense anger

Traditional Remedies

- Abstaining from killing any animal for a promised amount of time
- Offering one's own blood at the kill site (usually a small amount taken from a finger or the hand)
- Returning the kill back to the land along with additional offerings

Remediation Ritual: The Red Feast

To right this wrong, set out your feast at midnight on Tuesday (associated with Mars). Prepare as many different types of red foods and drinks as you can. Meats, vegetables, fruits, breads, desserts, wine—whatever you can find as long as it is naturally red or dyed using fruit or vegetable juices. Your offerings should be fresh, and homemade is best. Invite the wronged spirits to your table. Give them their own plate and cup at the table, piled high with a bit of everything offered. You can invite your family as well, especially if they are also under this curse. Eat, drink, and be merry. When you're finished, take the plate set for the spirits and distribute the food and drink offerings outside to be consumed by any critters that pass through. You can also take offerings to the original kill site. Repeat weekly if symptoms persist.

Orange: Fire Curse

The fire curse is sourced from disrespecting fire. Warnings against this curse can be seen culturally in the Ozark taboo against urinating on an open fire. I've encountered this folk belief among old-timers and younger generations alike. Younger folks often don't realize the silly "superstition" of their grandparents was once a very serious taboo. Little People are said to watch over the fire, seen as the life force of not only humankind but all beings. Other disrespectful actions include using the fire against others (e.g., starting forest fires and arson that affects the Little People). This curse can also befall humans who deny warmth and hospitality to their loved ones, strangers, and of course any faeries who have taken up residence in the home.

Symptoms
- "Cold sickness"—chills, cough, weakness, constipation
- Constant cold feeling in the body
- Pale complexion
- Inability to start fires or having fires easily get out of hand

Traditional Remedies
- Feeding the fire with offerings
- Candle- or fire-tending promised for a specific amount of time

Remediation Ritual: Fire Cleansing
Begin by lighting your fire. This can be outside in a firepit or a simple candleflame. Take care in tending to the fire. Use a new orange candle, or if you're working outside, build up the logs in an orderly fashion instead of just piling. While the fire burns, cut out a small doll from white paper. It can be any size. Say these words:

Fire, I give this curse to you. From fire it was born, and in fire it will die.

Then spit three times on the paper doll and cast it into the fire. Tend the fire or candleflame until it naturally burns out. Repeat as needed.

Yellow: Gold Curse
The gold curse is bestowed specifically upon stingy or greedy humans. Actions include denying offerings to the Little People or excluding them from festivities in the home. This curse also results from not fulfilling a promise made with the Little People. For example, one woman I met was cursed after she promised her house brownies a cup of coffee every Sunday, then got busy after a few months and forgot. This curse links to the Ozark belief in hospitality toward others. As I was taught, you always treat a stranger

with loving kindness because you never know if the Little People are watching. In general, showing compassion to all the seen and unseen beings around us is a great way to avoid this curse.

Symptoms
- Bad luck
- Loss of wealth (or finding it hard to retain money)
- Constant unemployment
- House problems (sudden, unexpected, and strange)

Traditional Remedies
- Throwing a party in your home just for the Little People
- Burying a gold item underneath the house or in enclosing inside a wall as an offering—giving gold to the Little People

Remediation Ritual: Keeping Promises
As this curse results from breaking promises of offerings, a great remedy is to get back on schedule. Write up all your promises on a piece of white paper with red ink (symbolizing blood). Make sure these are actions you can actually perform! This is a new contract, so old promises should be disregarded unless you'd like to have another try at them. When you're finished, roll up the paper and tie with a red ribbon. Place it on your home altar or somewhere near the kitchen (the heart of the home). Stick to your new promises! Or else don't make any at all.

Green: Field Curse

The field curse results from dishonoring the earth, including crops, fields, and forests. Abuses include chopping down old trees, lumbering, and destroying villages of the Little People housed in natural land features. Old-timers still warn land and road developers to go around old trees and other auspicious sites lest they incur faery wrath. Denying the Little People their share in crops can also cause the field curse. This is especially true if they were ever petitioned for the health or bounty of the crops. These offerings are generally small, unless something larger was promised. A small section of the field, maybe just a few plants, would be left unharvested at the end of the season as a gift for the Little People. Or if the crop produces throughout the season, a few of the first ripened fruits or vegetables would be picked and then left in a pile in the field or orchard.

Symptoms
- Crops wilting when they should be producing otherwise
- Wilting (or wasting) body and symptoms of malnourishment
- "Live things"—magical parasites that cause the sensation of crawling creatures inside the body
- Insect invasions inside home, barns, or on the land
- Loss of luck and wealth related to agriculture

Traditional Remedies
- Offering your first fruits next year
- Offering a small amount of blood to the fields
- Burying a silver item in the field for the Little People
- Herbal purgative remedies in the case of "live things" (flushing out the curse)

Remediation Ritual: Cleaning the Green
The simplest path to remediation is to take care of the land. Go out to a park or forested area on a Friday (associated with Venus). Take some trash bags with you and go around and clean up any waste that might be in the area. While you're cleaning, think to yourself that by this action, you're cleaning all the trash in the entire universe. Each piece is expanded to the size of galaxies and solar systems. The microcosm connects to the macrocosm. Continue cleaning until you're tired—a bit of a sacrifice for the offense. Repeat weekly until the symptoms subside.

Blue: Water Curse
The water curse results from polluting waterways through actions like urinating or defecating in the water, throwing trash into creeks, and destroying natural springs. This can also include causing waterways to become polluted through land development, sewage, building runoff, and so on, as well as swimming in a faery pool without giving offerings first. Those who still hold to this faery faith will often leave some food items as an offering every time they visit a natural body of water just in case it might belong to the Little

People. Offerings traditionally include bread, cake, cooked meats, or loose grains like oats, barley, and cornmeal. It's also traditional to leave an offering of loose tobacco, a practice influenced by Indigenous sources.

Symptoms
- "Wet sickness"—congestion, vomiting, diarrhea
- Extreme thirst or dry feeling in mouth
- Dizziness and blurred vision
- Anxiety or a racing, anxious mind
- Drowning or constantly getting choked while drinking water

Remedies
- Cleaning up waterways
- Restoring natural springs
- Leaving offerings at bodies of water

Remediation Ritual: Taking a Bath
Go out on a Monday (associated with the Moon) to a natural body of water that you can swim in. Take with you twelve dried corn ker-

nels, twelve dried beans (any kind), and a small amount of milk. Throw these in the water when you arrive. Then, step into the water and face west. It's most auspicious if the water itself flows west. Say,

Water take this watery curse back! Let it flow into the west. Let it flow back home and never come back.

Repeat this three times, and after each time, dunk yourself fully under the water. Dry off and return home. Repeat weekly as needed.

White: Pale Curse

The pale curse derives primarily from killing an all-white animal. These creatures are considered auspicious by Ozarkers and have direct connections to the Otherworld. Because of their magical nature, these animals are never killed. According to many of the old stories, all-white animals are also known to deliver specific quests to humans in return for good luck or magical power, as in the tall tale of the hunter who was asked by a white deer to bring him seven flowers from seven mountaintops in return for good luck in hunting. Failing such a quest can mean receiving the dreaded pale curse. This is, however, not such a straightforward curse and is sometimes thrown onto an individual by one of the Little People for seemingly no reason. It can also be delivered instead of one of the other rainbow curses for particularly serious offenses.

Symptoms
- Blindness or quickly failing eyesight
- Wasting diseases that make the skin pale and body weak
- Quickly graying hair
- Hauntings in the home or on the land (white animals can call in other spirits)

Traditional Remedies
- Offering your own blood at the kill site
- Purgative rituals to flush out the curse
- Pact promises (the magical life of a child, a faery marriage, etc.)

Remediation Ritual: Milk Offerings

Show your dedication to being forgiven through ninety days of milk offerings. Daily before sunrise, fill a small cup with whole milk or cream. Never use metal, as this material is offensive to the Little People. Leave your offering on the mantle above a fireplace, on your home altar, or in the kitchen on the stovetop (not on a burner). Pour the milk on the roots of a tree or in running water at dusk every evening.

Black: Death Curse

The most serious of the rainbow curses. This curse is only delivered for severe offenses against the Little People. Examples include killing one or more of the Little People; destruction of larges areas of land; and kidnapping, binding, or trapping a faery being.

Symptoms

- Cursed individual will waste away and die or watch those closest to them pass away quickly and in a short span of time from each other

Traditional Remedies

- Severe purging rituals to remove the curse from inside the body
- Petitioning for aid from angelic guides, deities, other faeries, etc.
- Lifelong pact of servitude to offended beings (can often span generations)

Remediation Ritual: Embracing the Night

Make a sacrifice symbolizing the darkness of the grave. Stay awake from dusk to dawn in a lonely, forested spot with no lights on. This can be out in the open (for extra penance) or inside a tent. The Little People will likely try to frighten you as punishment, but stay the course and you will be cured. At sunrise, take a bath in a body of moving water like a creek or river.

Temazcales

Laura González

One of my most treasured memories growing up in México City is going to steam baths with my mom. I was a preteen when she took me there at least once a month, and it was a great bonding moment. Both of us there sweating, detoxing, chatting, healing, naked. Later in life, I learned the deep significance that steam baths have for our Indigenous people, and those memories became even more valuable—the understanding that our bonding experiences happened in the belly of the mother and at the care of Our Grandmother Toci. After my mother passed away, she came to me in a dream, and we were in a steam bath when she told me, "You know we'll meet again." After I opened the metal-covered door of the steam bath, she was gone.

The steam baths of my youth are a modern and industrialized version of the sweat houses of our ancestors. In the Nahuatl languages, steam baths or sweat houses are called *temāzcalli*, and they are indeed an Indigenous practice that has survived colonization.

Native Practices

The Native practice of the temazcal that we'll explore in this text is indigenous to Mesoamerica, and we must remember that as much as we want to put together Native practices and Paganism, they are not the same. Native American/Indigenous practices are very similar to Pagan ones in context; however, the living people of these tribes, because of the historic wound of colonization, don't like to be referred to as Pagans. Let's not forget that the majority of people in Mesoamerica were detribalized, and most of us modern-day Mexicans were stripped of our tribes, customs, and language. I have the privilege to practice both the Native philosophies and Paganism, so I have no problem with being called a Pagan. However, it is very important that we understand that distinction.

What Is a Temazcal?

The *temazcal*, or sweat house, was a square or round domed building consisting of two chambers and traditionally built of clay or stucco. The large chamber that would house people needed to be large enough for people to gather, so builders would calculate the radius and height to be the length of one adult lying comfortably (roughly six feet). The smaller adjacent dome was attached to the large one by an opening facing the west. This smaller dome would hold the fire and heat rocks that were drenched with herb-infused water, thus producing the steam that would go into the big chamber. People would go in and out of the chamber through the main door, which faces the east, the site of the rising Sun.

Our oral traditions share that it's believed these steam houses existed about six thousand years ago. Some people go so far as to believe that the temazcales were created as early as fire was created. In either case, it's believed to be a very ancient tradition, and it's certainly a tradition that is spread throughout the world. We found them in the northern land, which is modern-day Canada and the United States. The steam house of the Lakota people is called *inípi*, or sweat lodge. Inípis follow a similar principle and are a single rounded dome created from different materials.

Nowadays, Mesoamerican peoples, modern-day Mexicans, and Mexican-Americans follow the design of the inípi, a direct influence from the Lakota tradition and its exportation of the Sun Dance to México in the 1970s. The single chamber dome is created with similar dimensions, and a hole is dug at the center where volcanic rocks heated outside the temazcal are deposited, to then be drenched with herb-infused water.

Ancient Philosophy

What happens when you put together fire and water? *Atlachinolli!* From the Nahuatl *atl*, "water," and *tlachinolli*, "to burn," this word roughly translates to "burning water." When you have that incandescent volcanic rock and you add water to it, it is going to produce vapor, and this vapor is called atlachinolli—the beginning of life on

Earth. And if you look at science, our people were not mistaken. What gave life to Earth was heat and water, and from their combination came steam, creating the atmosphere of Earth. Thanks to the atmosphere, we evolved into humans. So of course, the concept of atlachinolli is the concept of life: when we come in and out of the temazcal, we are born anew.

The hole dug in the ground is the belly button of the Mother, and the dome is indeed our Mother's pregnant belly. It is Our Grandmother Toci who cares for us while we are inside the temazcal. There are two different schools of thought when it comes to these Native practices. Some folks believe that Toci and Tlazolteotl are forces of nature or that they were people realizing certain chores and practices, and they were not gods and goddesses. The second school of thought says that of course they were gods and goddesses, that there are plenty of temples, ruins, and remnants of religious practices. The truth of the matter is we don't know because a lot of this history was destroyed by the colonizers, unfortunately lost from our oral traditions due to genocide.

If you search Toci and Tlazolteotl online, you'll probably obtain as a result "Grandmother and goddess of steam baths" and "goddess of sexuality, vice, purification, lust, filth, and a patroness of adulterers. She who eats filth and sin." Worry not—we will learn why Tlazolteotl was labeled in such a way in the next section.

Uses of the Temazcal

Please keep in mind that this content is provided for informational purposes only and does not intend to substitute professional medical advice, diagnosis, or treatment.

Oral tradition suggests three main uses for the temazcal. The first was hygiene. Our people were very passionate about two things: timekeeping and hygiene! It is believed that some would use the temazcal up to twice a day. Keep in mind that this does not involve the abrasive soap and water we use nowadays. These folks will cleanse themselves with the steam, which cleans and hydrates the skin. Some would use cold, soft rocks such as pumice or herb bunches to slap or rub on their skin to rid of dead cells. Our ancestors believed that the temazcal not only cleansed our body but also helped with the cleansing of anxiety and any and all mental uneasiness.

The second common use of the temazcal was conflict resolution. In any given argument, both parties will enter the temazcal and talk it out until a solution is found. I personally believe conflicts were solved quickly because who would like to have a discussion to no end in that heat? I'll say, don't sweat it!

The third and most common use was for women's healing. Women who were pregnant visited the temazcal regularly for hygiene; however, it was during the traditional quarantine after

A Little Bit of Magic

MEXICANS' OBSESSION WITH BEING CLEAN AND PRESENTABLE RUNS DEEP WITHIN OUR ANCESTRY.

giving birth that they were encouraged to visit at least every other day to bring healing to their bodies after the traumatic experience of pregnancy and birth. Temazcales were often adorned with images of Tlazolteotl and Toci. Tlazolteotl symbolizes rebirth and renewal of oneself and the earth's seasons, vitality, sexuality, and pleasure, while Toci symbolizes purification, the Grandmother, the wise woman, and the healer. It is believed that people would visit the temazcal for hygiene before or after intercourse and to prevent any sexually transmitted diseases. Our ancestors viewed sexuality, birth, and death as natural aspects of life and not taboos. However, colonizers interpreted things throughout the filters of their culture, equating sexuality and vitality with lust and filth, thus deeming Tlazolteotl and Toci as "eaters of filth and sin"—so far from the truth. Mesoamericans had no concept of "original sin" as defined by Christianity, and the human body was not considered filth—quite the opposite.

Modern-Day Temazcal

My purpose in sharing this information is not only to share the information of our people's practices but also to invite you to find about your own people's traditions and the land in which you exist. Do they have any steam bath or other bath and wash traditions? Nowadays temazcales are being used for both physical and spiritual purification, and it is easy enough to find a group of people who can facilitate a ceremony. Please find within your local community Indigenous practitioners who may provide this practice, and make sure that you have done thorough research, ensuring that they are not appropriating the culture of Indigenous people. Support Indigenous cultures not only for what is beneficial to you but also for what is beneficial for them. There are so many Indigenous peoples around the world who need our help, not only in a way that brings attention to their struggle but also to contribute to their financial stability and work, paying fair wages for the goods and services they have to offer. So if you're going to get into any type of ceremony of this kind, make sure you're giving back to the Indigenous communities.

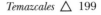

Practice a Steam Bath at Home!

If you are unable to find local practitioners, you may consider trying a steam bath at home. Please keep in mind that if you're going to try this, do it with somebody else who can help you, and follow these instructions as closely as you can.

You will need:

Big pot (at least 1 gallon)
Pot holders
Bathroom with a shower big enough to put a chair on it
Chair
Plastic shower curtain
Cotton bedsheet

Fill the pot with water and bring it to a boil.

Put the chair in your shower, and then use the bed sheet to cover the chair, leaving easy access to the bottom of it. Sit on the chair and cover yourself with the rest of the bed sheet.

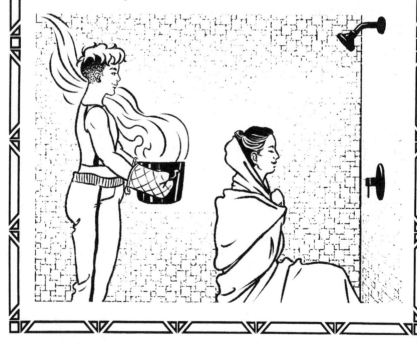

Have your helper, using the pot holders, bring the pot of boiling water to the bathroom shower and carefully put it under the chair.

Ask your helper to then cover you completely with the plastic shower curtain. Some people get very claustrophobic and don't want to cover their head. If you feel that way, it's fine to leave your head uncovered.

Sit back and relax, letting your physical and spiritual bodies be cleansed with the steam. Feel the essence of Tlazolteotl and Toci there with you. The work is done.

How long should you stay there? As long as you can breathe without having to strain yourself, and of course, when you feel that it is getting a little too intense, call on your helper so they can remove the shower curtain, and then you can come out of the bath. If you wish, you can take a shower after the steam bath. Using warm water is best, for if you take too cold of a shower, you can shock your body. Some people like that shock, but I don't, so I take a warm shower when I feel I have to shower after the temazcal.

Foot Soak: Steam Bath Alternative

There is an alternative way to do this on your own:

You'll need:
Big pot (at least 1 gallon)
Pot holders
Towel
Bucket in which you can soak your feet comfortably
Cool water

Fill the pot with water and bring it to a boil.

Set the bucket in a place where you can sit comfortably for a few minutes. Keep your towel near you.

Using the pot holders, bring the pot of boiling water and carefully pour it into the bucket. Pour some cool water in the bucket to temper it, but keep it as hot as you can safely take on your feet.

Soak your feet and relax, letting your physical and spiritual bodies be cleansed with the steam. Feel the essence of Tlazolteotl and Toci there with you.

When the water has cooled off completely, you can take your feet out of the bucket and gently pat them dry with the towel. The work is done.

Herb Use

As I mentioned earlier, a traditional temazcal will include the use of herbs. You can add those fresh or dried to the boiling water just before you bring it to use. The possibilities are endless. I recommend you research those you would like to use to infuse your water, to better suit your needs at any given moment.

Here are some of my favorites:

- Arnica (*Arnica montana*) to ease muscle pain
- Basil (*Ocimum basilicum*) to ease sinus symptoms
- Chamomile (*Chamaemelum nobile*) to ease inflammation, reduce stress, and promote sleep
- Eucalyptus (*Eucalyptus globulus*) to ease cough and promote good respiratory health
- Rosemary (*Salvia rosmarinus*) to ease muscle tension and headaches

• • • ☽ • • •

Whether you're able to attend a temazcal ceremony or do a steam bath or foot soak at home, I invite you to connect with the energies of releasing, renewal, and vitality with your internal cycles and the magic and cycles of Mother Earth with Tlazolteotl and Our Grandmother Toci.

Resources

Gutiérrez, Arturo Meza. *Mosaico de Turquesas*. México: Ediciones Artesanales Malinalli, 1994.

Martínez Sánchez, Ángela María. *Temazcal: Una disciplina ancestral*. Morelia Michoacán, México: City Council of Morelia Michoacán, 2010.

Creating and Running a Pagan Festival or Event

Stephanie Woodfield

As a priestess, I serve both the gods and my community. Part of my service as a priestess has led me to create and run Pagan events. I approach it keeping in mind how ancient Pagans gathered at different points in the year. Their festivals were religious in nature yet also included feasting and merrymaking, the selling of goods, and building bonds within the wider community. Most modern events are much the same. We have rituals, maybe a drum circle or potluck dinner, and vendors. Not much has changed, yet there is a lot of red tape that modern festival creators must consider.

The first event I created, which now has grown and been running for over ten years, I was pushed into starting by an Irish goddess who doesn't really take no for an answer. The Morrigan wanted her people to gather, and so I started a yearly retreat in her honor. I really didn't know if it would be a one-off event, but it turned into something that created a thriving community and forged lifelong friendships.

When I moved from Connecticut to Florida, I started smaller local events. There was a large community in central Florida, yet there wasn't much going on other than one or two big events a year. The rest of the year no one did anything together. I missed the localized gatherings, sabbats, Full Moon rituals, and events I had experienced in Connecticut. So I started my own event that met in a local park every couple of months.

A great deal of work and planning happens behind the scenes of any event. Whether it's a single-day or multiple-day event, chances are someone has spent a year or more planning to make everything run smoothly. The reward is well worth the effort, but there are a lot of things to consider. The following are just some of the challenges you will have to solve if you wish to create your own Pagan event.

Finding a Purpose and Sticking to It

The events that last the longest and tend to be the most meaningful are the ones that have a vision and stick with it. Why does your event exist? What purpose does it serve? Is there an overall theme?

The Morrigan's Call Retreat focuses solely on the Morrigan, with each year having a different theme related to her. The local events I run have a unique theme for each event, revolving around a different type of magical practice, a holiday, or a deity. Whatever your theme is, stick to it and weave it throughout everything that goes into the event. Events that have no clear theme can be fun, but they don't always have enough appeal to keep people coming back or for attendees to get anything very meaningful out of it. You may also be called, as I was, to create something to honor a specific deity and allow others a chance to explore that deity in a deeper, more immersive way.

You may even wish to formally ask that deity or a set of spirits to be the guardian of the event and guide its creation and evolution. There are a lot of practical and everyday things involved in running an event, but that doesn't mean you can't add your magical intent into it as well. It may also be useful to create a mission statement, write it down, and keep it on your altar so you can infuse it with your magical intent for your event. Whatever your goal, don't lose sight of that core purpose behind what you are creating.

Permits and Other Requirements

This is the not-so-fun part. Whether you are on public property or are renting a private venue, you will have to consider the cost of the rental in your overall budget. In addition to the rental, there may be other things you may have to buy or rent, such as porta-potties, pavilion tents for dining, tables and chairs, and so on. All these big-ticket items will influence what your ticket price will be. If you are having a bonfire, you may also have to apply for a single-use fire permit for the day or days of the event. You will also have to purchase event insurance, possibly with a specific amount of coverage per your contract with the venue. If there is alcohol at the event, of course the venue must approve it, and your insurance will have to include it in your coverage.

I know of one event that was held on private property, and the owner didn't think they needed any permits to hold a festival on their own land. The day of the event, as hundreds of cars drove down the road to their property, the local police realized there was a large unpermitted event happening and shut the festival down. Not knowing what is required to host an event can kill a year or more of planning on your part. Be open and honest about the event you are setting up with your park and rec or local permitting agencies. Pagans tend to be secretive, but for a successful event, you need to be upfront about what you are doing and acquire the proper permits to make that event run smoothly.

> **A LITTLE BIT OF MAGIC**
>
> *Creating and running Pagan events challenged us to use both mundane and magical skills to forge something meaningful for our communities.*

If vendors or other merchants will be selling food or products at your event, you may need additional permitting. For private events at a rental venue, this is less likely to be a problem, but for events held in public parks or open to the public, most cities and towns will consider it a special event and require permits to allow the selling of food in addition to whatever other permits you will be required to have for running the event.

Last, you should consider creating an LLC or a nonprofit for the event. You will need to have some kind of plan for filing your taxes. That also means being organized and keeping track of all expenses and receipts for tax time.

Staff and Delegation

You can't run an event alone. Trust me—I've tried. You will need help and a lot of it. You will have to recruit staff or volunteers. You will also need to make sure your staff are reliable. Be clear with them about what tasks you will need their help for and how much of a time commitment it will be. You will need a wide variety of skills: some people who are strong enough to move things, someone

trained for medical emergencies, someone who can coordinate with a food vendor or cook food, and many other roles. Will these volunteers be paying to attend? How much of the admission will be credited back to them, or will they pay a smaller ticket price as a volunteer? You will also have to have staff meetings so that everyone is on the same page, know their duties, knows how to handle emergencies, and so on.

Rain and Cancellations

There will always be things outside of our control. You may have an outdoor ritual planned and it rains. There might be a drought and your fire permit is not approved. Things will happen and you must be able to pivot quickly. Having a rain plan or cancellation

plan if the event cannot happen will help you navigate these issues. During the COVID-19 pandemic, I found myself in a place where I had to pivot and turn a longstanding in-person event into an online format. All our staff meetings were done through Zoom, so we were already familiar with the program, and it made sense to switch to something we already used.

Ritual Coordination and Creation

Rituals are always the highlight of any Pagan event. Having a skilled ritual team and rituals that are planned out and executed well are essential to a successful event. In the events I am part of, we have dedicated ritual staff that tend the temple space we create at events and who write and perform the rituals. This also includes the priests of this group spending the time to connect more deeply with deity and hone their ritual and skills at moving energy in the months leading up to the event. Leading this group might be something you delegate to another event coordinator, as it tends to form its own little unit of the staff.

It is also important to consider how you will bring people to the ritual space. Are there those present who have mobility issues? Are there people in wheelchairs, or do they need additional help getting to the ritual space early perhaps? It may be a good idea to have these folks lead the group to the ritual area so they can set a slower pace and not be left behind. You might also invite them to be led down first by a staff member so they can make themselves comfortable before the rest of the group arrives.

Funding

Funding and how well you handle money can make or break an event. Before starting an event, you will need to do a lot of research. Get quotes for your venue, additional things you will need to rent, catering, and the little things like tablecloths, décor, and decorations for ritual or temple space. All these things need to be accounted for before you can create a budget. Before you begin, you need to have an honest conversation with yourself or your organizers about how much it will cost to run your event and how much you will need to

make to be able to put down deposits and fund future years. This can also influence when you begin to market and sell tickets to your event so you can begin to recoup money or make enough to pay final balances by their due dates before the event.

Not all the events I run are ticketed; some are free events. These shorter, single-day events are much less expensive to run, and we have been able to fund them through selling vending spots at the event. For events such as these, vendors make the event enjoyable for those who attend. It also means for these events to run smoothly, it is up to the event organizers to promote the event well enough that enough vendors sign up to cover the costs of the event and that enough people show up to make it worthwhile for your vendors to return for the next event.

Learning from Old Leaders and Cultivating New Leaders

Perhaps the most important thing that helped me create my first event was sitting down with one of the organizers for a large Pagan festival in the area and picking her brain. We had dinner one night and talked about all the things that worked and didn't work for her event and different practical things to consider.

The simple truth is there aren't enough people who want to take on this kind of leadership role. It demands a lot of time, effort, and money. Leaders get burnt out, and unfortunately that sometimes means when they are too tired to continue, the event dies with them. Listen to the organizers in your community. Pick their brains about how an event you love works. Find out how they made it such an enjoyable experience. I guarantee it didn't happen by accident. Ask if you can help be part of organizing something that is local to you so you can gain the skills to run something in the future.

If you are a current organizer for an event, it's important to consider how long you plan on staying in that leadership position. Who will take your place? Is there someone who you need to take on as a protégé so they can learn what you do? These are all important things to consider both when creating an event and thinking about the future of a long-running one.

The Magical Side of Things

So much of running an event is mundane work, but there is a magical side of things too. An event that is dedicated to a specific deity may involve divination and devotional work to see what that deity would like for a given year. The themes and rituals for the Morrigan's Call Retreat are all crafted based on divination and journey work with the Morrigan. For other events, I may simply see what deity or theme I get a magical nudge from. It also doesn't hurt to use your Witchcraft when asking to find the best possible venue for an event or to help raise funds. Magical and mundane efforts should work in tandem with one another.

· · · ☽ · · ·

These are just a few of the things you will have to consider and plan around when creating a Pagan event. Even this short list may seem like a lot, and it is, but I can tell you it is well worth it. I hope this inspires you to create something beautiful and meaningful that you can share with your local community.

Hearth Magic

Elizabeth Barrette

Hearth magic is all about making the home a comfortable and productive place to live. It spans a collection of different ideas for home decorating, energy balance, and convenience. It's not fancy; it's practical. It can include spells and rituals but doesn't have to; much of it lies in the setup of the home itself. You can make it work with almost any combination of colors, materials, or techniques based on your personal tastes and traditions.

Hearth magic is some of the oldest magic known. We catch glimpses of its history through archaeology. It's there in the family altars, the incense burners, the tiny charms lost in the corners of a room. It's in the mosaics and frescoes decorating the walls, pictures of old gods and folk heroes and food. Each room of the house has its own associations that we can enhance. Whenever we work hearth magic, we connect with our ancestors.

The Foyer and Porch

The foyer is the entrance to the home, which sets the tone for everything inside. Porches that have both an inside and an outside door serve a similar purpose. These areas give you a chance to keep good things in and bad things out, much like an airlock. So use them mindfully.

You want to attract positive energy and repel negative energy. For instance, some people believe that a red door attracts good fortune while a blue ceiling—sometimes called "haint blue"—blocks evil spirits. Anchor your protective wards in this part of the house with a stone or statuette. You might hang a coin charm from feng shui for prosperity. Artwork, especially nature art, helps make the space welcoming and personal. If you're out of the broom closet, consider Pagan art featuring any of the deities related to gates or passageways.

Pay particular attention to the thresholds. Make sure they are secure, not loose, and won't easily snag on anything. Some folks believe in sweeping inward so you don't sweep away your good luck; others believe in sweeping out the bad luck. Either way you should do it intentionally. Likewise, the entryway should guide people gracefully into the home. Use rugs, art, or other décor to suggest a path pointing inward, so folks don't wind up opening all the closet doors looking for the way in.

Accommodate practicalities. A rack for coats or keys makes life easier by keeping necessities at hand; if you get one with a star or some other magical motif, then you can anchor your home wards to it. This is especially important with doors that open directly into main rooms such as the living room or kitchen. A hall tree encourages people to take a moment and transition from outdoors to indoors a little more mindfully.

Houseplants create vital energy and represent the element of earth. As many porches have primarily glass enclosures, they make ideal places for a collection of plants. If you have sidelights on your door, consider placing one plant on each side in those narrow little windows. Protective plants such as cacti help keep out unwanted influences too.

The Kitchen and Dining Room

Both the kitchen and the dining room revolve around food, from storage through preparation to eating. Consider the layout of your home and work with it, not against it. Some homes are designed with these spaces as major social areas, while others keep them out of the way. A hidden kitchen allows for more prosaic items like a potato keeper, while a more open one requires more support for socializing. An enclosed dining room might suit a china cabinet and an open one a games cabinet. A large mirror reflecting the stove or dining table will reflect and enhance the heart of these rooms.

Warm, bright colors like sunshine yellow, pumpkin orange, and scarlet add energy and stimulate the appetite. Yellow works well on walls or cabinets. Orange and red may do better as accents, such as small appliances or curtains. These all speak to the fire aspect of cooking. You can bring in the abundance of earth with artwork of a cornucopia or harvest deity.

Store items based on use. Rarely used items can go down low or up high. Commonly used items should go in the middle, easy to reach. Only those you use the most often, like knives in a knife block, should live on the countertop. Empty stretches of counter don't just make it easy to work; they keep the energy flowing smoothly.

Unless you have a huge family, consider a round or oval dining table instead of square or rectangular. Similarly, choose rounded chairs with comfortable cushions. Curving shapes support eye contact, conversation, and domestic harmony. A genuine wood table provides a grounding earth influence, while a glass tabletop offers the clarity of air. Balance energy flows with wind chimes, bells, or a distinctive chandelier over the table. Always keep something on the table, preferably edible, like a bowl of fruit, to promote abundance.

The Living Room

The living room is usually where people spend the most time awake at home. It's also the part of the home most accessible to guests. That means you need to balance relaxation with things to do. Lay out the furniture to support diverse ways for people to interact with each other.

Use colors to set the scene. For a large room, earthy blues, greens, and browns may evoke a cozy forest grotto or ocean beach. For a small room, open it up with pale colors like sky blue, mint green, or sunshine yellow. If your favorite furniture doesn't quite match, you can use dust covers or throw pillows to connect it better. Green plants add to the harmony, with examples like jade plant, lucky bamboo, and graceful climbing vines.

The living room is the most likely to have a fireplace or wood-stove, followed by the dining room. The literal hearth is the best place for hearth magic! Choose the finest fireplace tools you can find and afford, preferably with a Pagan motif like dragons or cats. When a woodstove is not in use, its flat top makes a great place for fire symbols such as candles or incense burners. With a fireplace, use the mantelpiece above it to house icons of fire or hearth deities.

The living room is also the most popular place for a family altar, although some people prefer the bedroom. This may consist of a whole altar table or cabinet, but many people just make a casual shrine by collecting meaningful objects. Family photos, souvenirs from vacations, favors from weddings, bronzed baby shoes, and other memorabilia all support the family spirit. Ideally, place the family altar near the hearth if you have one; a mantelpiece is perfect.

The Bedroom

The bedroom is a peaceful refuge from the rough-and-tumble of everyday life. Aim to create a sense of sanctuary. Try to avoid bringing in busy elements like a work desk or video game console. Windows should have good curtains, preferably thick ones that can block outside noise or light if necessary.

Choose soothing colors like purples, blues, browns, or grays. Hot tones in a bedroom can make it hard to unwind and fall asleep. Textures matter a lot here too. Think how good it feels to sink into a fluffy rug or poofy comforter. While natural fibers are often best, do consider modern marvels like microfiber or sherpa blankets, especially if you can find one with a witchy design. Some people like to bury their bed in pillows, while others only want a few. Promote mystical aspects like dreamwork or yoga nidra with embroidered pillows, wall art, or statuettes.

Place furniture for calm and balance. Ideally, put the bed with its headboard against a wall, although under a window can work with a low headboard if the outside is not too noisy. Even if you sleep alone, put a nightstand on each side of the bed to promote balance through symmetry. If you are single, honor that with strong solitary art such as a lone oak tree or a sea turtle. Conversely, if you share with a life partner, this is the best place for icons of deities specializing in love, romance, or sexuality. You could also use art showing pairs of animals, such as swans or seahorses.

If you are somewhat closeted about your magical practices, the bedroom is the most private place in the home, making it a good location for your altar. The top of a dresser is one convenient option, but some people like a jewelry chest or wall cabinet that closes. Include iconography of all your patron deities along with the tools for your magical specialties.

The Bathroom and Laundry Room

The bathroom relates to water, cleansing, and banishing. If you also have a laundry room, or even a washer-dryer set tucked into a laundry closet, then that area serves a related function and has similar parameters for magic and decor. With multiple rooms of this type, consider obtaining a set of matched art prints or statuettes to help link them together in a network that will keep your home's energy refreshed.

For these rooms, pale, clean colors like white and light gray work well, as do watery purples, blues, or greens. Unless you have a lot of natural woodwork, avoid earthy colors like brown, black, or dark gray for their associations with dirt. Themes like a beach, river, rain, fish, or other aquatic décor support the energy. Genuine glass fishing floats are intensely magical, as are driftwood, beach glass, and seashells. If the room gets enough light, add damp-loving houseplants such as ferns or air plants. Otherwise, consider artwork of water lilies, irises, willows, cattails, and similar aquatic flora. You could also choose mermaids, sea dragons, or water deities.

Water is the element of purification. Support this by keeping your cleaning supplies in the bathroom; under the sink is a good location. Your magical cleansing supplies can stay here too. Handmade soap and a salt scrub with purifying herbs such as mint or lavender are helpful choices.

These rooms also get rid of things you don't need. Liquid residues from spells or rituals can usually be dumped down a drain or flushed down the toilet. Make sure your garbage can is big enough, preferably solid metal, to handle any solid remains. Keep your banishing supplies here too, such as salt, asafoetida, and charcoal dust. Not only are they helpful in general, but if your washer-dryer gets gremlins, be prepared to dispel them with sea salt and asafoetida.

For a laundry room in particular, you may also want to invoke air. Think how often such products use words like *fresh* or *breeze* in

the name. Light, gauzy curtains over a window can add a billowy effect. Artwork may show open, airy places like prairies and mountains or delicate flowers such as baby's breath and Queen Anne's lace. Anything with flyaway seeds such as maple or milkweed also serves this purpose.

Conclusion

Hearth magic spreads throughout your space, customized for each room. It's part of what makes a house or apartment into a home. By spreading out your magical supplies and fitting the décor to the heart of each room, you always have what you need within easy reach. It also keeps you from making a big pile of magical materials that is hard to dig through in search of one thing. The mood of each room suits its purpose, creating balance in the home as you move from one to another. It's not fancy, but it works. Give it a try!

The Magical Nature of Natural Hair

Stephanie Rose Bird

Back in the day, my ma did my hair. I sat on the ground between her knees and put my trust in her loving hands. She'd grease her hands and give me large twists, braids, and Afro-puffs. It was my cousins who made the more elaborate cornrow styles. Cornrows are three-strand braids braided closely to the scalp. This ancient Indigenous African style made a cultural comeback in the 1970s and is having another revival today. I learned from my ma and elder cousins how to create Afro-puffs, braids, twists, and cornrows, and I use all of those skills on myself and my children, if they are so inclined, to this day. Sub-Saharan Indigenous Africans have a lengthy history of treating their locs with scented pomades of animal- and plant-based oils. Today, Africans in the Americas, like myself, continue these practices, which we learn at too early an age to remember.

Ancient through contemporary cultures, language groups, and tribal groups have been cultivating the magick of their locs and tresses through the ages. This article encourages the modern-day Witchcraft, Hoodoo, and Pagan practitioners to extend their power and essential beauty through their body to the hair, by using a variety of braiding, twisting and loc techniques enhanced with botanicals and herbs.

The Power within the Tresses

I used to think, being a Black woman, that it was only my people who were obsessed with hair. Then I opened my ears and started looking cross-culturally at hairstyling, adornment, and the mythic stories of the power of hair. From Medusa, the Gorgon of ancient Greece with wings and living poisonous snakes as hair, whose very

steely gaze could turn a human to stones. In Greek myth, Pterelaus had a magickal golden hair that made him immortal and difficult to conquer. Then there is the Christian biblical figure Samson. As long as his long hair was left to its own devices, he had tremendous strength and was able to perform feats that surpassed human strength. Finally, all are probably familiar with the fairy tale "Rapunzel" of the Brothers Grimm fame and her long, long braid, which gave her power over who entered her tower.

From these and other stories, I realized hair's significance to our general culture to our history and collective story. Hair and its beauty, symbolism, and implied power are of great concern to all of us and have been for a very long time.

Recently, I was a presenter, one of the "Queen Mothers," or elder women, at Sacred Waters Retreat in Tennessee, a retreat that caters to approximately 100 women of African ancestry and people of color. Before even packing my suitcase, I called my neighborhood florist and ordered a headdress. I would wear a baby's breath and green-leaved laurel each day of the event, atop my TWA (teeny-weeny Afro), matching a vision I had. Hair and its adornment is of utmost importance in the Black community. I knew that with flowers and leaves in my hair, the energy and strength I felt within would be on the outside of me too.

Only weeks before the retreat, I had what is called a "big chop," meaning I had my shoulder-length hair cut off. I had decided it was time to go 100 percent gray. I had been growing my hair out and found myself to have a stark, two-toned look, much like a skunk. I had distinctly black and white hair and this displeased me to no end. My salon is a place that caters to all types of curly hair, specializing in such things as Deva and Rezo cuts. I sat down in the cushioned chair and had the big chop; that move set my curly blue-gray and white tresses, and me, free. Now, I wash and condition my hair, finger-comb it, and then I'm good to go.

Years ago, I had locs. I wore them for about fifteen years. They'd grow to my butt, I'd cut them to my shoulders, and then they'd grow there again. This to say, long hair comes naturally to me, and I enjoy it. Cutting it short was a *big* change!

Loc Traditions

When I first thought about beginning a loc journey, I thought about the regal hair some called *dreadlocks* worn in certain parts of Africa or in the Caribbean, most notably Jamaica. Being interested as I am in cultural anthropology, I looked into the history of this type of hair we call *locs*. It didn't take long to determine that for the Rastafarians of Jamaica; the Shaivas (devotees to Shiva) and Vaishnavas (devotees to Vishnu) of India; and numerous tribes and groups in Africa, including the Turkana, Maassai, and Samburu of Kenya, Himba of Namibia, Fulani of Senegal, and the Baye Fall (Black Muslims), loced hair is not simply a hairstyle—it is a way of life. The locs are anchored by culture, traditions, and most of all spirituality.

The spelling of *loc* is an intentional reclaiming of the word to describe this style or way of life as it actually is. *Dreadlock* sounds negative. It is negative. It's institutionalized racism, and we deny its hold over our beautiful locs. By renaming, we reclaim locs and put them in the positive light they deserve to be within.

Just as many different cultures have hair-locing traditions, so too does this distinctive way of wearing the hair have diverse names, including natty dreads (Rastafarians), *ndiagne* (strong hair), and *jaṭā* (gurus of India).

With the many immigrants from Jamaica and sub-Saharan Africa in the United States, several decades ago the loc culture began to transcend its specificity with relation to various traditions and belief systems to become a cultural phenomenon. Acclaimed author Alice Walker has worn locs for many years and so have other creative artists, including the very high profile ancestor-loc-donning Bob Marley, Lisa Bonet, Lenny Kravitz, and Whoopi Goldberg.

Different Ways of Starting Locs

Organic Loc: Curly hair comes together and stays that way.

Sister Loc: A process done in the hair salon, where locs are instantly created on your head, and these can come out without leaving your natural hair loced.

Two-Strand Twist-Out: The hair begins in small parts and two-strands are twisted around each other until the end of the hair is reached. A setting solution is applied during this process. Then, in a few days, you untwist your dried hair, and you can either wear that style, which resembles locs, or let your hair come together, allowing permanent locs to form.

My locs grew fast and easily, and I applied aloe vera gel to them. After thanking the plant for sharing its life juices with me, I made a slit in it with a sharp knife to release the natural gel within. I squeezed this into a small cup or bowl. While I no longer have locs, aloe vera gel is 100 percent natural and my go-to for an easy herbal styling gel that I use on the short, curly Afro I have now. It works just as well if you segment your hair and apply in small portions to a fuller Afro to set, soften, and hold the curls.

Adornment with Flowers, Scents, and More

I adorn my hair as much as possible. As an eclectic Pagan, that includes a desire to reflect the days of old in my styling. I sought to play up the notion of the crown, what we call our hair. I have several headdresses that I purchased online. A few feature silk flowers in different color patterns, and one is golden with fake pearls. It is my true crown.

I also wear real flowers and leaves in my hair, à la the great blues singer Billie Holiday, but also as a salute to Orisha Oshun, a Yoruba being of the Ifá path. Her attributes are love, sensuality, and beauty. I also seek to invoke Venus and other Roman and Greek goddesses, as well as to salute the Hawaiians, Tahitians, and Indigenous peoples worldwide.

As a magickal herbalist and aromatherapist, I know the scent that emanates from aromatic flowers has specific power over the wearer and those around them. Here are a few favorites that you can get from the garden or your local florist:

- Gardenia
- Roses
- Carnations
- Lilies
- Orange blossoms
- Orchids
- Baby's breath
- Green leaves

Do some legwork—go out in your garden or to your flower shop and see what is available and what works best for you. You can then try these styles:

- Braid your hair if it's long and affix flowers to it with bobby pins or a rubber band.
- Pin a large, showy flower over your ear or use it to accentuate a chignon.

- If you have an Afro, you can make a magnificent crown by randomly sticking baby's breath in your hair. You hair should hold it. If not, use bobby pins.
- Get three strands of eighteen-inch ribbon. Braid it tightly, then stick smaller flowers in between the strands. Wear this as a band around your head.

Scented hair can easily be traced back to the Egyptians. The unguents and pomades used often had an animal oil base like lanolin made pliable through the application of fragrant essential oils from flowers.

Folks have done a lot of what I call "botanical defiance" using their tresses. For example, enslaved Africans under extreme duress, chained and transported on ships, hid okra seeds and other soul food seeds in their cornrow-styled hair so they could be nourished by their motherland foods, once they made it to their destination, wherever that might be. Their magickal thoughts paid off, because now we are blessed with these soulful foods.

Shells, a tribute to Venus, Aphrodite, Yemaya, and other sea-loving beings, make a great ornament for the hair. If you have small braids or small individual twists, you can slide cowry shells up the shaft of each one until they won't go any further. Cowry shells are so beloved in sub-Saharan Africa that you can find them in many fabric prints and on mud cloth, and they were even used as currency.

When Africa Comes Home

We all learn from our people, like it or not, especially generationally. We can also learn from others. As I said, I learned a lot of what I know about natural hair from my ma and cousins. Recently, though, I learned firsthand of the deeply spiritual connections that can go into hairstyling.

In between my cuts and big chop, I found a braider. She was born in Senegal but lived mostly in Mali. I knew that the great griots and kora players came from these countries in West Africa, so I was very excited. She and her cousin who worked with her, however, were Muslim—deeply religious practicing Muslims. Pagans know that under the skirts of Abrahamic religions live the ways of the days of old. This is what I found to be true with my braider.

Now, let me set the stage. Braiding is an epic event. It is not a short stage performance but a lengthy endurance sport like a marathon. Depending on the style, it can take up to eighteen hours to complete, so something like this is done over a two-day period. My braider is a Queen Mother—in other words, she is an elder. She is also very fastidious. She takes few breaks, hardly ever eats, and only talks if it strikes her fancy.

To my delight, once or twice, she has taken me back to her homelands in West Africa with stories that deserve a stage of their own. She began braiding at an early age, using local shea butter as a styling aid, sitting under mango trees with her cousins, all of whom were braiders, but she was the best and ended up making her way to America with her talent.

She loves telling me all of the uses of shea butter: hair pomade, skin treatment, arthritis treatment, joint pain relief, skin condition relief, and so on and so forth—things I know but thoroughly enjoy a firsthand account of from her. Then she started speaking about the great griots (oral storytellers who preserved much of our history through folktales), magickal mudcloth, and the great kora players, and tears flooded to my eyes. I got much more than I paid for: she shipped me back, if only for a little while, to my people's homeland, from which I was so harshly removed, decades ago.

Alas, there was more. This speaks to me, very closely to the heart. At first I was confused, like we all get. Did I hear what I think I just heard? I had to ask myself this several times. Before any of the extension hair was braided into my own, she talked to it. She sang to it. She prayed over it. This was animism in action, from one whom I share ancestry with, and it brought chills up and down my spine. I don't know the nature of her prayers but whatever she said, the hairstyle turned out beautifully. Blessed be!

Water Magic

When Meditation
Becomes Shadow Work

Diana Rajchel

My meditation practice started in 1996, and I often bemused my friends with my "weird" practice of withdrawing from everyone to go sit on the floor and do nothing for twenty minutes a day. One especially curious friend, who enjoyed reading a mix of topics skeptical and superstitious, sent me an article about the pitfalls of meditation printed in the *Utne Reader* around 1998. The article highlighted "meditation's dark side," reporting that some individuals experienced panic attacks, increased heart rate, headaches, and emotional meltdowns.

The article arrived in the mail just after my first-ever unpleasant meditation session, one that caused me to recognize my deep unhappiness with my family dynamic. Even with the pain, I continued my practice, officially informed that the potential rabbit hole might cost me mental health. My choice did both harm and good. I was aware of things boiling within me; I just didn't have adequate, affordable support available.

The risk of meditation lies within its key benefits. It lowers blood pressure, reduces anxiety, increases brain plasticity, improves self-awareness, lowers your resting heart rate, and helps you sleep better. Most neurotypicals can get most of those benefits after forming a simple sitting meditation habit over three weeks. One phrase in that list pinpoints the danger: *self-awareness.* Knowing your own mind and motivations can be painful. We notice that itch that our inner noise had crowded out or that tiny twinge in the neck from sleeping wrong that now demands attention. Then, as we work through those physical notes—

and sometimes even find ways to use energy work developed during meditation to relieve them—our brain moves on to the deeper layers. We arrive, sooner or later, to that point where we must hear ourselves think and feel ourselves feel.

About Spiritual Bypassing

Spiritual bypassing refers to people skipping the more painful aspects of personal growth and development. Those that bypass use purity-culture language to excuse a refusal to acknowledge their pain and unresolved troubles, often framing it as a spiritually superior approach ("good vibes only," "raise your vibration," and so on). Some espouse a program of forced forgiveness: one where the forgiveness is announced without expectation of accountability or amends. Others deny even feeling anger. People look at grief and reach for all the offensive platitudes that comfort no one in a loss.

Seeking authentic bliss in meditation calls you to walk through your inner boneyard. You may never predict what your body-mind tosses up from your inner dirt—but once it appears, your deepest self is asking you to deal with it even if you don't have the right tools for the job. Wherever you are at, when it happens, assess: First, recognize the injury. Second, find a way to cleanse the wound and check its depth. Identify the source of the injury, if possible. There are no shortcuts here, not if you want improved mental health to be one of the benefits of meditation.

What to Do If Your Meditation Session Dredges Up Your Shadows

When you have an intense emotional experience—even a positive one—give that experience time and space. Allow yourself to experience the emotion, communicating to it and to any spiritual guides "as is healthy for me right now." Allow the mix of inner vision, sound, and bodily sensation.

As you experience meditative intensity, create a measure of intensity tolerance. For example, if your heart rate accelerates, or you have shortness of breath and dizziness, ask your guides and your body-mind to gently dial down the reactions. If an overly distressing image or memory cycles, get up, play music, or smell something that disrupts the energy of that mood.

You may want to use a measure to recognize when to back out of a difficult meditation. If it works, start keeping a small notebook or note-taking app nearby. At the beginning of a meditation session, sketch (with pen or finger, as appropriate) a line. The left side of the line indicates less discomfort. The right side of the line indicates more discomfort. Mark a hash in the area that feels appropriate. If the hashmark you make veers too far to the right, ask your body-mind to stay gentle as you go within.

When you practice next, make two lines. On the first line, mark where you feel your intensity tolerance is for that day. If it's to the right, verbalize an intention to meditate to relax. State a limit: you can go x far into discomfort today. If you're comfortable, go where you need to. Once you get into that meditative state (some people can take a moment for pen and paper without destroying the whole session, contrary to popular belief), see where you feel discomfort. Over time, as you encounter more intense meditations, you may find your average comfort level inching left on your lines. When that happens, celebrate processing your inner life!

Other Shadow-Management Techniques

In addition to creating a comfort line, you may consider additional techniques. The first is the "pre-set" method, which I adapted from advice given by Ivo Dominguez Jr. He advises psychics state, in prayers and meditations, "Show me only what I can do something about." I sometimes add a rider to his statement: "whether that's within or without."

Creating a *yes, focus here, look for the following information from the astral and ether* for my brain, works far better than *no, don't show me*. If pain arrives, I accept that it needs immediate attention.

Journaling both before and after meditation sessions can prove helpful. While for me the act of writing in a notebook works best, typing, voice recording, and taking video all make valid journals.

But What If It Gets Really Bad?

Should you find these emotionally packed moments starting to disrupt your life, seek help. If your meditation focuses on a heavy trauma from this lifetime, your body-mind is asking you to seek healing. As much as magical folk often would like to, most of the time we can't heal inner wounds without outside support.

What supports are available are, unfortunately, limited in the United States by access to money. Most people with state-supported or standard insurance now have at least access to an insurer-provided mental health support phone line. The advantage of these is that they are often low or no cost; the disadvantage is that the people answering the calls are limited in what they can do. These lines work well for coaching in on-the-spot coping skills and offering referrals—never bad, just not a long-term solution. If you have the means, seeking a therapist for recurring traumatic memories surfacing is ideal. Depending on where you live and how connected your magical practice is to your identity, this can be stressful in and of itself. In some areas, the only affordable mental health care clinics are run by conservative Christian agencies; some professionals aligned with these philosophies uphold that magical thinking is a disease while simultaneously encouraging their Christian clients in prayer practice. The flaw in the logic is in no way a criticism of Christianity, but it is a criticism of the health care practitioners that do this and can present a concern to magic practitioners in need of care.

An alternative source of support is to seek a spiritual counselor. Spiritual counselors are not always required to obtain degrees (check your state regulations), which makes it difficult to assess someone's qualifications. A spiritual counselor can assist within the frame of a specific religion or practice but cannot prescribe medical treatments, provide cognitive or dialectical behavior therapy, nor supply medications. A spiritual counselor will, however, be able to offer compassionate support and, depending on whom you find, may be able to help you develop magical tools to address the spiritual side of what you're experiencing. If you practice a magical religion, Witch shops in nearby cities may direct you to someone if you don't know of a person already in your community. If that fails, sometimes Unitarian Churches have all-inclusive clergy with spiritual counseling certification, as do some synagogues and more liberal Christian denominations. If you go this route, you may want to attend a few services to get a feel for the community that the clergyperson leads and what that particular clergyperson is all about. Buddhist monasteries also sometimes have individuals who can offer spiritual counseling, and the quiet ubiquity of these temples in American cities is surprising. For those with religious trauma, skipping a suggestion of seeking out mainstream clergy is absolutely understandable.

If you live in the US and can't find affordable mental health support through these means, dial 211, and someone from the United Way will help you navigate your local resources.

Even after experiencing intense unpleasantness, I believe meditation is worth pursuing as a lifelong habit. That self-awareness, in the long run, makes you better at *being* a person because you can identify what causes you pain that you would not otherwise recognize. I also believe that when those traumas and anxieties become overwhelming, it is not just appropriate but an act of moral and ethical strength to seek help for them. Whether you meditate through stillness or movement, I wish you healing, peace, health, and insight on that journey.

Queer Ancestral Connection

Kir Beaux

Every single ancestral lineage on Earth is queer. Every family bloodline and spirit lineage is made up of some queer and trans people. This is what I know, but it's not always what I believed. Just like so many of us, I believed the story of the supposed "modernity" of queer and trans life. Of course, there are countless stories of same-sex lovers and gender rebels throughout world history, and the quickest Google search will turn up stories of Achilles and Patroclus, Sappho, and many more. But even after I learned more about queer history and understood that we've been here all the while, I still subconsciously believed that I was the first queer person in my line.

When I was called to ancestor work in my practice, one of the many fears I had was about my being queer. I really resisted this strong and deep call inside of me out of fear of rejection by my lineage, but ultimately I wanted to know my ancestors. I wanted to feel connected to the land and to history. I wanted to feel the pulse of belonging in my heart. I wanted my birthright, and so I began anyway. It was a surprise to me that when I called upon my well and well-intentioned ancestors, they actually showed up. It was intense and visceral but sweet at the same time. A spirit whom I thought my whole life was my grandma told me she was my actually my aunt, and I confirmed that with my family as the truth. Of course, as a well and well-intentioned ancestor, she turned out to not be homophobic. Homophobia is not a quality of wellness. My relationship with her is one of guidance, gentleness, and care.

I am so grateful to her. She taught me, of all the Witch's allies, the ancestors come first. They are meant to be our medium, our connection to the invisible world. They are our first line of spiritual and energetic defense. They are guides with a vested interest in our evolution. The well and well-intentioned ancestors are the ones constantly rooting for our success and well-being and working in our favor to make it a reality. They want us to thrive and they are there to help. Most importantly, I learned the power they have to intervene and assist us increases tenfold when they have our continued enthusiastic consent. June, my auntie, changed my life before I knew she was there, but when we started working together? That's when the real magic happened.

First Meeting

As I continued my journey connecting with ancestral spirits, and saw so much of them in myself that I knew I wanted to find someone like me in a queer way. So one day I lit up my altar; burned my sacred smoke; called in the elements and my spirit allies; did my breathing, grounding, and centering; and traveled to my astral ancestral meeting place. I called upon my well and well-intentioned queer ancestors and I waited. To my utter astonishment, nothing happened. No one came. I was crushed. I was so disappointed and unsure of myself. I knew I wasn't the first one in my line. I couldn't be. Were they all unwell? Did they all lead horrible lives of suffering that caused them to not become helping spirits? I knew that wasn't the only reason someone may not be a helping spirit, but I was focused on that, because I was still afraid. I was afraid that a queer life meant only suffering. I was afraid that being trans automatically excluded me from becoming a good ancestor. By this time, my ancestor practice had become so fulfilling that I really wanted to be a part of them after this life. So you can imagine my relief a few days later when I received a vision in meditation.

I saw a rocky path down into a gorge. I saw a path lined with menacing trees, gnarled and twisted with thorns and stickers big enough to take me out. I was rushed along the path closer to them and stopped where the trees came together across the path to block the way. An overgrown tangle of branches wove together to block the path, growing from the ground to above my head. I saw a hand (my hand?) reach out and touch the terrifying branches. They began to quiver before withdrawing to reveal the open path before me. I was zoomed along again until I came upon a diverse group of people around a fire. There were Africans, Celts, Indigenous Americans, and people of the diaspora. They were all of me, and they were at peace together in this place. They brought me into their circle, everyone reaching out to touch me, some ruffling my hair, some hugging me, and some just placing their hand on my shoulder or back. With every touch, I was more present and the world around me more vibrant.

We sat together, and they spoke to me about the value of the truth. They spoke about "chosen" over "found" family and how chosen denotes the intentional building of a community. They spoke about history and the many lies I believed about queerness and transness with an emphasis on my own family history. They reassured me that I was perfect in my multitudes, that my many lineages blended well even with the truth of violence and oppression. And of course, many of my ancestors did not, in fact, get along, and there was absolutely healing to do in the spirit and physical world

of my family line, but I was not a mistake. It was revolutionary to me. After so many years of hating myself on behalf of my ancestry, the truth was I was not hated by my own history. I no longer had to live on Earth feeling like I didn't belong. I am natural. They showed me the kind, creative, blessed vibrancy of the queer spirit, and though it did not heal me in an instant, it gave a foundation to begin the work of self-acceptance.

After our deep, insightful, and frankly hilarious conversation (our spirit kiki, if you will), we all stood together around the fire. We clasped hands as one of my Choctaw ancestors began a blessing in their language. Everyone began to hum as a bright, beautifully multi-colored light energy from inside of us coursed through our bodies. It traveled through us, and when it reached me, I began to cry. I cried tears of joy and release as the hard buildup of hate and pain inside finally began to shake loose. It was excruciating and ecstatic. I was humbled and grateful. When that blessing and cleansing was done, I was held in their arms again. All these people, my people, just loved me. Even the parts I was convinced were unlovable. I returned to my body renewed and determined. Then I did what practical Witches do, and wrote down the details of my experience.

Reaching Out to the Ancestors

I crafted the Queer Ancestor Revival Ritual as a container for continued connection and mutual support with the past. This ritual is not just for queers but for everyone. Many of our queer ancestors lived in hiding or were erased completely from family histories. While there are those who certainly did not live or die well, there are many who did. Many of them are ready to take their place as our guides and guardians. They have so much wisdom, care, and love to share with their descendants. This ritual may have to be repeated several times before making any contact and that's okay. Again, many of them have been disconnected for a very long time, but connecting with them is worth the effort.

Repeatedly call to them, make offerings to them, live in their honor. Build a container to receive them, and eventually they will arrive. I know that many of us do not know the details of our ancestry.

When you are selecting the offerings or touchstone items for your altar, I ask that you pull from your cultural heritage. Maybe you know you are generally Celtic but your family has lived in Ohio. You can look to the foods and rituals that were important to the ancient Celts, or you can pull from the general knowledge of Midwestern culture. Maybe you are separated from your birth family but know you are part of the African diaspora via the transatlantic slave trade. You can pull from Black American or Pan-African culture and practices that feel resonant to you.

Ultimately, I suggest you start with yourself. You are the most direct source of ancestral information because you are them. You are the physical continuation of their DNA and part of their spiritual lineage. We all know stories of people being near exact copies of their family members, so just start with what you like. What makes you sing, what makes you feel alive and vibrant? You can use your favorite music, your ultimate comfort food, or your special interests. This will work! I know because it is what I did to connect with my people. You have all the information you need to begin. Trust and believe that if your offerings or practices don't resonate with your ancestors, they will let you know! In their own way and by their own means, you will be told. Your first attempts to reconnect will not be judged harshly by them, nor will you be punished. Just try. Open your heart, your spirit, and your altar to them in any way you can, and the rest will come out in the wash.

Before beginning this ritual, I recommend contemplating your thoughts and feelings on queerness, your own ancestry, and how your queer ancestry may fit into the story of who you are.

These prompts may be useful:

- What role does queerness play in my life now?
- Do I see myself reflected in my current understanding of my ancestry? Where?
- What gifts and challenges have I inherited, and how do I feel about them?

The Altar

Your altar for this ritual is highly personal. The only requirements I insist upon are a glass of water, a candle, a protective element, and an offering. The glass of water acts as both an offering and a conduit of energy. The candle illuminates your altar in the spirit world and provides life force energy. Even though we are only calling in our well and well-intentioned ancestral helping spirits, I still like to have some protective force when I'm working with magic, especially spirits. This can be a stone, a blade, a talisman, your favorite protective herbs, a spell, or a protective spirit. As for your offering, this is where you can get a little creative and personal!

It is common in many cultures to offer some kind of food, and I too recommend it. It can be a full plate of the same meal you had or just a small, teacup-size portion. You can use hot, cold, and even dried food. It can be whole fruits or special treats. Candies are often appreciated, as well as coffee, wine, and other spirits. This is one of those moments where you want to look to your cultural roots for relevant offerings. Again, if you're stuck, choose what you like! These food offerings do not have to stay out longer than the ritual if that is not realistic for you, and when it's time, dispose of them in the trash outside your home. If it is safe for it to be returned to nature, that is an option, but I do not condone any illegal dumping or polluting of waterways. Our environment is not the same as it was in ancient times, and so the old ways of disposing of magical materials are usually not appropriate. Remember, the earth is our parent and our original ancestor, so their well-being comes before any of our magical needs. On top of a food offering, I recommend an offering of smoke, song, dance, poetry, or art. You don't have to have written the

A Little Bit of Magic

THE MOST UNDERRATED OF ALL THE MODERN WITCH'S TOOLS IS A FIRE EXTINGUISHER. STAY SAFE!

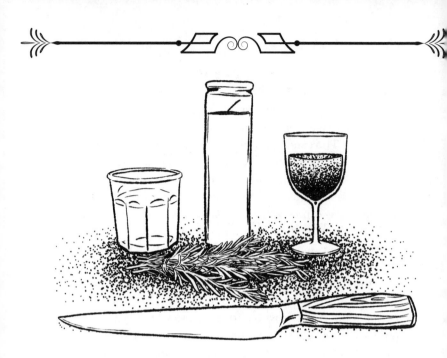

poem or song, but you do want to put your heart into the performance of it.

Other than these, fill in your altar with items that have meaning to you and your ancestry. I call these touchstone items. If you identify as queer, also include anything that represents your connection to your own queerness.

Queer Ancestor Revival Ritual

Begin by cleansing yourself and your space and building your altar.

Light your candle, and if using, burn your sacred smoke.

If casting a circle and calling in the elements is part of your practice, please do so now.

Breathe, settle in, ground, and center yourself.

Begin moving in a clockwise circle while reciting the following incantation. Repeat for a total of three circles with three recitations of the incantation:

I, [your chosen name] of the [any and all of the family names you have] family lines, have crafted this container of love, protection, and connection.

I am here with a humble and grateful heart and the intention of connecting with my well and well-intentioned ancestral spirits that self-identify under the queer umbrella. I invoke thee. Be with me in this time.

Benevolent queer and trans ancestors, I call upon you now. Imbibe of these offerings and strengthen yourselves as you have strengthened me. Come close, be here, be known.

When you have completed the circles and incantations, come to a place of stillness. If you are offering a performance, begin now. After we invite the spirits, we must be available to receive them, so we give the offering of time. Sit, stand, whatever is comfortable, and listen. Write down any feelings, encounters, questions, or answers you receive. When you are finished, move in three counterclockwise circles and release the spirits by reciting,

Spirits that have gathered here today, thank you for your presence. It is with so much respect and love that I now release and dismiss you. Thank you.

This ritual is intended to be repeated. Do not be discouraged if you don't experience anything groundbreaking immediately. Commit yourself to the practice. Add any other elements that call to you to this ritual. Important information can and will come through your body and instincts. Not all spirits communicate through the clairs, so you must pay attention to any encounters, symbols, energies, and synchronicities that feel related in your mundane and your magical life.

I hope that this has been valuable for you, and I hope that your queer ancestry connection journey is fulfilling. And to the queer Witches out there, you are seen and you are loved. You are as natural as a miracle and your ancestors are holding you in love.

Will the Real Medusa
Please Stand Up?

JD Walker

Greek mythology has given us many enduring figures. Some are deities who can be appealed to for any number of benefits for those of us who are earthbound. Others are archetypes—models of rulers, heroes and adventurers, both good and bad. Somewhere in the middle is Medusa.

Most of us know Medusa as a beautiful mortal woman who was variously seduced or assaulted by Poseidon or was his willing partner. Regardless, the act takes place in Athena's temple, which evokes her wrath. Medusa is transformed into a Gorgon with the power to turn anyone she looks at into stone. She eventually ends up on a remote island somewhere to the west of Greece with two others of her kind.

Why did Athena target Medusa and not the instigator, Poseidon? Some people reason that Poseidon was one of the original Olympians and therefore outranked Athena. Other people point to Zeus's golden rule—the gods do not attack each other with violence. Trickery and pranks were okay. Out-and-out warfare was strictly forbidden.

For modern people, Medusa is either a vengeful seductress or a sympathetic victim. For the ancients, she could be an apotropaic symbol, both terrifying and protective. For artists and writers of the same period, Medusa could be little more than a convenient plot point.

Regardless, from the time we have evidence of her existence in the archeological record up until today, Medusa seems to be never far from the imagination of those who behold her. The question arises, is Medusa an entity who can be incorporated into the daily practice of modern Pagans? Certainly, some women might be drawn to her because of what they have seen in current tellings of Medusa's myth. But do the modern interpretations of Medusa's story give us a true picture of who she is and what she might be capable of?

To answer that question, we have to go looking for the real Medusa.

Medusa in the Modern World

Technically, the name *Medusa* means "the ruling one." On the other hand, the word *Gorgon* variously means "terrible," "fierce," or "frightful," writes Dr. Miriam Robbins Dexter. This is how modern writers and artists have presented her.

Consider, for example, the 1981 movie *Clash of the Titans*. In this feature, Ray Harryhausen (1920–2013) worked a masterful bit of stop-motion animation to create a Medusa that had the upper body of a woman with a coiffure of loud, hissing snakes and a lower body that was serpentine. Medusa's face in this feature is recognizable as human, but it is still hideous.

The script didn't do much for Medusa's image. Writers played fast and loose with the Greek myth by having Medusa constantly on the prowl for victims in her cave labyrinth. She even carries a bow and arrow. This seems a little redundant considering she has the power to turn people into stone, but Hollywood must have its drama. This is in contrast to certain myths pertaining to Medusa that portray her as less of an aggressor and more of a recluse, hiding in the caves and trying to stay away from the world.

In the movie, Harry Hamlin, who played Perseus, engages in a cat-and-mouse game with Medusa that mostly has him looking for a large stalactite to hide behind. He had to use stealth and cunning (plus Athena's magickal shield) to sneak up on Medusa and render her head from her body with his adamantium (diamond) sword.

Medusa doesn't fare any better in the 2010 remake of *Clash of the Titans,* although actress Natalia Vodianova does make a much more fetching monster than Harryhausen's Claymation figure—at least until the moment she strikes. At that point, her lovely face becomes a horrible grimace that reinforces Medusa's association with snakes.

In the book series Percy Jackson and the Olympians, author Rick Riordon makes Medusa a challenge that his twelve-year-old hero, Percy, must outwit in the first book of the series, *The Lightning Thief.* In the movie of the same name, actress Uma Thurman plays Medusa, wearing a turban to hide her snaky locks until the moment she strikes. She isn't called Medusa. Riordon hides her identity by calling her Aunty Em (*M* for Medusa—get it?). Thurman is perhaps the comeliest Medusa to date, but she still meets her end through beheading, like all of those before her.

This image of Medusa as a beautiful if vengeful woman can be seen all around us in tattoos and modern art. But it took her a while to get from beastly to beautiful. In artworks up until about the nineteenth century, Medusa might have a human face, but it is grimacing and terrible. The Italian artist Michelangelo Caravaggio (1571–1610) designed what we might perhaps call the "typical" portrayal of Medusa: severed head adhered to a shield, face tormented, snakes flaying, and blood flowing from her neck.

By the time of Percy Bysshe Shelley (1792–1822), Medusa was getting a makeover. In his poem "On the Medusa of Leonardo da Vinci in the Florentine Gallery," Shelley finds beauty in the horror of Medusa's decapitation when he writes,

Its horror and its beauty are divine.
Upon its lips and eyelids seems to lie
Loveliness like a shadow, from which shrine,
Fiery and lurid, struggling underneath,
The agonies of anguish and of death.

And so it is today, the lovely Medusa is an aggressor, at least partially justified in her rage because of the circumstances behind her curse. But what were those circumstances? We have to go back in time to the days of Ovid, Hesiod, and Apollonius to find the origins of today's Medusa.

Medusa in Ancient Greece

Ovid (43 BCE–17 CE) was a Roman poet in the time of Augustus. It is his account of Medusa that most closely aligns with modern interpretations. In book 4 of *Metamorphoses*, the hero Perseus explains that Medusa had once been a beautiful maiden with "marvelous hair," which "was her crowning glory." Neptune (Poseidon) sees her and takes her in Minerva's (Athena's) temple. Minerva is deeply offended and transforms Medusa into a Gorgon.

How did she look? Most representations of the time show her with a human body and a head of snakes; some add wings. In Ovid's telling, there is no mention of a serpentine lower half.

Later Perseus, one of Zeus's many offspring, brags that he will bring Medusa's head to Polydectes, a suitor for his mother's affections. Why Medusa? Probably for the same reason brave knights went off to slay dragons. They were monsters, fair game for any man who wanted to prove his worth. Perseus manages to kill Medusa while she sleeps, something that gets lost in modern movie retellings of the myth. Her two sisters also have wings and attempt to pursue Perseus after his attack, but he gets away because he has Hades's helmet of invisibility and Hermes's winged sandals.

On his way back to Polydectes, Perseus saves Andromeda by using Medusa's head to turn a sea monster into stone. Polydectes meets his end when Perseus reveals Medusa's head to the him and people in his court. This isn't a bad thing. Polydectes isn't a very sympathetic character.

In Apollodorus's[1] telling in *The Library*, published around the first century CE, Medusa is mortal and presumably mortal in appearance except for her hair and her stoney gaze. Her sisters,

---

1   While modern sources refer to the author of *The Library* as Apollodorus,
    technically scholars believe Apollodorus of Athens could not have written
    the book. It was probably written roughly 100 years after the original
    Apollodorus died. Still, modern convention is to continue to call the book
    Apollodorus's *The Library*.

Stheno and Euryale, "had heads twined about with the scales of dragons, and great tusks like swine, and brazen hands, and golden wings, by which they flew; and they turned to stone such as beheld them."

It is Apollodorus who asserts that Medusa was targeted by Athena as much for the sin of claiming to be more beautiful than the goddess as for her dalliance with Poseidon. The Greek gods hate nothing more than human hubris.

Going back even further to Homer's telling in the *Illiad* and *Odyssey* sometime in the eighth century BCE, there is no Medusa. There is only one Gorgon—or rather, a Gorgon's head set on the shield or breastplate of Zeus. Athena is also said to wear the breastplate. The Gorgon's head is believed to inspire terror. There is no mention of decapitation by Perseus; the Gorgon just exists. It is fierce and fear-inducing. Even Odysseus dreads the possibility of Persephone sending a floating Gorgon head to petrify him while he journeys to the underworld in Homer's *Odyssey*.

A Protective Talisman

Writing sometime between 750 and 650 BCE, the Greek poet Hesiod recorded that there were three Gorgon sisters who were children of the sea-god Phorcys and of Keto. Keto may have been Gaia's daughter or one of many sea nymphs. According to Hesiod, the Gorgons "live beyond famed Oceanus at the edge of Nyx where the clear-voiced Hesperides dwell: the immortal and ageless Sthenno and Euryale, and the mortal Medusa, who met a foul end." The foul end is her run-in with Perseus during his hero quest.

As terrifying sea monsters, the faces of either of these three creatures could and did serve as talismans to ward away evil. Archaeologists have found plenty of examples of the *gorgoneia*—the Gorgon face with bulging eyes, open mouth, fangs, and protruding tongue—on temple pediments, urns, plates, cups, and more. They served the same function as the evil eye talismans we see so often on jewelry today. They kept bad things away because even the worst monsters were afraid of the Gorgons.

It is in this function as talisman that Medusa specifically or the Gorgons in general can be of use in today's practices. Just as we evoke certain creatures of legend or tradition to help defend us, we can ask Medusa for protection.

It should be kept in mind that this is a passive protection. I am frequently asked what the best herb or stone for protection is. My response is always to ask, what kind of protection do you need? Do you need a sword or a shield? Are you actively going out (either magickally or in reality) to do battle with a problem or opponent? Or are you trying to stay out of sight, living on the down-low, in modern parlance?

If you are gearing up to do battle or simply sallying forth with as much armament as possible, Medusa is not for you. The Gorgons didn't foray out into the world like Marvel Comics superheroes. They pretty much kept to their island at the end of the world. If you showed up on the island and tried to mess with them, they would certainly invoke their defenses. But they didn't go looking for trouble. They mostly tried to make short work of any troublemakers who came their way.

In a more direct understanding, neither Medusa nor the Gorgons could be considered champions of women. That is above their calling and beyond their powers. Use any version of Medusa's face you like as you ward your home or protect your personal space wherever you go. Just don't ask her to save you from a bad relationship or take vengeance on an abusive authority figure.

There are better resources for that kind of assistance. The Mesopotamian she-demon Lilith comes to mind as a good example. Now, here is an aggressor who has little compunction about dishing out a big plate of just desserts—especially if she is directing that aggression toward deserving male figures.

But that is a story for another day.

Resources

Apollodorus. *The Library*. Translated by James Frazier. London: William Heineman, 1921. Page 157. https://archive.org/details/apollodorus 00frazgoog/page/n4/mode/2up.

Dexter, Miriam Robbins. "The Ferocious and the Erotic: 'Beautiful' Medusa and the Neolithic Bird and Snake." *Journal of Feminist Studies in Religion* 26, no. 1 (2010): 25–41. doi:10.2979/fsr.2010.26.1.25.

Hesiod. *Theogony*. Translated by Michael Heumann. Self-published, 2021. Page 13. https://archive.org/details/hesiods-theogony-translated -by-michael-heumann/page/40/mode/2up.

Homer. *The Iliad*. Translated by A. T. Murray. London: William Heinemann, 1928. Page 249. https://archive.org/details/iliadmurray01 homeuoft/page/n7/mode/2up.

———. *The Odyssey*. Vol. 1. Translated by William Cullen Bryant. Boston: James R. Osgood and Company, 1871. Page 300.

Ovid. *Metamorphoses*. Translated by David Raeburn. London: Penguin, 2004. Page 170.

Shelley, Percy Bysshe. "On the Medusa of Lenardo da Vinci in the Florentine Gallery." Academy of American Poets. Accessed July 25, 2023. https://poets.org/poem/medusa-leonardo-da-vinci-florentine-gallery.

Tuning In to the Presence
of Ancestors

Angela A. Wix

It was the tail end of winter, that sweet point when the Sun starts to whisper its promise of spring. Warmth was spreading, but as the Sun set on another day of thaw, it seemed the freeze had found me again, knees on a cold bathroom floor and face in my palms. Tears streamed down my cheeks as I finally submitted to the storm that had been building behind all that sunshine.

In the days and weeks leading up to this moment, waves of grief had been washing over me with increasing frequency. I was headed into a season of significant family celebrations that I wanted only to be excited for, but it was kicking up dust around things I'd normally been able to tuck away in my hidden world. I desperately wanted to keep focus on honoring and showing up for the ones I loved, but I worried over the numerous hurdles I might end up throwing in the way, accommodations I needed that could end up being . . . complicated. I was struggling to determine where I needed to set boundaries or ask for support, and where I needed to just lean in and simply be present as best I could.

I'd become used to isolating in order to avoid the full depths of this body grief and its accompanied anxiety. I was accustomed to taking care of my own needs, adjusting as necessary day to day, and even moment to moment, in order meet those ever-changing needs. What I *wasn't* used to was asking other people to meet those needs for me. Even with loved ones, it was still incredibly difficult, especially when the coming celebrations were to be about *them*. How could I ask for anything to be catered to *me?*

I felt vulnerable in my need and grief-stricken for the lack of ability to simply *be* in a typical body that didn't need so much specialized care.

These were the thoughts that ran through my mind as I rocked myself back and forth in the night, letting the sobs cascade out of me. As I rocked, I suddenly sensed my grandpa in Spirit, in front of me to my right. Then my older sister was at my center, and my great uncle (my personal patron saint of cheer and fortitude) was to my left. As I tuned in to their faces, watching in my mind's eye as they became clearer, I felt and saw a hand at my back, then another, and another. It was my family and friends, my cherished ones, all branching out like an unfolding flower, a mandala spreading in a veil behind me. They held space as I wept the pain of so many years of isolation, loss, and fear. Each tear was attuned to the frustrations of a limited body, but my ancestors were there, and they wanted me to know they had my back as I let every one of those tears fall.

Being human is hard. Sometimes it's really, *really* hard. Our ancestors know this; they've been through it themselves, after all! If you're receptive, you might be surprised to realize who in Spirit is ready to catch and lift you back up when you're in the midst of falling. Learning how to invite them in to hold space for you and witness your experience can be powerful. The following will guide you in making these connections. To practice, you could have someone read this for you, or you could record yourself reading the instruction and play it back. Alternately, you can read through to get a sense of the steps and then naturally flow through it on your own. Or you might even practice as you're reading it, suspending yourself between consciously reading and existing in that intuitive inner space of engagement. Go with whatever works best for you.

Exhale Winter: Rocked by the Ancestors

While this first practice can be especially supportive during moments of grief, you can apply it at any time, perhaps even starting out each day with this ancestral connection. I've expanded on each step in detail for you, but know that this can be very fluid and could even be a quick practice that you play out naturally in your mind in moments of need.

Here you'll learn how to tune in and receive support for letting out difficult emotions, processing what may feel like the dark depths of winter caught within you. Let's start by defining your goals before you dive fully into the practice.

Set Your Request and Intention

Think about (1) the request and (2) the intention you want to set for this practice. Is there a certain emotion, challenge, or situation that you're facing and want guidance with? Is there something you're feeling really alone in handling, or is there a goal you're striving toward that you could use some reassurance with? What is it that you want to let go of?

For example, a request could be "I'm feeling really alone in handling the details of this chronic illness, and I'd like to know who's here to guide me in asking for what I need." From this request, an example of an intention could be to release fear around setting healthy boundaries with others.

Whatever initially comes to mind, focus in on that. Speak it out loud, think it in your mind, or write it out in your journal.

Rock, Breathe, and Center

With your request and intention defined, you'll move on to allowing yourself to be held in the presence of your ancestor(s). Settle in now by getting into a comfortable position and closing your eyes. You might sit in a rocking chair to assist this practice, you can simply sway your body, or you can cross your arms (as though hugging yourself) and alternate tapping your left arm with your right hand and your right arm with your left hand. Alternating tapping your right foot and your left foot can be another way of capturing this rocking motion in the body when you're trying to be subtle in a more public space. You can continue your rocking now or hold off until it comes up more specifically later in the practice.

If you're okay with deep breathing, take a few deep breaths now. When you exhale, feel the air exiting fully. The deeper you exhale, the deeper you'll inhale. Repeat this deep breathing until you feel your body and mind relax. Once you hit that point, settle into a more natural breathing pattern and focus in on your energy.

Tune in to whether or not it feels as though your energy is reaching out externally. For example, while you're trying to relax, you might notice that you're also anticipating someone needing your attention or that you're trying to time your practice so that you can move on to your next task. If you find these types of reaching-out energies, envision pulling the energy all back inward until it is centered. Then progressively relax all areas of your body. Focus in on your head, neck, hands, arms, shoulders, and so on, and move on to the next step when you feel ready.

Inviting Your Ancestor(s)

You'll now move on to allowing your ancestor(s) in Spirit to make themselves known to you. Go into this practice without anticipation of who specifically you're going to connect with. Allow the individual(s) to reveal themselves. This way, you can meet whoever is most important for you to be aware of at this time.

In your mind's eye, see yourself standing before a beautiful door. Light coming from the other side seeps out around its edges. You take a step forward and rest your hand on the handle. Twisting the knob, you open the door, letting the light spill completely around you.

Stepping across the threshold, you find yourself in a favorite meditation space. See what this looks like. Maybe you're on a tropical beach, in a clearing on the edge of the woods, or at the top of a mountain with a fantastic view. Walk deeper into this space and find a place to sit down. Settle in and take in the details of the space. Notice what you see, hear, feel, smell, or taste. Touch the surface you're sitting on with your fingers and notice the details there.

Enjoy the scenery for a bit before moving on.

When you're ready to continue, scan the space around you once again. As you do, this time you notice another door nearby. On the other side your ancestor(s) in Spirit is waiting to connect with you. Go to that door now and, with your hand on the knob, pause and repeat the request you formed at the start of this practice.

With your request made, you open the door. Your ancestor(s) steps over the threshold toward you. Notice the details of their appearance and the feeling you get from them. Sink into the rocking motion (whichever form you chose earlier) and feel the love passing to you as your ancestor(s) holds space for your experience.

Ask any questions you might have for them and share the intention you set earlier for whatever it is you want to release. As you continue your rocking motion, and with each deep exhale, your ancestor(s) connect with the flow of your energy, helping you eliminate what's ready to be released.

As you continue rocking, perhaps seeing your ancestor(s) as the one(s) rocking you, receive the message they have for you. This could be verbal, visual, or a feeling that's imparted to you. Take time to soak in the energy and simply be with them.

When you sense your meeting has come to a close, say your farewell. If it feels right, lean in for an embrace before you watch them exit through their door. Move back to the door you came through and gently come back to your physical space by wiggling your fingers and toes, stretching, and opening your eyes. Take a drink of water and do anything else that you like to do to ground back into your physical space. Jot down any details that were significant to you.

Inhale Spring: Recharged in the Presence of Ancestors

Now that you've let go a bit, are you ready to recharge and shake off the dust even more? I note this next practice as one of "spring" because it carries that kind of seasonal energy, but as with the previous exercise, you can do this in any season. In fact, this can be especially helpful to practice in the dark of winter, when many of us are most craving the Sun's charge. Throughout, you can envision the details of spring and summer vibrance, energy, and life. The brain often believes what's imagined, so take advantage of that magical ability!

Breath, Intention, and Affirmation

While we focused on the exhale in the previous practice, here our attention is on the inhale. Ignite and let in! Think about the intention you want to set for this practice, focusing on whatever it is you want to breathe into your life. Speak it out loud, think it in your mind, or write it out in your journal. In addition to your unique intention, we'll also engage with an affirmation focused on safety and healing. If it feels right to you, you can also hold the intention that, in addition to this practice being for yourself, the benefit is also meant for anyone who has ever been connected with you, who has also needed healing.

Once you have your intention defined, settle in by getting into a comfortable position and closing your eyes. Inhale deeply and feel the air in your lungs energizing your body.

Inviting Healing Down the Line

This practice came to me on a first true spring day, on its way to 70 degrees Fahrenheit here in the Midwest. The Sun was renewing, setting life into the stirring heart of awaiting seeds. See this moment as your own. The song of frogs chirping in a nearby pond cascades over you, serenading the moment, calling in the Sun to warm you to your core. You feel the heat soothing on your skin, filtering through to deep layers, all the way to your bones. There's

a slight breeze, a gentle caress across your body. You're rocking in a rocking chair, the comforting motion, back and forth, a sensation of being held to and fro.

Rock your body now in whatever way you choose. You are the rocking chair, soothing.

Envision a seed at your center. A drop of sunlight touches your skin, seeping through your pores, trickling deeper and deeper, winding through your body until it finds your core. The center seed vibrates, waking to the light. It breaks open, the hint of life unfolding, and soon it's a blooming flower reaching for the sky.

You dig your toes into the damp earth, grounding into a balanced energy as roots move downward, taking hold in the dirt under your soles. The earth below you is an ancestor, the skin and bones that have held the spirits of every person who's come before you. She has created your own body, housed and helped your being, nurtured you to this point of existence, witnessed the hardship, and nurtured the joy. Your eyes fall to the trees before you, and in them you see your ancestors. You feel your kin in Spirit drawing close.

Rest one hand on your belly and the other on your chest. Close your eyes and sink deeper into this moment. Breathe in.

In your mind or out loud, say to yourself and to your body, "I am safe." (You can also speak your personalized intention here). In your mind's eye, see the resulting pulse of electricity burst and expand outward from you, like a shock that sends energy out along electrical wires. It's the message rippling through your mind, your brain, your body, reaching every part of your nervous system. It is the energy moving through the wiring and connection to your ancestors.

Repeat again, "I am safe." The pulse bursts again, a defibrillator recharging the physical, reaching all corners of your mind, and dusting out the cobwebs that have collected in your spirit.

Once more, repeat, "I am safe." The light electrifies your core, rippling out in lines of wires to the edges of places unknown, a message expanding to anyone—past, present, and future—who needs it.

Working in the presence of ancestors can be so powerful, and you're likely to find that after you intentionally engage, those in Spirit you're connected with will naturally show up for you unbidden when you could use their support, as they did for me in my moment of grief. When I first did this second practice, tears filled my eyes and a feeling of ecstasy ran through me. I was so lit with joy and overwhelmed with gratitude for the love I was feeling. I hope these practices help bring to life that magical connection for you as well.

Rest and Dreaming:
A Portal to Power

Shana Nunnelly

As your eyes begin to softly scan the page, continue to read and feel your body relax into ease. Allow yourself to read and become aware of your eyelids hovering over your pupils. Take deep breaths. Feel any tension in your shoulders dissolve. As you're reading, become aware of any sensations you feel in your feet. Imagine your breath moving up and down from your belly, down to your feet, and back up again. Find where your body feels most rooted to the earth. Take another deep inhale and slowly exhale—you are in no rush. Now feel where your body is asking for more attention, and imagine you're breathing life into those parts. Allow your awareness to notice the ease you feel in the present moment. Right now is the only moment that matters. This is where your power lies.

In your now-relaxed state, you are able to access dimensions beyond measure. You're able to access those worlds because your body is being nurtured and recharged and there is no conflict in your mind for Spirit to fight against. You are open, trusting, and at ease when you are present in the moment. This same space of trust and presence is accessed when you relax into sleep. When you relax, you are able to live freely in your imagination. In rest, meditation, and sleeping, you feel safe and your fight-or-flight instinct is dismantled, allowing access to the deepest truths within yourself. The act of sleeping is a powerful portal to send and receive messages from Source or Spirit. Dreams, sleep, and meditation can be considered ancient technologies as they allow you to access your subconscious mind and work out any blocks that impede you from your highest destiny.

If you follow your dreams—literally and figuratively—you are living out your purpose with a flow that guides and magnetizes you toward those goals being fulfilled. Dreams and dream states (or "d-states") have been deciphered since ancient times with prophetesses and shamans. To the Mojave, dreams granted spiritual powers and general skills, sent to them by Mastamho, the chief deity, writes anthropologist Dr. Trudy Griffin-Pierce. In today's world, with dream therapists and lucid dreaming apps, dream interpretations are easier than ever to receive. With these services, anyone is able to decode their dreams so that they are able to master their life's journey with power and joy.

Roadblocks to Sufficient Rest

My ancestors, and many other folks throughout antiquity, have a history of chattel slavery. In this institution, our bodies were used for capitalist gain, meaning we were mules, used only for work. The memories of this brutalization are in our bones. This ancestry implanted a "survival code" that teaches us to work hard and worry beyond our human capacity in order to feel worthy and whole. My grandfather would regularly say, "There is no rest for the poor one." He sang this as a mantra for hard work and perseverance. Many poor people hold this mentality as true, keeping them in a vicious cycle of back-breaking labor for generations to come. We can see this in athletes and entertainers. Many stories are told of a young person becoming a professional athlete at a young age, working their body tirelessly in the professional sport, and going bankrupt after their short careers, once again facing the poverty they were so tirelessly working to bring themselves and their family out of. The capitalist system gives them no rest or reprieve to truly learn abundance and break the chains of poverty. What people recall as slavery, and its father capitalism, is a cruel infliction on a population by a system that is designed to capture and corrupt the human spirit through stress, work, overproduction, and capitalistic gain.

This system thrives as we speak, and many believe they are free—until they are asked about meditation. When asked about rest, stillness, and meditation, some people report that they find these practices to be difficult, recalling that they became frustrated rather than being able to discover the benefits. However, there are studies that show that there has been an increase in the number of people who say they have meditated. In results published in 2017,

the Center for Health Statistics found that "the use of meditation increased more than threefold from 4.1% in 2012 to 14.2% in 2017." Statistics for how many people maintain a regular meditation practice are harder to come by.

According to estimates by the National Heart, Lung, and Blood Institute, "50 million to 70 million Americans have chronic, or ongoing, sleep disorders." Embracing the power of resting is such a foreign concept that some people are terrified to even attempt intentional silence for twelve hours out of fear of what their minds might show them. Capitalism and its offspring consumerism—be it television, telephones, or work—cause a cycle that takes us out of our natural and most optimal state. The Sleep Foundation reminds us that "checking social media, sending emails, or looking at the news before bed can keep us awake, as nighttime use of electronics can affect sleep through the stimulating-effects of light from digital screens." In particular, "the blue light emitted from electronic screens has the greatest impact on sleep. Blue light stimulates parts of the brain that makes us feel alert, leaving us energized at bedtime when we should be winding down."

Depriving one of rest, sleep, or calm is an invitation to anxiety that can and does lead to insanity and depression. Many of us experience this insanity as workaholism, becoming overly ambitious, experiencing excessive worrying, and overusing our logical analytical brains instead of using our powerful intuitive guidance. Having no way to rest, our bodies become unaware of their innate intuitive cues. Without a meditative practice to empty our brains, we overstimulate ourselves with thoughts and lose connection with our easeful innate senses. These senses are what guides us, what lifts us, and also what protects us. In ease, we find a wholeness that is able to answer all our pressing wants and needs just by being present. Exhaustion doesn't leave time to reflect on a day and learn from the experience. Exhaustion crashes us from one problem to the next with heavy eyelids and a hungry ghost of desire that is always searching for the next thing to be satisfied.

Inspiration and Restoration through Sleep

Quiet connection practices have been taught for thousands of years, from the daily practice of praying five times a day in Islam to the peaceful messages of Jesus, the Hindu prince of peace and mediation Krishna, and the Buddhist goddess of peace Kwan Yin. Every voice of any spiritual tradition will teach a method of going within to access universal truths beyond logical thought. Genius is found in stillness, as exemplified by the prophecies Harriet Tubman received during sleep as well as Albert Einstein's walking and nap meditations. Both had rest practices that lead to extraordinary and revolutionary changes in humanity and history.

Clearing anxiety to access power comes naturally through rest. We all sleep: it's a practice that connects us all to every living thing. Within rest, there is a connection to Universal Source, commonly referred to in the East as chi. There is recharge of your Source energy when you rest that heals your body. When people are ill, the first thing a doctor will do is find a way to relieve the body of pain, tension, and disharmony. The majority of healing medicines are designed to allow your body to rest so it can naturally restore itself. Have you ever asked yourself, in a coma, in deep sleep, where does the mind go? When a person or animal doesn't get enough sleep, the results are stress, unhealthy eating, and a lack of empathy for others. This is a constant disconnect we find in society. Think about being tired and driving home in traffic! Exhausted, you find yourself angry, tense, and unable to be present in the moment. Allowing yourself to rest, breathing deeply in the moment, you will find yourself grateful that you are not in an accident or delighted that your partner wants to tell you about their day while driving home, and now you have more time to chat uninterrupted before taking on the evening routine once you arrive home.

As described before, sleep, dreaming, and visionary meditation are ancient practices that have been revered as holy for thousands of years. Shamans and other spiritual facilitators practice a form of sleep to guide their clients and themselves into deeper realms of

consciousness. This is exactly what happens when I use my crystal singing bowls in a sound bath meditation. Vibrationally, the bowls emit soundwaves that sync with the nervous system, allowing the body to rest. The music and guidance allow the client to let go of their thinking mind, and as I play, I am able to let go of the thinking mind as well. We travel together into a vibratory realm of healing and access universal consciousness.

I know this all sounds wonderful, but you aren't in front of my sound bowls, and you aren't asleep. But I can give you a practice that you can use at home to simply feel what conscious rest feels like, connect with your heartspace, and access your power. As you practice and when you are ready, you can ask Spirit any question you want and receive an answer. Practice the following meditation and receive a symbol, a vision, or a feeling in your body as an answer to any question you have.

Yoga Nidra Practice

Let's practice a restful yoga nidra practice that you can read and feel at the same time. Yoga nidra is the yoga of sleep, and we'll use a body scan to relax the body. It is commonly performed in *savasana*, or corpse pose. This practice will aid you in clearing and easing your mind, while sending rejuvenating energy to your entire body and auric field. Afterward, feel free to go to sleep or set a timer in order to take extra time to rest your body and allow yourself to access the dream space safely.

Once you have practiced one time, you can add any question you would like to ask Spirit or your ancestors. Then, you can jot down in a journal any messages you received in the form of colors, visions, feelings in your body, smells, tastes, sounds, and so on. You will have access to all your senses as an antenna-like connection for spirits messages.

All you have to do is read and take a moment to journal how you feel afterward. I suggest trying this for nine days straight at any time of the day that you can dedicate to it consistently. Once you have mastered nine days, allow yourself to upgrade to a twenty-one day practice. When you are feeling like you need to make a profound change, feel depressed, or want to manifest something specific, a forty-day meditation combined with an *I am* mantra will reveal truths and align you with an energetic flow that will truly change your life and awaken your inner power.

Let's begin.

Move your body so that it can rest with your entire body feeling supported. You can lie on your back, on your side, or on your stomach. You can sit up in a chair. Make sure your back and head feel supported. You will be moving your awareness through your body rapidly as you read.

Take a slow breath and ask your body what it needs to be comfortable and to surrender. Take a breath and move your body into that comfortable place.

Allow your eyelids to soften or close.

(Pause.)

Breathe in and count 1, 2, 3, 4. Hold for 1, 2, 3, 4. Breathe out 1, 2, 3, 4. Hold 1, 2, 3, 4. This is called a box breath.

Repeat this box breath four more times. Allow your breath to flow naturally, in and out.

Allow yourself to think of a statement that affirms you. Begin that statement with *I am* . . . As you take your next breath in, say to yourself, *I am* . . . and breathe out your affirmation word. Repeat this three times and let it go.

On your next breath, begin to become aware of a soft light at your third eye, allowing the awareness of that soft light to move to different places in your body as you read them.

Begin to feel or sense a soft light in these places:

In the middle of your head, back of head, inside mouth, right cheek, left cheek, point where lips meet, throat center. Envision soft light. Right shoulder. Right elbow. Right wrist. Soft white light moves to thumb, first finger, second finger. Third finger, pinky finger. Up right arm, envision soft light. Right shoulder blade. Middle of back. Left shoulder blade. Left elbow. Soft white light at left wrist. Lefthand thumb. First finger, second finger. Third finger, pinky finger. Left arm. Left shoulder. Center of your chest. Center of chest. Center of chest. Soft light moves down to the top of your stomach, soft light at belly. Soft light between your legs. Right hip, soft light, right thigh, right knee. Soft breath in right knee. Soft light down to the ankle. Right foot. Bottom of foot. Soft light up to ankle, up right leg, middle of hips. White light at left hip. Soft light left thigh, left knee. Soft breath in left knee, soft light to ankle. Left foot. Bottom of left foot. Soft light up to left ankle, up left leg. White light at center of the belly. The whole back. Soft light in the center of the chest.

(Pause.)

Deep breath in. As your breath deepens, the light intensifies. Breathe out and the light spreads.

(Pause.)

Deep breath in and the light intensifies throughout your body. Deep breath out and the light spreads.

(Pause.)

Final time: Deep breath in, light intensifies. Deep breath out, light spreads through the body.

Allow yourself to feel and see whatever comes up in your body. Allow yourself to just be and feel relaxed for two to three minutes or more without direction. When you are ready, write down everything you can remember!

Your rest practice is complete.

Resources

Griffin-Pierce, Trudy. *Native Peoples of the Southwest.* Albuquerque: University of New Mexico Press, 2000. Pages 242–43.

National Center for Health Statistics, "Use of Yoga and Meditation Becoming More Popular in the US," Centers for Disease Control and Prevention. Last modified November 8, 2018. https://www.cdc.gov/nchs/pressroom/nchs_press_releases/2018/201811_Yoga_Meditation.htm.

National Heart, Lung, and Blood Institute. "What are Sleep Deprivation and Deficiency?" National Institutes of Health. Last modified March 24, 2022. https://www.nhlbi.nih.gov/health-topics/sleep-deprivation-and-deficiency.

Newsom, Rob, and Anis Rehman. "Sleep and Social Media." Sleep Foundation. Last modified December 15, 2022. https://www.sleepfoundation.org/how-sleep-works/sleep-and-social-media.

Coloring Magic

Color Correspondences

Color magic uses various hues to influence energy. It can attract or repel, strengthen or weaken. It expresses thoughts and feelings that don't fit easily into words. People choose colors of clothes, jewelry, walls, and carpet to create desired effects. In magic, we use altar cloths, candles, gemstones, bowls, and other altar tools to channel this energy. Coloring pages help people relax.

Different cultures may use different correspondences. Western cultures associate white with life and black with death; Eastern cultures tend to reverse those. It comes from interpretations. Red is the color of blood, which can suggest vitality or danger, depending on how you look at it. So there is no "right" or "wrong" meaning. Use the color associations that resonate with you.

Maroon: Crone, drama, respect, sensuality

Crimson: Determination, righteous anger, survival

Scarlet: Action, female sexuality, vitality

Red: Fire, strength, danger

Orange: Creativity, addiction, opportunity

Gold: God, Sun, justice

Topaz: Male sexuality, memory, fast effects

Yellow: Air, joy, charm

Lime Green: Growth, speed, end frustration

Green: Envy, money, health

Teal: Acceptance, abundance, happy home

Turquoise: Work-life balance, guilt, receiving

Blue: Water, truth, family

Indigo: Will, spirit, psychic

Purple: Wisdom, emotions, power

Lavender: Knowledge, intuition, divination

Violet: Calm, gratitude, tension

Coral: Mother, nurturing, emotional energy

Pink: Love, compassion, partnership

Fuchsia: Fight depression, self-direction, self-worth

Rose: Maiden, romance, friendship

Brown: Earth, stability, memory

Tan: Construction, food, past life

Black: Dark Moon, defense, grounding

Gray: Balance, loneliness, rest

Silver: Goddess, Moon, dreams

White: Crescent Moon, purity, peace

Ivory: Full Moon, luxury, animal magic

Activating the Magician's Manifestation Tools

Melissa Tipton

The Magician depicted in the tarot uses their will to channel divine energy into the here and now, and in the popular Smith-Waite imagery, the four tools of successful manifestation are on display: the pentacle, sword, wand, and cup. This spell pairs the Magician's tools with Jungian psychology to enhance your innate creative powers.

C. G. Jung developed a theory of typology that categorizes different attitudes and behaviors into four functions. When we link these functions to the Magician's tools, *sensation* tells us that a thing exists via the physical senses, making it a good corollary to the earthy pentacle; *thinking* interprets what we perceive in order to generate meaning (the airy, mental sword); *feeling* evaluates what we're perceiving to determine its subjective value (the watery, emotional cup); and *intuition* perceives possibilities that are not yet realized (the fiery, inspired wand).

Jung observed that we typically have one, or perhaps two, finely honed functions, and we tend to rely on them exclusively, like someone who is perhaps more at home wielding the sword of reason, whereas tapping into the cup of emotion feels uncomfortable. The infrequently used tools reside in our unconscious where they undergo little development. Why does this matter? Well, if circumstances invoke one of these undeveloped tools *for* us—such as a crappy day conjuring the cup of emotions—we're less skillful at wielding it, so we might experience its powers as overwhelming or even destructive. This can make us even less likely to develop this particular tool, furthering the imbalance.

The Magician reminds us that we need all four functions to unlock our creative potency. And sure, we may never be *experts* at all four, having a favorite that feels more natural, but even small increases in tool flexibility can spell a big difference when it comes to manifestation!

You will need:

Coloring medium of your choice

Take a few moments to ground and center yourself, then raise your non-dominant hand to the sky and point your dominant hand to the earth, adopting the Magician's power pose. Draw energy from the sky through your body and into your downward-pointing arm, but don't release it yet. Feel yourself existing as a magnetic channel of divine energy, able to transmute pure thoughts and desires into tangible forms.

Color in the four tools (choose colors that feel personally meaningful), starting with the sword and moving clockwise, allowing the channeled energy to flow into each image, activating it. Color in the circular border connecting the tools in a clockwise motion, generating a magical container in the center of the page. When done, place your palms on the ground and release any excess energy, if needed.

Moving forward, you can place your manifestation goals within this container, be they in the form of worded intentions (written directly on the page or on slips of paper), photos, drawings, or physical objects. Then, be on the lookout for cosmic nudges in the form of synchronicities, dreams, quotes, and the like that point you toward using the four functions effectively to manifest your goal. Bonus: whichever color(s) you used for each tool, wear clothing or jewelry to match to intensify that tool's powers when needed.

The Self-Care Menagerie Meter

Natalie Zaman

Setting boundaries and expressing and loving yourself are necessary to nurture (not spoil) your body and soul. Tap into the energies of symbolic animals and the power of the chakras in this ritual coloring page to boost your self-care habit. Meditate on each animal and chakra point to motivate acts of self-care. Once you've colored in an animal (in any order you wish!), perform the act of self-care it inspires before moving onto the next.

Capybara of the Root

The capybara is the embodiment of peace and grounding. As you color, visualize a soothing connection with the earth. Feel the capybara's comfort provide a safe haven for rejuvenation. Breathe in the stability of the natural world and exhale unsteadiness. Feel your energy align with the serenity of the capybara and say aloud, "I am secure."

Spider of the Sacral

The spider represents creativity and ingenuity. As you color, imagine the threads of your creativity coming together. Embrace the spider's ability to transform challenges into opportunities. Breathe in inspiration of the natural world and exhale any thoughts of "I can't." Feel your energy align with the creativity of the spider and say aloud, "I live a creative life."

Peacock of the Solar Plexus

The peacock exudes self-expression and confidence. As you color, allow the peacock's majestic plumage to mirror your beauty and radiance. Envision your self-confidence blossoming. Breathe in your authentic self and exhale expectations and "norms." Feel your energy align with the brilliance of the peacock and say aloud, "I am confident."

Dog of the Heart

The dog's energy is loving and loyal. As you work, be enveloped in the essence of unconditional love. Reflect on the joy and comfort that companionship brings, and let the dog's image remind you to nurture and cherish your own being. Breathe kindness into your heart and exhale pain. Feel your energy align with the dog's devotion and say aloud, "I love myself unconditionally."

Whale of the Throat

Dive into emotional healing with the whale, the ambassador of clear communication. As you work, visualize the gentle sway of the ocean cleansing your spirit, leaving you with a deeper connection to your intuition and inner wisdom. Breathe clarity into your heart and exhale misinformation. Feel your energy align with the whale's wisdom and say aloud, "I am heard."

Eagle of the Third Eye

The eagle symbolizes vision and perception. Embrace the eagle's ability to rise above challenges, gaining a broader perspective on your journey. Breathe in vision and freedom and exhale mental clutter. Feel your energy align with the eagle's clarity and insight and say, "I see all that I need to see."

Butterfly of the Crown

The butterfly is transformation. As you color, visualize the process of shedding old layers and embracing the divine within. Allow the butterfly's grace to remind you to see wonder in all things. Breathe in change and exhale fear. Feel your energy align with the butterfly's majesty and say aloud, "I am divine."

• • • ☽ • • •

Use this coloring ritual often—self-care is a practice that needs consistency!

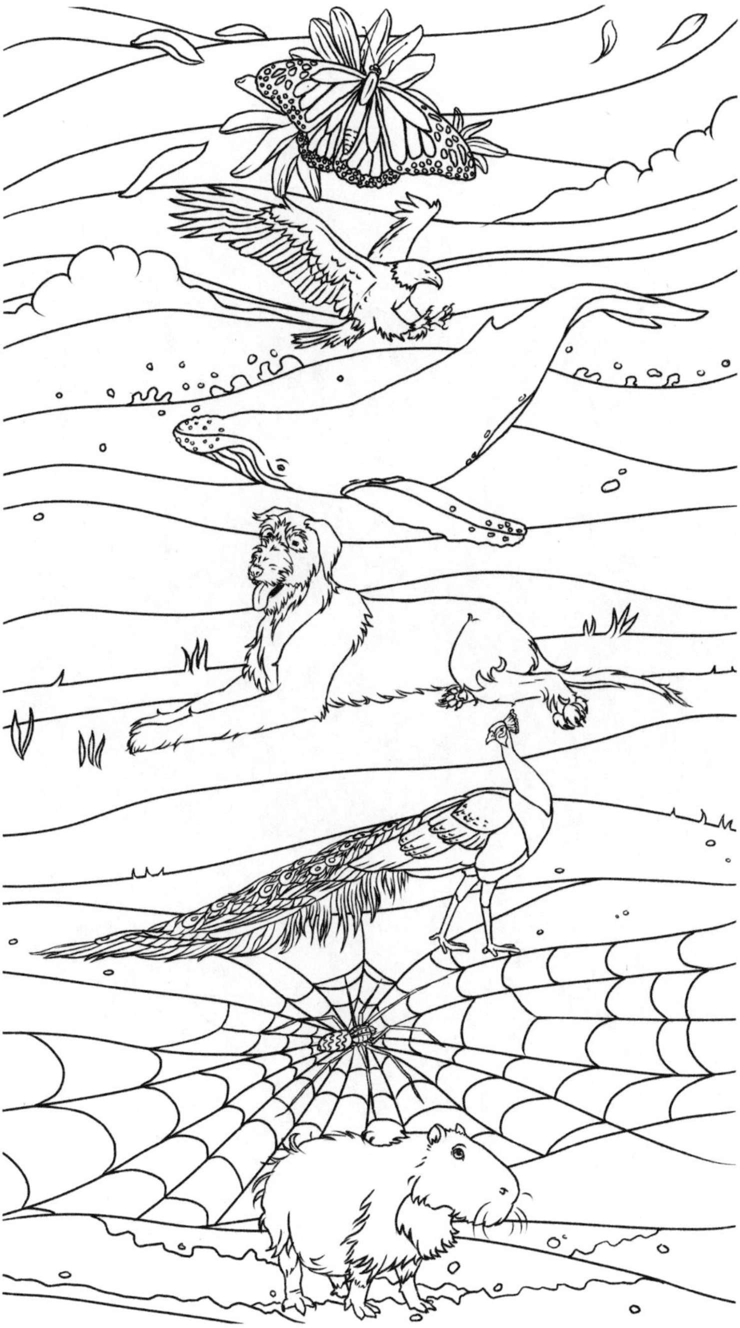

One Beautiful Thing Each Day

Angela A. Wix

Not long ago I experienced a health event that had me pondering the fragile and fleeting nature of life. I have a naturally anxious mind and quickly recognized I needed to give myself something else to focus on in order to not get caught in the negative spiral of what may be. I decided to focus on finding at least one good thing each day. Regardless of that days' circumstance, curiosity held at least a part of my focus as I awaited that day's beautiful thing to reveal itself.

Looking through this new lens can put life into a different perspective. Not only can it refocus where your daily attention is most drawn, but it can also empower you when you have days, weeks, and even months of findings to look back on. When you track each day's detail, you're left with a collection of beautiful things you've experienced.

It can be so easy to get stuck looking down, but with intention and curiosity, we can choose to find the things that help us look back up.

Find the Magic of Your One Beautiful Thing

Get caught in the upward spiral of the things that are simply *magical* to you! Take part in this mindfulness practice to identify at least one beautiful thing each day for a designated amount of time. Will you aim for a week? Two weeks? A month? More? What's inspired you today? What held you captivated or left you feeling thankful? The first step in this gratitude practice is to start noticing.

If you feel so inspired, color in the illustration, track your own beautiful things by writing them along the meditative spiral winding toward the center, or weave doodles of your own into the image. If you prefer, you can also keep a separate journal or sketchbook to track your journey alongside this coloring page entry. Get creative and go where inspiration takes you.

I find nature and the changing seasons to be a magical part of life, which is reflected in this coloring page. Pets also top my list! Maybe your list will overlap with the items I identified as I went through the practice myself, or maybe yours will look entirely different. That's part of the splendor. We all find beauty through our own lens. You might find it in a scientific equation, computer coding, or the functioning of machinery. That's not my cup of tea, but you do you! Whether it's a moment, event, thing, person, process, or location, keep your attention on the lookout for whatever holds you in wonder and watch how the practice potentially shifts your mood . . . goodness manifesting goodness.

To take your practice a step further, think about what those beautiful things mean to you as you see them unfolding. For example, do you notice a threaded message emerging from the synchronistic connection of each individual beautiful thing? Consider them as individual symbolic words connecting to form a sentence. What is the universe communicating through your attention? Tune in and observe the magic that's revealed to you.

ONE BEAUTIFUL THING

Contributors

ELIZABETH BARRETTE has been involved with the Pagan community for more than thirty-four years. She has served as managing editor of *PanGaia* and dean of studies at the Grey School of Wizardry. Her book *Composing Magic* explains how to combine writing and spirituality. She lives in central Illinois. Visit her blog *The Wordsmith's Forge* (ysabetwordsmith.livejournal.com) or website PenUltimate Productions (penultimateproductions.weebly.com). Her coven site with extensive Pagan materials is Greenhaven Tradition (http://greenhaventradition.weebly.com/).

KIR BEAUX (they/them) is a trans, nonbinary queer, neurodivergent, psychic Witch, and tarot reader based in Los Angeles, CA. Kir offers spiritual support and education via It's Queer Magic. You can find them featured on Pride.com, *Refinery 29*, and *The World According to Jeff Goldblum* on Disney+. Heart-centered, open-minded, and an ever-changing Gemini, Kir is here to root you down and help you fly.

STEPHANIE ROSE BIRD is the author of the COVR award–winning *Sticks, Stones, Roots & Bones*, as well as *The Healing Power of African American Spirituality*; *A Healing Grove*; *Light, Bright, Damn Near White*; *Four Seasons of Mojo*; *Mama Nature's Spiritual Guide to Weight Loss*; *365 Days of Hoodoo*; *African American Magick*; and *The Healing Tree*. Bird

holds a BFA cum laude from Temple University, Tyler School of Art, and an MFA from University of California at San Diego, where she was a San Diego Opportunity Fellow.

BLAKE OCTAVIAN BLAIR is a shamanic and Druidic practitioner, ordained minister, writer, Usui Reiki Master-Teacher, and musical artist. Blake incorporates mystical traditions from both the East and West with a reverence for the natural world into his own brand of spirituality. He is an avid reader, knitter, nature lover, and member of the Order of Bards, Ovates, and Druids. He lives with his loving husband in New England. Visit him on the web at www.blakeoctavianblair.com.

CHIC AND S. TABATHA CICERO are Chief Adepts of the Hermetic Order of the Golden Dawn as re-established by Israel Regardie. They have written numerous books, including *Golden Dawn Magic, The Essential Golden Dawn, Self-Initiation into the Golden Dawn Tradition, The Golden Dawn Magical Tarot,* and *Tarot Talismans.* Both are Rosicrucians: Chic is Chief Adept of the Florida College of the SRICF and Tabatha is Imperatrix of the SRIA in America.

MONICA CROSSON is the author of *A Year in the Enchanted Garden, Wild Magical Soul, The Magickal Family,* and *Summer Sage.* She is a Master Gardener who lives in the beautiful Pacific Northwest, happily digging in the dirt and tending her raspberries with her family and their small menagerie of farm animals. She has been a practicing Witch for thirty years and is a member of Evergreen Coven.

MAJORIE GATSON is the intuitive force behind her esoteric business, the Punk Priestess. She is a tarot reader, evolutionary astrologer, and reiki practitioner. Majorie began her witchy spiritual path at a young age by studying astrology. Her astrology practice eventually led her to the esoteric art of reading tarot a decade later. Majorie's passion is to inspire and teach others the art of tarot and astrology to uncover their soul's evolution.

LAURA GONZÁLEZ is a Pagan priestess, minister, practitioner of traditional Mexican folk magic and Native philosophies, and

priestess of the Goddess. Her community activism is an extension of her spiritual practice: she advocates for the Latin American, Pagan, and LGBTQIA+ communities; women's rights; suicide prevention; and diversity inclusion. She is also a popular podcaster and producer of her shows, *Lunatic Mondays* and *Paganos del Mundo*, on Circle Sanctuary Network Podcasts.

JAMES KAMBOS has contributed to Llewellyn's annuals for over twenty-five years. He has written many articles about folk magic traditions, spellcraft, and herbs. He's also an artist and has designed cards and calendars. A gardener, he raises a large variety of herbs and wildflowers. He lives in the beautiful Appalachian hill country of Southern Ohio.

OPAL LUNA is a crone, priestess of Minerva, and fiber magician. As the author of *Fiber Magick: A Witch's Guide to Spellcasting with Crochet, Knotwork, and Weaving,* she has enjoyed being a guest on podcasts and headlining at Pagan festivals. As the president on the board of Abelina's Grove, she has enjoyed presenting many topics, including an annual Hurricane Protection Ritual each June. She lives in South Florida with her husband and two cats.

LUPA is an author, artist, and nature lover in the Pacific Northwest. She has written several books on nature-based Paganism and is the creator of the Tarot of Bones. More about her work may be found at www.thegreenwolf.com.

SARA MELLAS is an artist and writer living in Nashville, TN. She's authored three books and written about food, music, comedy, and astrology for several media outlets. She holds a master's degree in music education and vocal performance and works as a performer and food stylist for television, commercials, and live events. Outside of her creative pursuits, she can be found reading, spending time with horses, and practicing astrology. Her website is saramellas.com.

MO OF AUSTRAL-TAUR is a traditional astrologer who specializes in Hellenistic and medieval timing techniques. In particular,

she focuses on utilizing the lesser dignities such as triplicity, bounds, and decans to provide extra nuance when delineating natal charts and giving timing advice. She is also versed in the symbolism of tarot and astrological correspondences via the Golden Dawn tradition. She hopes to inspire people who connect with her work to appreciate the layered meanings across different systems of divination. Visit austral-taur.com.

SHANA NUNNELLY is a sound bath facilitator and wellness entrepreneur who offers space for healing and rest. As a practicing Buddhist and a West African priestess, Shana's connection with spirit is passed down from her ancestral lineage. After twenty years of being a salon owner and healer, she sought a deeper way to serve clients. From years of devout training and mentorship, she began to teach sound meditation and healing to others.

DIANA RAJCHEL is an animistic Witch who interacts with spirits cultivated and uncultivated. As a result, people ask her for spirit work when they discover roommates they weren't aware they had consented to. She is the co-owner of Golden Apple Metaphysical with Nikki Jobin and the author of *Urban Magick* and *Hex Twisting*. Book her for consultations or see what she's come up with this time at dianarajchel.com.

MHARA STARLING was born in North Wales, raised on the Isle of Anglesey, and is a native Welsh speaker. She is a *Swynwraig*, or Welsh folk Witch, and a leader of the *Sarffes Goch* Coven based along the Northern Welsh marches. Mhara teaches at various conferences, classes, and events across the United Kingdom and has appeared in numerous Welsh and English documentaries.

MELISSA TIPTON is a Jungian Witch, Structural Integrator, and founder of the Real Magic Mystery School, where she teaches online courses in Jungian Magic, a potent blend of ancient magical techniques and modern psychological insights. She's the author of *Living Reiki: Heal Yourself and Transform Your Life* and *Llewellyn's*

Complete Book of Reiki. Learn more and take a free class at www.real magic.school.

JD WALKER is an avid student of herbalism and gardening. She has written a regular garden column for thirty years. She is an award-winning author, journalist, magazine editor, and frequent contributor to the Llewellyn annuals. Her first book, *A Witch's Guide to Wildcrafting*, published by Llewellyn Publications, was released in spring 2021. Her book *Under the Sacred Canopy* was released in spring 2023.

CHARLYNN WALLS is an active member of her local community and coven. A practitioner of the Craft for over twenty-five years, she currently resides in Central Missouri with her family. Charlynn draws on her background in anthropology, archaeology, and her own personal experience to help shape her daily practice. She continues to share her knowledge by teaching online and at local festivals and by continuing to produce articles for publication with Llewellyn Worldwide.

BRANDON WESTON is a folklorist, spiritual healer, and writer living in the Arkansas Ozarks. He is the author of *Ozark Folk Magic: Plants, Prayers, and Healing* and *Ozark Mountain Spell Book.* He is the owner of Ozark Healing Traditions, a collection of articles, lectures, and workshops focusing on traditions of medicine and magic from the Ozark Mountain region. He comes from a long line of Ozark hillfolk and works hard to keep these traditions alive for generations to come.

ANGELA A. WIX is an acquiring editor for books on wellness and spirituality. She's a Certified Medical Reiki Master (CMRM), ordained interfaith minister of spiritual healing, and lifelong intuitive medium-in-training. She is also an artist, a poet, and the author of five books: *Llewellyn's Little Book of Unicorns, The Secret Psychic, Your Pain Is Real, I Am Strong (and other things i tell myself),* and *One Beautiful Thing.* Visit her at AngelaAnn.Wix.com/arts.

CHARLIE RAINBOW WOLF is an old hippie who's been studying the weird ways of the world for over fifty years. She's happiest when she's got her hands in mud, either making pottery in the Artbox or tending to things in the "yarden." Astrology, tarot, and herbs are her greatest interests, but she's dabbled in most metaphysical topics in the last five decades, because life always has something new to offer. Charlie lives in central Illinois with her very patient husband and her beloved Great Danes.

STEPHANIE WOODFIELD has been a practicing Pagan for over twenty years. A devotional polytheist, teacher, and priestess of the Morrigan, she is an organizer for several Pagan gatherings. A long-time New Englander, she now resides in the Orlando area with her husband, two very pampered cats, and various reptiles. She is called to helping others forge meaningful experiences and relationships with the gods.

NATALIE ZAMAN is the author of *Color and Conjure* and *Magical Destinations of the Northeast*. A regular contributor to various Llewellyn annual publications, she also writes the recurring feature Wandering Witch for *Witches & Pagans* magazine. When not on the road, she's busy tending her magical back garden. Visit Natalie online at nataliezaman.blogspot.com.